BANKING

TRENDS & PRACTICES

BANKING
TRENDS & PRACTICES

Edited by

M.C. Pande
Subodh Kumar

ANAMIKA PUBLISHERS & DISTRIBUTORS (P) LTD.
4697/3, 21A, Ansari Road, Daryaganj
New Delhi 110 002
Phone: 23281655

First Published 2005

ISBN 81-7975-000-0

PRINTED IN INDIA

Published by Anamika Publishers & Distributors (P) Ltd.,
4697/3, 21A, Ansari Road, Daryaganj, New Delhi 110 002.
Typeset by Phoenix Computer Centre, New Delhi and
Printed at Nagri Printers, Delhi.

FOREWORD

Management of Banks and Financial Institutions has always been vital for the efficient functioning of the country's economy. But the focus of attention has been changing from time to time depending upon the societal needs and aspirations. The years 1969, 1975 and 1991 are landmarks in the Banking history of India; 1969 for changing focus from class to mass banking by nationalising 14 major commercial banks; 1975 for the implementation of the Tandon Committee recommendations relating to norms, methods, styles and follow-up of bank credit and 1991 for ushering the country into a new era of economic liberalisation and implementation in phases of the financial sector reforms based on the recommendations of the Narasimhan Committee Report. Some of the major recommendations of the Committee such as Capital Adequacy, Income Recognition. Asset Classification and the provisioning norms, which were implemented by Indian Banks from 1992-93, aim at making the Indian Banking System more transparent, efficient and competitive so as to enable it to face successfully the emerging challenges triggered by the forces of deregulation, liberalisation, and globalisation.

The policy of economic liberalisation being pursued by the country since last few years, led to the emergence of the variety of new players in the financial sector like Non-Banking Finance Companies (NBFCs), high tech private banks, subsidiaries of public sector banks and more branches of existing and new foreign banks. It also resulted into appearances of new and innovative instruments of money and capital markets such as Commercial Paper (CP), Certificate of Deposit (CD), floating notes, zero rate bonds, deep discount bonds, fully convertible debentures (FCD), partly convertible debentures (PCD), Non-Convertible Debentures (NCD), etc. resulting into acute competition amongst banks on the one hand and banks and NBFC's, corporate sector, banks subsidiaries on the other. Further, the triple rated corporates and blue chip companies have started sourcing capital market directly for their financial needs, both domestic and international. Hence, demand for bank credit of these high rated companies has become feeble and their demands on banks for low interest rates, quick, good and personalized service tailored to their individual requirements have increased manifold. In contrast, the low rated borrowers, who would always face problems in accessing capital market, will be almost fully dependent on bank for their credit requirements even at higher interest rates. This pinpoints the need for upgrading the credit appraisal skills of bankers to enable them to segregate between low and high credit-risk and take prudent credit decisions.

Due to these and other emerging developments the concept of "Credit risk" and "Credit worthiness" of borrowers has now occupied the center-stage of credit management and appraisal. Keeping this in view, it is widely felt that there is urgent need to bring out some Journal, periodical or books which may throw latest thinking of knowledgeable people within the country or outside periodically.

It gives me great pleasure to know that Dr. M.C. Pande and Dr. Subodh Kumar of Department of Commerce, P.G. College, Rudrapur have decided to jointly edit and bring out a special number on latest development in banking within the country and abroad. I extend a hearty welcome to this innovative effort and wish it all success.

Dr. S. Singh
Principal
New Delhi Institute of Management,
60-61 Tughlakabad Institutional Area,
New Delhi-110062
and former Executive Director, Allahabad Bank

PREFACE

Commercial banks operating in India have been facing tremendous challenges as also opportunities in the new millennium. Liberalization, privatization and globalization have brought about remarkable changes in the way banks and banking personnel work. Entry of well-equipped foreign banks and new wave private sector banks has made the banking business highly competitive. In the rapidly changing economic scenario, banks are becoming increasingly vulnerable to the changes that are taking place in the other parts of the world. Banks are revamping their working systems and improving their work-culture under the close supervision of Reserve Bank of India. Everyday new instructions from higher offices are facilitating avenues that may pave the way to achieve international standards.

At present, Banks are in quite a comfortable position with regard to profit earning position. The profits of Public Sector Banks increased by 46-25% from Rs. 84.07 bn in 2001-02 to 122.95 bn in 2002-03. Present day's challenge lies in maintaining the profits in years to come without much help of high interest bearing government securities, which form a sizable part of profits these days. Asset Quality Management, Risk Management, Asset-Liability Management, Management of Business Spread, Customer Relationship Management, Human Resource Management, Technology Management, Management Information System, Corporate Governance etc. are newer areas which are the main concern of today's bankers. Business strategies are also changing. Now banks are eager to finance for consumer loans, which was termed as 'Non Productive Loans' in recent past.

New trends and practices in banking sector have changed the face of banking. Various innovations have been observed to cope with the threat of profitability. Research Paper 'Innovative Banking: Techniques and Practices in Selected Banks' is a combined effort of Mr. B. Satya Swaroop, B. Satyanarayana and Prof. D. Prabhakar Rao. It is a study of various banks providing innovative services to their customers. Research Papers 'Trends and Developments in Indian Banking Industry' by Dr. A.B. Thapaliyal and 'Innovative Banking: A Challenge before Indian Banking' by Dr. N.P. Singh, Parimal Kumar also analyze the same aspect, but with a different treatment. Issue of corporate governance is gaining importance day by day. Dr. J.D.S. Negi and Dr. A.B. Thapaliyal in their paper 'Corporate Governance in Banks' have dealt the matter very carefully. Infrastructure Financing has emerged as an important segment of our banking system. Mr. Manoranjan Sharma, in his paper 'Infrastructure Financing in India: An Appraisal of Shifting Gears' has presented it in an analytical manner. Mergers, acquisition and re-organisation have become inevitable in the present age of cutthroat competition. Research Paper of Dr. P.C. Kavidayal on 'Merger of ICICI with ICICI Bank: Its impact on the value of shareholders' is an efficient effort of peeping into the facts of merger and its role in the interest of investors.

Banks are now entering insurance sector for spread in business with increased profits and reduced risks. Prof. M.N. Mishra has presented 'Bancassurance: An Innovative Step' to discuss the entry of Indian banks in insurance sector. In fact, Risk Management is an area where a lot of changes are expected in future. Dr. M.C. Pande and Lalita Prasad discuss risk management in depth in their articles 'Risks in Banking' and 'ALM: An emerging trend in banking sector'.

In India, Banking Sector Reforms were initiated in 1991. Dr. B.K. Agarwal, Dr. Subodh Kumar has discussed probable and possible effects of reforms in their paper 'Banking Sector Reforms: Retrospect and Prospect'. Prof. R.P. Bharati has suggested 'Market-Oriented Strategies at Bank Branches' in the context of changing scenario of Indian banking. Market share of a bank will increase automatically, if it has proper business strategies, which include excellent customer service. Dr. Subodh Kumar in 'Panorama of CRM in Commercial Banks' and Dr. P.K. Garg in 'Customer: An Unpaid Salesperson (A study of public sector banks)' have dealt important issues like Customer Relationship Management and Customer Satisfaction. Human Resource Management has always been the most important task for service-based industry like banks. Getting work done is not merely an administrative assignment; it needs psychological treatment at every step for making management successful. Dr. R.K. Srivastav in his paper 'HRD in Banking: Few Psychological Inputs' has touched this issue in a sophisticated manner. Dr. Mohd. Younus Ali Khan has highlighted the need and importance of Human Resource in 'Planning for Human Resource Development in Banking Industry'. Now-a-days, strategic Human Resource Management is getting more and more importance. Dr. S. Hussain Asraf has carefully described this issue in his paper 'Strategic Human Resource Management: A Panacea for Commercial Banks'.

Technology, in the time to come, will bring sea changes in the Indian Banking. In the next two years, major banks are poised to spend Rs. 3,500 crore on technology. Research papers 'Management Information System (MIS) in the commercial bank's perspective' and 'Entering of Banking Industry in Information Age' by Dr. S.K. Sharma and Dr. K.K. Varma respectively are based on the role and importance of information system in banks.

Regional and sectoral issues have also been raised in this volume. Social control on banks, nationalization of banks, RRBs, Lead Bank Scheme, IRDP, DRI scheme etc. are the steps which have been taken time to time for all-round development of our economy. 'Indian Rural Banking in Next Decade' by Mr. R.C. Pande — Dr. P.C. Kavidayal and 'Regional Rural Banks in India and their role in Rural Development' by R.K. Agrawal are two sketches of rural financing in Indian economy. 'Cooperative must succeed in India' is not just a saying but also a truth. Nasrullah Bhat and Dr. Rais Ahmad have presented a study of cooperative movement in some villages of J & K in their joint paper 'Business Performance of Central Cooperative Land Development Bank of J&K State'. Dr. K.S. Ramola's study is based on the role of banks in development of the secondary sector. His paper 'Role of Commercial Banks and Financial Institutions in the Development of Small Scale Industries (SSIs) in India' gives an account of financial assistance provided by various financial institutions and its utilization by their customers.

This book is the outcome of the combined efforts of all the contributors, who responded our call within expected time frame. Their positive response enabled us to present this book in its present form. We express our sincere thanks to all of them. Our family member had to feel neglected for the sake of this poise work. Their sacrifice is the backbone of this work. Publishers of this book Anamika Publishers

& Distributors (P) Ltd. do deserve our thanks for promoting such academic work. We wish to express our gratefulness to all of our friends and well-wishers whose contributions in different forms enabled us to bring out this volume.

M.C. Pande
Subodh Kumar

CONTENTS

1

INNOVATIVE BANKING: TECHNIQUES AND PRACTICES IN SELECTED BANKS

B. Satya Swaroopa*, B. Satyanarayana* and D. Prabhakar Rao**

For paying a telephone bill or paying the LIC premium the consumer used to take half day leave and spends his time and energy. Now, banks effect such payment at almost no cost on standing instructions from his depositor. These solutions are provided by the innovations in the banking business.

Innovative banking means application of new methods and techniques, new and novel schemes for deposit mobilization and credit deployment and in the area of bank management.

In order to meet the challenges of emerging competitive environment the banks reoriented their strategies to bring innovations in their products and diversification in their services. The banks are now no merely deposit and lending institutions but they are going to be developed as complete financial service centers where a client can depend on his bank for any financial service and counseling too.

The authors give an account of innovations in the leading banks —Indusind Bank, UTI Bank, ING-Vysya Bank, IDBI Bank, Canara Bank, CITI Bank, BoB, State Bank of Punjab, SBI, Hongkong-Shanghai Banking Corporation (HSBC).

*Research Scholars.

**Professor, Dept. of Commerce & Management Studies, Andhra University, Vishakhapatnam and, General Secretary, Indian Accounting Association.

INTRODUCTION

In primitive days, people used to carry bags of coins for the purpose of shopping or purchasing any article or any service. Later the invention of paper money and its varied denominations made the process less burdensome. He used to carry the money with him for his daily activities, which was also a risky and uncomfortable process. The invention of plastic money, i.e. credit cards and debit cards made the man free from carrying lots of money. These credit and debit cards are the latest innovation by which the customer can go to any member establishment and purchase whatever he needs though he is not having money in his pocket. It is also a secured form of transaction.

For a businessman who needs funds in other areas/cities where he has no bank account, has to go for taking demand draft and post it to the concerned person. But now with the innovation of Electronic Funds Transfer System, this problem has been solved and this facility is accessible without much cost. Customers used to wait in long queues for long hours to deposit cash or withdraw cash. For the purpose of paying bills (electricity, telephone, house tax, water tax, income tax, professional tax etc.) also the customers used to take half day or full day leave and forego their pay and energy. Now the banks offer payment of such bills at free or nominal cost on a simple standing order given by the customer. All these solutions are provided by the innovations that have taken place in the banking sector of India, more so, after the introduction of New Economic Policy. These innovations are popularly known by the name 'INNOVATIVE BANKING', which saved a lot of time, money and energy and made the customers hassle-free.

Innovative banking means the application of new methods and techniques, new and novel schemes in the field of deposit mobilization, deployment of credit and bank management. For example, in order to attract deposits the banks have introduced retirement schemes, perennial pension plans, Akshayanidhi schemes. Various innovative schemes for money-lending such as education loans, car finance, home loans, household goods finance etc. Besides these, many banks have started Sunday branches, anytime anywhere banking and round the clock facility, mobile banks, computerized banks, internet banks etc., for the benefit of the customers.

Economic liberalization and growing deregulation along with radical reforms in financial sector, technological expansion and fierce competition and sharp acceleration in the pace of innovation and structural changes in international financial markets brought tremendous changes in the corporate policies and strategies and so also in the business mix of Indian financial system. The changes so occurred raised the distinction between money and capital market institutions by changing their bank character from mere lending institutions to catalytic agents of growth.

In order to meet the challenges of the emerging competitive environment, the financial corporations along with banks re-oriented their strategies to bring innovation in their products and diversify their activities. This time these institutions operated primarily as term lending institutions confining themselves to few developed regions of the country. They used to perform the role of a channeliser rather than a financial intermediary. However, on sensing the ferocity of competition the financial institutions ushered in by change in government policy surpassed their traditional role to assume the role of a full-fledged financial institution to render financial services to the needy customer and entrepreneurs in addition to project finance.

As a financier, term financial corporations/banks have decided to bring about innovation of new products, diversify into new business and improve the quality of products and services. These are done in order to attain internationally accepted standards which are the links to become overseas market participants and face competitive challenges more effectively.

Banks, now-a-days, are no more a mere lending and depositing institutions, they have become more than a financial intermediary by which it undertakes every activity of its varied customers in order to show how useful are the banks in every walk of life. If the customer is an entrepreneur, the bank provides loans and advances as a primary function, besides these the bank also supplies management advices through merchant banking system, gives project financing, renders loan syndication facility if it is a big venture, assure working capital finance, tax payment facility and other subsidiary facilities relating to day-to-day transactions in the business. If the customer is a salaried person or a senior citizen the facilities rendered by banks includes special savings accounts, pension schemes and other subsidiary facilities like home loans, household services, credit and debit cards, etc.

Innovation in banking emerged through priority sector lending and with the most important phenomenon of computerization. Computerization in banks solved many of the problems in banking sector and this has become the accelerator for the banking activities. So, 'computerization of banks' has been termed as Innovative Banking. Computerization and technological upgradation in the field of communication through electronic devices enhanced the growth of banking business. With this, the banks could innovate new products and services to satisfy their customers. One of the most important innovations is 'Cyber Banking' which is a mixture—an interactive structure of E–Commerce and E-Banking. E-Banking means banking through computers. Virtual Banking which is also known as Remote Banking or Home Banking which uses extensively the information technology without direct recourse to the bank by the customer. We would like to discuss the era of pre-innovative banking and the emergence of innovative banking, before presenting various techniques of innovative banking.

PRE–INNOVATIVE BANKING

The period after 1964 may be clearly described as the phase of 'innovative banking' or 'revolutionary phase'. After 1964 there was a significant change in Indian politics. In fact, it is the period (1964–67) where there was an increasing concern about the problem of concentration of economic power in few hands. Several official reports investigated into these problems such as —

1. The Committee on Distribution of Income and Levels of Living (Mahalanobis Committee) 1964.
2. The Monopolies Inquiry Commission, 1965.
3. The Managing Agency Inquiry (Patel) Committee, 1966.
4. The Industrial Planning and Licensing Policy, 1967 (R.K. Hazari).
5. The Industrial Licencing Policy Inquiry (Dutt) Committee, 1969.

These reports formed the basis for significant policy changes in Indian Banking. The central issue of debate was that the large scale industries, large borrowers, big established business houses had monopolized bank credit whereas the small business houses and such priority sector could not get their due share. This provided a platform for the revolutionary changes in the structure, operations, polices and practices of commercial banking in India. However, bank financing of the priority sectors was not entirely ideological. These enterprises had no access to capital market and their need for funds could only be met through bank credit. The main features of pre-innovative banking phase are:

1. Social control
2. Follow-up of social control
3. Nationalization
4. Bank credit to priority sectors

1. Social Control

The Indian banking structure had grown in strength and stability in the phase of consolidation as a result of rigorous control of RBI. Yet, it suffers from coverage and credit gaps. This is due to the fact that network of bank branches could cover only the urban areas and totally neglected the rural areas containing the agriculture sector, small-industries, artisans, retail traders and so on. Still major reason was that majority of the banks were lead by business houses. So, the scheme of Social Control was introduced at the end of 1967.

According to this scheme the bank credit was an instrument for the attainment of the socio-economic objectives of state policy. The main objective was, to achieve a widespread of bank credit, prevent its misuse, direct large volume of credit flow to the priority sectors. Through the reformation of management it sought to remove the control of business houses without removing private ownership of banks. The main elements of Social Control consist of:

(a) Organisational Changes
(b) National Credit Council
(c) Agriculture Finance Corporation Limited.

(a) *Organisational Changes*: Social Control introduced organizational changes through the reconstitution of Board of Directors of Banks, with the persons who had specialized knowledge and experience of agriculture, rural-economy, small scale industries and banking. Likewise industrialist chairman was replaced by the person who is specialized in banking finance, economics and business administration.

(b) *National Credit Council* : NCC was created in February 1968 which symbolizes the role of credit planning in development for the purpose of assessing credit priorities on all-India basis. Its functions are:

- To assess the demand for bank credit from the various sectors of the economy.
- To determine the priorities for the grants according to the availability of resources and requirements of priority sectors.
- To coordinate the lending and investing policies of commercial banks, cooperative banks, specialized agencies and to ensure optimum utilisation of resources.

(c) *Agriculture Finance Corporation Limited* : AFC limited was set up as a joint venture by the leading banks to finance agricultural projects as well as to stimulate the banks to participate actively in development of the agricultural sector.

2. Follow-up of Social Control

This exists of the two study groups appointed by NCC in October 1968.

(a) *Organizational Framework for the implementation of Social Control Objectives under the chairmanship of Prof. D.R.Gadgil* : The report identified the major territorial and functional credit gaps and recommended for adequate institutional credit to neglected sectors of the economy and weaker sections of the community. It commented upon the urban orientation of the banking system and drew attention to the problem of small farmers. As a follow-up, it identified a number of weaker sections to be brought within the scope of bank credit.

Suggestions of the report include an area approach wherein individual banks select a particular area for intensive development to expand deposit mobilization and area of finance to agriculture and small scale industries. Dynamic relationship between the banks, the cooperative institutions, short-term and long-term lending institutions and government machinery at state level to integrate credit and banking activities have been formulated. Later a committee of bankers, appointed by RBI in August 1969 under the chairmanship of F.K.F. Nariman, adopted the area approach and advocated a Lead Bank Scheme (LBS). Under this scheme the banks were allotted specific districts to take lead in surveying the potential for banking development, extend their branchcs after identifying growth centers and potentially viable propositions and mobilising deposits out of the rising levels of income. Accordingly, RBI finalized LBS in 1969 with 336 districts in the country excluding metropolitan cities and some union territories to play a lead role, mostly in public sector.

(b) *The extent to which credit needs of industry and trade are likely to be inflated and how such trends can be checked by under Shri. V.T. Deheja* : The conclusions of this report submitted in September 1969, were:

(i) The organized sector of industry was over relying on bank credit.

(ii) The credit limits were related to security offered and not to cash flow analysis and there is no uniform procedure.

The recommendations include a study of industry-wise norms of minimum inventory levels in order to determine the important element of cash credit account. These measures may enable the banks to release more funds for meeting the requirements of priority sectors. Report of All India Rural Credit Review Committee, 1969 which was appointed by RBI for reviewing agricultural programmes envisaged a positive and active role for the commercial banks in the direct and indirect financing of cultivators through suppliers of inputs, marketing or processing of produce and government procurement operations.

3. Nationalization

Even though the banking system had taken several measures for achieving the objectives of social control, still there were serious reservations of political leadership. Social control measures without deteriorating the framework of profit-oriented private ownership of banks were undertaken. Accordingly fourteen major banks with individual deposits exceeding Rs. 50 crores were nationalized on 19th July 1969. Again on April 15, 1980, six more commercial banks (now five, New Bank of India was merged with Punjab National Bank in September 1993) were nationalized.

The post-nationalization period yielded significant changes in the operational policies and practices of the banks. The changes include the introduction of New Bill Market Scheme (NBMS) in November 1970, guidelines for follow-up of Bank Credit, 1974, review of cash credit system and replacement of Credit Authorization Scheme (CAS) by Credit Monitoring Arrangement (CMA).

4. Bank Credit to Priority Sectors

The flow of bank credit in the priority sectors was considerably accelerated after the nationalization of banks. Advances for retail trade and education which received negligence before were well developed. The government advised the public sector banks to make efforts to increase the proportion of advances to the priority sector in their portfolio to 33% in March 1979. Later, priority sector accounted for two-fifths of the bank lending. The facilitating schemes of the government of India included Integrated Rural Development Program (IRDP), Twenty Point Economic Program (TPEP) and Drought Prone Areas Program (DPAP). The priority sectors have received the conceited attention of the banks particularly after nationalization.

EMERGENCE OF INNOVATIVE BANKING

The present banking system was basically evolved to cater to the financial needs of trade and industry and also to satisfy the institutions of the country. The constituents of the banking system today in India have varying origin and sizes. At the apex is the Reserve Bank of India, the Central Bank of the country. It is the bankers' bank and lender of last resort. Besides it acts as the fiscal agent of the government, manages the currency and controls the credit in the national interest. State Bank of India was created in July 1955 by nationalizing the Imperial Bank of India following RBI's nationalization. Followed by this are the subsidiaries of SBI, twenty major nationalized schedule banks, other joint stock banks that formed in India in the later half of the 19th century, Cooperative Banks which had their first existence in 1904 in the grab of Cooperative Credit Societies, nidhis and chit funds, which have been in existence since the last quarter of the 18th century. Along with these there are indigenous banks and bankers who are centuries old. Later Regional Rural Banks were formed to assist the rural folk. Thus, the banking sector in India comprises of the Commercial Banks (both in public and private sector), Cooperative Banks and Regional Rural Banks.

Banking system in India has passed through five stages.

1. Evolutionary Phase (Prior to 1950)
2. Foundation Phase (1950–1968)
3. Expansion Phase (1968–1984)
4. Consolidation Phase (1984–1990)
5. Reformatory Phase (1990–till now)

1. Evolutionary Phase (Prior to 1950)

Enactment of RBI Act, 1935 gave birth to Scheduled Banks in India, and some of these banks had already been established around 1881, the prominent one is Allahabad Bank established in 1865. The first bank with Indian ownership and management was Oudh Commercial Bank (1881) followed by Ayodhya Bank (1884), the Punjab National Bank (1894), etc. During 1901-1914, twelve more banks were started, prominent among which were Bank of Baroda (1906), the Canara Bank (1906), The Indian Bank (1907), the Bank of India (1908) and Central Bank of India (1911). In 1921, three presidency banks were amalgamated to form the Imperial Bank of India to extend banking facilities to industries in all parts of the country. It used to play the role of central bank and regulatory authority of banks. Later in 1935 RBI came into existence as the Central Bank of India and operated as a regulating authority of banks, bank to the government, lender of last resort and also a note issuing authority.

2. Foundation Phase (1950–1968)

The banking scenario during the period 1950–1968 presented a strong focus on class banking on security rather than purpose, being the emphasis to have sound banking system in India. Banking Regulation Act was passed in 1949 to conduct and control operations of the Commercial Banks in India. Later Imperial Bank was transformed into State Bank of India, redefining its role in the economy, to strengthen the cooperative credit structure, provide long-term finance to agriculture and industry on institutional grounds. During 1951, the number of commercial banks had been declined to 566. Before 1968 only RBI and Associate banks of SBI were mainly controlled by the government. Some of the associates were fully owned subsidiaries while some had a very small shareholding by individuals and rest by RBI.

3. Expansion Phase (1968–1984)

This phase witnessed socialization of banking in 1968. Commercial banks were taken as agents of change and social control on banks. As all the banks except SBI and its seven subsidiaries were in private sector they could not be influenced to serve social interests. So banks were nationalized in two stages. The 1st stage of nationalization was taken up in 1969 with fourteen banks and 2nd stage in 1980 with six banks. This period was characterized by the death of private banking and dominance of social banking over commercial banking. During this period only, i.e. in 1975 Regional Rural Banks were set up and in 1982 NABARD came into existence with priority sector as its focus. There were number of ups and downs in the number of commercial banks existence. In spite of the unparalleled growth in banking industry in terms of reach, business parameters and employment the banking industry had hardly anytime to consider other issues such as support systems required for efficient operations, control mechanisms and profitability.

4. Consolidation Phase (1984–1990)

A series of policy initiatives were taken with the objectives of consolidating the gains of branch expansion undertaken by the banks, and so relaxing the regulations. Serious attention was paid to improve house-keeping, customer services, credit management and staff productivity and profitability of banks. By this time 90% of commercial banks were in public sector and closely regulated. Indian Banking Association along with RBI regulated the composition of assets of banks, Cash Reserve Ratio (CRR) and Statutory Liquidity Ratio (SLR) and directions towards priority sector lending and small loaning facility.

5. Reformatory Phase (1990–till now)

Due to the economic crisis in 1991 the economy suffered from serious inflationary pressures, emerging scarcities of essential commodities and breakdown of fiscal discipline. Various macro-economic, structural, reformatory measures were undertaken in the field of foreign trade, tax system, industrial policy, financial and other sectors. During the last decade banking sector in India has gone metamorphosis.

In the banking industry there has been an unexampled growth and diversification. During the last thirty years since nationalization, tremendous changes have taken place in the banking industry. The banks on shedding their traditional function innovated, improved and came out with new types of services to cater to the needs of their customers. Massive branch-expansion in rural and underdeveloped areas, mobilization of savings and expansion of credit facilities particularly in priority sectors resulted in widening and deepening of financial infrastructure and which transferred the basic character of class-banking into mass-banking.

Considerable innovation and diversification in the business of major commercial banks was found. Some banks were engaged in the areas of consumer credit, credit cards, merchant banking, leasing and mutual funds etc. Subsidiaries for merchant banking, leasing and mutual funds were already set up by some bank and many are in progress. Later factoring and securitization were commenced. The banks also have business venture into project financing. Venture capital schemes are basically introduced to inculcate entrepreneurship among the qualified technocrats.

A new scheme of 'working capital financing' was launched by the financial institutions and banks to focus more on short-term lending for their high exposure to infrastructural projects. They reduce their average credit maturity by emphasizing on short-term lending not exceeding a period of three years as a precautionary step for asset liability mismatch. Merchant banking services have been started for the purpose of rendering services to professional advice and services to enterprises in formulating and implementing projects and helping them to raise capital from the market and avail financial assistance from various financial intermediaries. The concept of 'consortium financing' has been introduced by the institutions and banks which were later replaced by an informal system of loan syndication. Next to these banks also added 'life insurance businesses' to the existing product range.

Despite this laudable progress, certain serious problems have emerged in the form of downfall in productivity and efficiency and profitability erosion in banking sector. The quality of loan portfolio was an obstacle for income generation and enhancement of capital funds. Inadequacy of capital was accompanied by inadequacy of loan loss provisions. Due to fast and massive expansion of branches mainly in rural and un-remunerative places and inadequate progress in the upgradation of work technology, profitability of banks has been eroded. The deterioration in financial health of banking system reached such a point that remedial measures were to be taken soon so that it could not further erode the real value of return on savings, that could show adverse impact on depositors and investors confidence. Thus Narsimham Committee was set up to check the condition of Banking sector and recommend measures for its improvement in the year 1990.

Diversification of ownership of public sector banks (PSBs) has been permitted. Out of twenty-seven banks, eight banks accounting

50.5% of assets of PSBs have been diversified. Later domestic and foreign banks are allowed into the game. Further banking environment in terms of deposits and lending rates have been deregulated, statutory conditions have been reduced and banks have been provided freedom to decide their operations at their discretion. Certain prudential norms relating to income recognition, asset classification, provisions, capital adequacy norms, and exposure limits etc., have been subjected to commercial bank bearing upon international standards. One of the important developments in the recent past is that banks have entered into the arena of 'project financing' which is used to be the exclusive domain of financial institution. The banks along with other banking services, seeks to offer short-term lending and other services. This development has brought a step closer to Universal Banking. Thus commercial banks have become the financial supermarkets with a wide variety of services besides its traditional services, such as customer financing, leasing, credit cards etc. Investment banking, underwriting and other capital market activities, trading and broking etc., are now offered by banks as in-group services.

Commercial banks were also permitted to raise equity share capital from the capital market. Banking Companies Act was amended in May 1994 providing for the privatization of nationalized banks. As such, private individuals and companies including NRIs could hold shares in banks up to 40%. Next important development is the entry of Commercial banks into the Insurance business. With the passage of Insurance Regulatory and Development Authority (IRDA) Act 1999, Commercial banks have been permitted to enter into insurance business. The RBI has issued guidelines. RBI has stipulated that banks shall hold a maximum of 51% of the insurance venture. It has however, made an exception for the SBI. Further a bank to enter into insurance business must have a net worth of Rs. 500 crore and foreign partner is allowed to hold not more than 26%. Some of the private sector institutions like HDFC having tied up with 'Standard life' have received the licence. Likewise ICICI has tied up with 'Prudential' for life insurance clearance.

In November 2000, the government of India took a decision to privatize nineteen public sector banks by reducing its stake from 51% to 31%. Accordingly Banking Companies (Acquisition and Transfer of Undertakings) Act, 1970 and 1980 are amended. These banks will continue to be statutory bodies and will not be converted into companies under Companies Act. This amendment will not apply to State Bank of India which is governed by separate Act. The SBI will continue to hold a majority stake in SBI, which along with its associate banks, controls one-third of the country's banking business.

Along with these developments computerization of banks and its branches has been made such that almost all the banking branches have the facility of internet for the purpose of speedier and prudent activities. This is one of the most important innovations which changed the structure of banking sector today. E-Banking, Electronic clearing system, Electronic cash with Smart Cards, Credit Cards, Debit Cards etc., phone banking, Internet and Intranet banking have come into existence, and well functioning by now.

TECHNIQUES OF INNOVATIVE BANKING

The whole history of the development of banking system in India, since independence, particularly after the bank nationalization in 1969, is a story of numerous diversifications and innovations introduced in the functioning of banks with a view to expand and improve their performance in accordance with the changing needs of the economy. Important innovations in banking which have been introduced recently are as follows:

1. ***SOCIAL BANKING***: After nationalization, the commercial banks of India have adopted a new policy orientation to meet the socio-economic obligations of the country. The important aspects of social orientation are:
   (a) Alignment of credit policy with the overall objectives of the government.
   (b) Allocation of credit in accordance with the requirements of the planned economic development of the country.
   (c) Reduction of regional disparities in spreading the banks to achieve the balanced development of the country.
   (d) A lead role in the development of credit at district level.
   (e) Greater financial assistance to the priority sectors of the economy and weaker sections of the society on easy and convenient terms.

Changes in the functioning for the achievement of social orientation banking:

- ➢ Expansion of bank offices in the rural and unbanked area.

- Gradual decline in the security and guarantee oriented approach and laying more emphasis on the purpose, viability and credit worthiness of the project for which loan is required.
- Decline in share of bank credit to large and medium industries and rise in that to small scale industries.
- Lead bank scheme was introduced in December, 1969 to evolve a consortium approach on the part of the commercial banks to develop on the basis of area approach, formatted on districtwise plans for branch expansion, deposit mobilization and credit allocation.
- Efforts are being made to extend housing finance by the banks in rural and semi-urban areas.
- Increased flow of bank credit extended to smaller and poorer borrowers of weaker sections of the society and also for women borrowers.
- Greater provision of bank credit has been made to the priority sectors like agriculture, small and cottage industries, export, small road transport, etc.
- Bank credit is provided under IRDP which aims at removing imbalances in the rural areas and for alround development of rural population.
- Differential Interest Rate (DIR) scheme was introduced in 1972 to provide financial assistance to the economically weaker sections of the society, the physically handicapped persons and orphanages and women homes at nominal interest.
- For bringing about major change in the quality and productivity of rural lending, service area approach has been adopted.
- SBI has undertaken a village adoption scheme under which a village is selected for development by meeting complete financial requirements.

2. ***PARTICIPATORY APPROACH***: In 1970, the RBI introduced Participatory Certificates Scheme with the objective of greater mobilization of funds, less recourse to the RBI and diversifying the availability of financial instruments. The Participatory Certificates Scheme has now been replaced by two types of

inter-bank participations (IBPs) – one on risk sharing basis and the other without it. Their purpose is to even out short-term liquidity within the banking system.

3. ***CONSORTIUM APPROACH***: It was introduced by Reserve Bank of India in 1974. According to this approach more than one bank would finance a single borrower requiring larger credit limits. This approach —
    (i) Enables bank to spread risk of lending.
    (ii) Breaks the monopoly of big banks to have larger spread risk of accounts.
    (iii) Enable to share experience and expertise.
    (iv) Introduces uniformity in approaches to lending.
    (v) Evolves banks to pool their resources.
    (vi) Checks multiple financing of the same account.

4. CREDIT CARD FACILITY : Commercial banks introduced the credit card facility in the early 1980s. In the following years, this facility has become increasingly popular among the banks as well as the public. Credit card is a convenient medium of exchange which enables its holder to purchase goods and services from the member establishments without using money directly by hand.

5. NEW TECHNOLOGY : The commercial banks now are fast introducing mechanization, computerization and many new techniques in their operating with the objective of improving the customer service, productivity and operational efficiency. The facets of new technology consists of —

Internet banking : With the advent of internet, banking is taken to a place of convenience for its customers. The customer can directly access the branch database with the help of his PC and internet connection. The factors that made to adopt this may be easy accessibility reluctance to change, security, convenience etc.

Shared Payment Network System (SPNS) : Under this system we come across ATMs, i.e. Automatic Teller Machines which function as any time money accessors at particular centers. Through these the customer can get his account checked for balance and withdraw money without going to a particular branch of a bank.

Electronic Funds Transfer System (EFTS) : EFTSs are transfer of funds instantly in the same city, between cities and countries. They are known by different names such as ATMs, Cash Dispensers, Point of Sale Terminals (POST) and home banking, Mail Transfers (MT), Telegraphic Transfers (TT) etc.

Electronic Clearing System : A facility was made for the purpose of making single bulk payments to different beneficiaries like salary, dividend etc. RBI will process the data of the companies' payments and settle it by debiting the companies account and pass on credits to beneficiaries account. Similarly a system is also for debt clearing.

Electronic Cash : Electronic cash, e-cash, digital money or digital cash provider is the means to transfer money between parties over internet.

E-Credit : In electronic credit conversational credit cards may be used along with a PIN. The PIN is a secret code that the customer must enter while using the credit card on-line. The following are some of the types of credit cards.

(i) *Smart Cards* : Smart card is a credit card that can be carried in a wallet. These cards have a process and memory on the card and carried around by the customer. These cards are referred to PCMCIA cards, since the card may be designed to fit in the PCMICA slots of a computer.

(ii) *Memory Cards* : Contain space for data storage. These cards can be used to store passwords or PIN. Many telephone cards use these memory cards.

(iii) *Shared Key Cards* : Can store a private key such that these cards are used in public key crypto systems. In this way the users can plug in the card to a workstation and the workstation can read the private key for encryption or decryption. Some cards may also process encryption or decryption.

(iv) *Signature Carrying Cards* : These contain a set of pre-generated random numbers. These numbers can be used to generate electronic cash.

(v) *Signature Creating Cards* : These carry a co-processor that can be used to generate large random numbers. These numbers can be used for assigning as serial numbers for electronic cash.

6. DIVERSIFICATION : Since mid-1980s the commercial banks in India have diversified into many related areas, such as Merchant banking, Mutual funds, Venture capital and Equipment leasing, housing finance, Hire-Purchase credit, either on their own or through setting up specialized subsidiaries.

*7. **CONSOLIDATION PHASE*** : Since mid-1980, banks have also entered the phase of consolidation, sophistication and greater productivity. The principles of viability, efficiency, prudence and profitability are now receiving as much attention as social banking. Consolidations with moderate and selective expansions are the keywords in banking operations. Apart from social functions the banks would now pay greater attention to —

(i) Improvement in financial viability.
(ii) Selective modernization and computerization.
(iii) Better consumer service.
(iv) Better managerial culture.
(v) Adequate profitability.
(vi) Strong and healthy organizational structure.
(vii) Effective system of internal supervision, control, house- keeping and training.

*8. **MERCHANT BANKING*** : Commercial banks have entered into merchant banking business. They have set-up merchant banking division and are underwriting issues. Some of the banks have set up separate subsidiaries and offer wide range of merchant banking services. At the end of 1991 eight commercial banks have started their equipment leasing and merchant banking subsidiaries.

Merchant Banking in India: Merchant banking was formally initiated into the Indian capital markets when Grindlays Bank received the licence from Reserve Bank in 1967. It started with management of capital issues, recognized the emerging needs of entrepreneurs for diverse financial services ranging from production, planning and systems design to market research. Following Grindlays Bank, Citi Bank set up its merchant banking division in 1970. It took up assistance evaluation of new projects and management consultancy services. SBI started merchant banking division in 1972 to render corporate advice and assistance to small and medium entrepreneurs.

Services rendered by Merchant Banks :

(i) Organizing and extending finance for investment in projects.
(ii) Assistance in financial management.
(iii) Acceptance house business.
(iv) Raising Euro-Dollar loans and issue of foreign currency bonds.
(v) Financing local authorities.

(vi) Financing export of capital goods, ships, hydropower installation, railways and hire-purchase transactions.

(vii) Equipment leasing.

(viii) Mergers and takeovers.

(ix) Valuation of assets.

(x) Investment management and promotion of investment trust.

The Commercial Banks that followed SBI were Central Bank of India, Bank of India and Syndicate Bank in 1977, Bank of Baroda, Standard Chartered Bank and Mercantile Bank in 1978, United Bank of India, United Commercial Bank, Punjab National Bank, Canara Bank and Indian Overseas Bank in late seventies and early eighties. Among the development banks ICICI started merchant banking activities in 1973 followed by IFCI (1986) and IDBI.

Merchant banking activities are regulated by,

(i) Guidelines of SEBI and Ministry of Finance.

(ii) Companies Act, 1956.

(iii) Listing guidelines of stock exchanges and

(iv) Securities Contracts (Regulation) Act, 1956.

9. MUTUAL FUNDS : Mutual Funds are either open-ended or closed-ended financial intermediaries which obtain the resources by selling units or shares.

Open-End : Here, the fund itself is ready to buy back the shares surrendered and sell new shares. Thus, there are no fixed number of outstanding shares.

Closed-End : The mutual fund management sells a limited number of shares. It does not stand ready to redeem or repurchase these shares.

Several commercial banks in India have recently entered into the field of mutual funds namely SBI mutual fund – *Magnum*, *Can Share Fund or Can Stock Fund* of Canara Bank, *Swarnpushpa* mutual fund of Indian Bank, *Bank of India mutual fund* of Bank of India. This offers the banks to collect funds from untapped areas. They enable small investor to obtain high-return low-risk combination from the indirect holding of equities and other assets. They are either income-oriented or growth-oriented or income and growth oriented funds and offer many other financial services such as insurance, share exchange, housing and bank loans etc., to their investors. On the investment side, mutual funds may specialize in using their funds in different areas. Depending upon this, they may be called Common-Stock Funds, Bond Funds, Balanced (Mixed) Funds, Municipal Bond Funds, Money Market Funds, Real Estate Investment Funds etc.

Till 1986, UTI had a monopoly of mutual fund business in India. Now many other mutual funds have also come up in the market. In the banking sector, mutual funds have been set up mainly by the merchant banking subsidiaries of some public sector banks, such as the SBI, Canara Bank, Punjab National Bank, BOI, Indian Bank, Andhra Bank, LIC and GIC, also have set up mutual funds. Besides private sector mutual funds are also coming up. Most of the schemes of mutual funds in India are closed-end schemes.

10. HIRE PURCHASE CREDIT : Hire Purchase means purchase of goods on the basis of installments. Hire Purchase or Installment credit refers to term loans provided for the purchase of consumer goods, services and sometimes producer goods. These goods are repayed in installments during the specified period. In India, hire purchase finance is provided by retail and wholesale traders, specialized hire purchase finance companies and Commercial Banks, and financial institutions. Bulk of hire purchase credit goes to the road transport industry for the purchase of vehicles and their spare parts.

11. VENTURE CAPITAL : Venture Capital Fund (VCF) is a new type of financial intermediary which has emerged in India in late 1980's. Venture Capital Funds (VCFs) are mutual funds or institutional investors which provide risk capital, management and marketing expertise to highly risky and new private business, particularly in technology-oriented or knowledge-intensive industries. Venture Capital is high risk – high return business. It is a form of equity financing designed specially for funding high risk and high reward projects. It not only plays an important role in financing high technology projects, but also helps to turn research and development project into commercial production. Venture Capital, besides financing the technology is also involved in fostering the growth and development of enterprises.

Venture Capital Funds in India:

(i) Risk Capital Foundation was sponsored by IFCI in March 1975 later reconstituted as Risk Capital and Technology Finance Corporation (RCTFC) Limited in January 1988.

(ii) Venture Fund of IDBI, started in 1986.

(iii) Venture Capital Fund of SIDBI in 1992-1993.

(iv) Technology Development and Infrastructure Corporation of India (TDICI) by ICICI in 1988.

(v) Credit Capital Venture Fund (India) Limited (CCVP) and Venture Capital Funds set up by IDBI and UTI, and Commercial Banks.

In banking sector, Grindlays Bank has set up India's first private sector venture capital fund, namely, *Indian Investment Fund.* Among the Indian Banks, the subsidiaries of SBI and Canara Bank have floated Venture Capital Funds.

13. FACTORING SERVICE : Factor is a financial institution which manages the collection of accounts receivable of business firms and bears the credit risk associated with those account. Factoring Service implies the advance payment of credit by the bank to the customer. It is to be collected later on from the debtor. The bank charges commission for this service. Factoring service, thus, solves the problem of shortage of funds of small scale industrial units. The scope of factoring in modern times has considerably increased. It is a continued service arrangement under which a financial institution or a bank undertakes the task of recording, collecting and protecting the book debts for its clients and also purchases bills receivables.

Factoring Service in India : The first factoring service in India has been started by the SBI, namely the SBI Commercial and Factoring Services Limited. In India, the SBI and Canara Bank are the only two banks which have set up separate subsidiaries for undertaking factoring services.

14. OFFSHORE BANKING : Many Banks now have an international dimension in the form of Offshore or Overseas banking. The operation of offshore banking is truly international business in which bank and management groups in many countries participate. Ninety-seven branches including offshore branches and mobile agencies of nine Indian Commercial banks (which include eight public sector banks and one private sector bank) were operating in foreign countries as on 31-03-1996. These branches are spread over twenty-five countries and specialized in various areas of international banking including financing of foreign trade.

15. CUSTOMER SERVICES : A number of measures have been taken to improve the quality of customer services offered by the banks to depositors and borrowers. Important among these are given:

(i) Till June 1996 about 1400 branches have been computerized. Almost all the banks have started in many of the branches.

(ii) Facilities like passbook printing, self service terminals for customers, terminals at customer places etc., have been started in many of the branches.

(iii) Efforts were made to conduct SWIFT (Society for World Wide Inter Bank Financial Telecommunication) training courses for Indian banking community on regular basis.

(iv) In 1997, Shared Payment Network System (SPNS) was started at Mumbai. It is proposed to extend this Network to other cities.

(v) RBI launched the Electronic Clearing Service (ECS) in April 1995 at Mumbai and Chennai. Once this system is made available across the country, it will reduce the number of physical instruments that pass through the traditional clearing system.

(vi) RBI has also started the Electronic Funds Transfer (EFT) in Mumbai and Chennai for retail customers.

(vii) Banks are making an attempt to evaluate services rendered in terms of expectations and requirements of the customers and to redress customer complaints.

(viii) Customer service audit are being conducted periodically to ensure meaningful implementation of Goiporia Committee Recommendations.

16. BANKING OMBUDSMEN SCHEME Banking Ombudsmen Scheme was announced in June 1995 to provide quick and inexpensive facility to resolve customers' grievances. Eleven Ombudsmen are now functioning in the country. They hear and redress those grievances of customers which have not been resolved to their satisfaction within a stipulated period of two months. The complaints can come under the areas like:

(i) Deficiency in bank services like non-payment or delay in collection, handling of cash and currency, non-adherence to working hours, complaints from NRI and exporters.

(ii) Complaints concerning loans and advances relating to delay in sanction, non-observance of RBI directions on interest rates.

17. SERVICE AREA APPROACH : In 1988, the RBI has started the service area approach for rural lending. This approach refers to a system of assigning special areas to each bank branch in which it can concentrate for productive lending and thus contribute to the development of the area. It aims at making available adequate and timely credit for meaningful activities and ensuring effective recycling of bank funds. Service area approach intended to bring about a major change in the quality and productivity of rural lending.

The implementation of service area approach involves the following five stages :

(i) Identification of the service area for each bank branch.

(ii) Survey of the villages in the service area for assessing the potential for lending for different activities and identification of beneficiaries for assistance.

(iii) Preparation of credit plans on an annual basis for the service area by each branch.

(iv) Inter and Intra co-ordination between credit institution and field level development agencies on an on-going basis for effective implementation of credit plans.

(v) Continuous system of monitoring the progress in the implementation of the plans and individual schemes.

The merits that arise from this approach are,

(a) Concentrated attention to the development of the service area designated for each branch.

(b) Duplication of efforts is avoided.

(c) Instead of scattering over wide areas, planned and organized lending is possible.

(d) Effective monitoring of the end-use of credit and assessment of its impact on production levels.

(e) A sense of pride and motivation can be developed and use of credit can be optimized by establishing better linkages between production and productivity.

INNOVATIVE BANKING IN SELECTED BANKS

Innovative banking practices that started after 19th century has taken up boost during the end. Various types of activities are undertaken by the bankers to compete with the present situation along with technological development which added air to the fire of changing trends in almost all the commercial banks. The commercial banks set up several schemes not only to attract the customers but also for the survival of the fittest in the banking sector. Thus, we discuss here various schemes / financial services that were undertaken by the bankers in their regular activities.

INDUSIND BANK

IndusInd Bank is the first Indian commercial bank which was certified by ISO-9001 in the year 2000 for all of its branches, immediately after the completion of 10 years of operation. The various innovations that are dealt within the functioning of banks include phone banking, internet banking, mobile banking and inter branch banking etc.

The accounts by the names Privilege Savings Account, Business Current Account, Fixed Deposits Comfort account etc. are organized to attract various categories of customers. Similarly senior citizens scheme has been opened for the purpose of senior citizens and a number of facilities are available to them. Under privilege account several privileges are given to the particular customer like free out station cheque collection, discounted rates on foreign currency drafts, cheque return protection, filing of tax returns etc. Privilege home banking consists of delivery at door step, cash pick up from door step, foreign currency travellers' cheques, Privilege time savers in the form of demand drafts through correspondent banking arrangements at the place where the bank has no branch, anywhere banking, multicity cheques, Electronic funds transfer – instant remittances, courier-pick up and delivery etc.

Indusnet is the net banking arm of IndusInd bank which facilitates its customers to do banking comfortably from house or from office. This is the easiest way to access the account through the internet, over a secured platform with on line assistance from personal bankers and can obtained account balances, past transactions for each account, deposit and loan details, other queries etc. over the internet.

Other innovative services that are ensured to the customers are:

- *24 – Hour ATM Network access* : Automatic Teller Machines run round the clock assuring any time money to the customer at various branches spread all over the country.
- *Power card facility* : International debit card–power card facility is accepted at over 50000 merchant establishments in India and at over 800000 ATMs world wide.

- *Mobile banking / Phone banking* : It is nothing but accessing bank on mobile phone for the purposes of account balance, mini-statements, cheque book request, statement request, any where, any time. Certain local phone banking numbers are provided to customers by which get information by simply dialing.
- *Fast cash system* : The modern technology today enables the customers to bank at any IndusInd branch and access funds from any of their branches across the country.
- *Fast Forex* : Global funds transfer scheme is also available which moves the funds globally from and to the particular designated account within a minimum period.
- *Depository services* : Under this through a depository account a particular customer can manage securities electronically.
- *Credit cards* : Internationally accepted credit cards are issued by the bank.
- *NRI Services* : IndusInd bank offers NRIs fast, convenient and personalized services. On offer are a suit of deposit products with attractive rates of return such as NRE, NRO and FCNR accounts as well as instant remittance services.
- *Resident foreign currency account (RFC)* : This is for export of goods or services and foreign currency transactions to protect from exchange fluctuations.

UTI BANK

UTI Bank Ltd., was established in 1994 as the first private sector bank in the post-liberalization era. In five years, as on 31st March 2000, UTI Bank has 49 branches in all the main centres in the country. Each and every branch has been designed to offer a full range of services in corporate and retail banking, international banking, treasury management, merchant and investment banking.

The innovative techniques used in the bank for their customers are —

- *Salary power* : Under this innovative scheme the bank assures the business entities to spare themselves from the monthly hassle of making salary payments to their employees. They have all the facilities as that a customer has like debit and credit cards, ATMs, Tele-banking and net banking priority banking for selected employees facilities and also at par cheque facility to all of its account holders.

- *Power loans* : The bank offers personal loans in the name of personal power (to meet personal expenses, big and small), power home (regarding home loans), consumer power (regarding enjoyable facilities at home such as finance for purchasing a washing machine, refrigerator etc.) and power drive (for car loans etc.) study power (loans for education of children) to its customers.
- *Encash-24* : The bank's Encash–24 is a dynamic two-in-one account that combines the liquidity of a savings account with the high returns of a fixed deposit.
- *iConnect* : This is the internet banking facility of the bank by which the customer can get any information regarding demat holdings, transfer funds, review term deposits, online trading, mutual fund purchases and online shopping etc. by click of a mouse.
- *Priority Banking* : It offers a host of investment and lifestyle privileges to enrich the banking experience. A relationship manager caters to the needs of picking up and dropping of cheques and cash, free passbook updates and financial advisory services such as insurance, RBI bonds (taxable and tax-free), mutual funds, capital gain tax saving bonds etc.
- *Cash management services* : Through this the bank brings a wide variety of collection and payment services for improved liquidity through faster access to the funds and total control on fund movements through customized MIS reports. These include collection services that offer local cheque collection (LCC) payment / disbarment services whereby one can issue cheques payable 'at par' in the country, warrants payable 'at par' for dividend / interest payments and avail electronic clearing services (ECS).
- *Depository account* : A depository account is opened for dematerialization of shares. Under this system physical security holdings are converted into electronic format. This ensures corporate benefits, rematerialisation, pledge / hypothecation facilities of shares, freezing / locking of accounts, nomination facility, tele depository services for getting latest balances in the demat account, loans against these accounts etc.
- As a salute to defence forces the bank offers several facilities to the defence personnel who hold accounts in the bank and even after their retirement.

- *Pension account* : The senior citizens can grab the opportunity of pension account under EPFO offering host of facilities for convenient banking as the latest technologies also ensure that the pension is transferred on line and no body needs to wait for it. These account holders also enjoy all the facilities a normal customer holds.
- *NRI account* : The portfolio of NRI products and services includes:

  Non-Resident (External) Rupee Deposit, Non-Resident (Ordinary) Rupee Deposit, Foreign Currency Non-Resident (Banks) Deposit, Capital Market Services through Portfolio Investment Scheme (PIS) and Demat accounts. For higher yield without exchange risk Foreign Currency Triple M (FCTM) is one of the innovative scheme. NRI services hub solves the Queries of NRI account holders.

  Other innovative facilities like International Debit Card consisting of free personal accident cover, online shopping mall and utility bills payment facility, free family account to make internal transfers from NRE savings.

ING Vysya BANK

ING Vysya is a premier private sector Indian bank (formerly known as The Vysya Bank Ltd.) with a heritage of 70 years. ING Vysya is a part of ING Vysya group in India which is active in life insurance, asset management banking. It intends to bring to its customers a range of integrated financial solutions tailored to meet the needs of life insurance, mutual funds, financial services and banking.

Its Orange Savings Account offers its customers —

- Free Personal Accident Insurance cover of Rs. 3,00,000 for 3 years.
- Annual Hospitalization cover of Rs. 35,000 for 3 years.
- Free Sambandh international debit card which is powered by Maestro and Cirrus from Master card.
- Free Demat account to buy/sell/hold stocks and shares in electronic format
- ATM facility
- Internet banking, Phone banking
- Bill Pay facility
- Smart serve services designed exclusively for the customer

which provides the convenience in their personal and professional life, like home services, information services, travel, gifts, entertainment and emergency etc.

- It consists of ING Vysya Nifty Plus Fund which is an open-ended index linked equity scheme, enabling the investors to participate in the Indian Economy through investment in stocks.
- NIP Fund is an open-end fund. Monthly income is not assured and is subject to availability of distributable surplus. Investment is in government bonds and high quality debt instruments. Investment maturity is managed based on interest rate outlook or other considerations.

- *Relationship banking*

  Types of NRI accounts: It offers the convenience of maintaining account in both Indian and Foreign currency by Indian Rupee accounts like NR Ordinary (NRO) NR External (NRE), Foreign Currency NR account (FCNR) and Resident Foreign Currency account (to benefit those NRIs who have returned home for permanent settlement after a stay of minimum one year) can be held in any of the four specified foreign currencies.

- *Schemes to access Indian Capital Market*

  VYS Prime: Simplc way to access primary market through bank.

  VYS Invest: Easy access to secondary capital market in India.

- *Remittance facilities for NRIs*

  Remittances can be made in any of the designated countries by way of Telegraphic Transfer through correspondent banks, Mail Transfers, Demand Drafts, cheques etc., preferably pay abroad. In case of emergencies, SWIFT (Society for World wide Inter-bank Financial Telecommunication) transfer is also possible using the banks SWIFT code Vysya in BB. Through Western Union Money Transfer services sound rupee remittances from across the globe is also possible.

IDBI BANK

IDBI offers various facilities to its savings account holders like instant account opening, any branch banking, International debit-cum-ATM card, Internet Banking, Phone Banking and SMS Banking, Investment advisory service, Preferred customer banking, Utility Bill Payment,

Demat account, Prepaid gift card, Personal loans, loans against securities, easy fill service at ATM or through SMS for prepaid mobile phone anywhere anytime.

Investment advisory services includes offers regarding various investment avenues like mutual funds, fixed income investments like government bonds, fixed deposit options like MIP, Sweep-in FD, re-investment FD and Recurring FD, Birla Sun Life Insurance and well trained investment advisors to help in making right decisions.

- Roaming current accounts for availing doorstep banking where by customer can pick up cash and cheques everyday.
- Preferred customer banking service includes exclusive privileges like waivers on the charges for select banking transactions, enhanced limits on complimentary debit card, preferential rates on loans etc.
- An innovative service beyond banking is ATM Next which gives information regarding cricket scores, daily horoscopes and movie schedules etc.
- SMS Banking, a step ahead of Phone Banking, by which bank can be accessed for the purpose of balance inquiry, bill payment, demat information and many other innovative services.
- IDBI introduces World Currency Card which is a mixture of credit card, travelers' cheques and cash.
  - It can be used for withdrawing cash in local currency
  - Offers deal with air tickets, holiday packages, travel accessories and a comprehensive insurance package.
  - Easy replacement facility if the card is lost by just calling any Phone Banking number.
- Tax payment facility for paying taxes like Corporation tax, Income tax, Wealth tax, Dividend distribution tax and other TDSs by simply calling a representative from the bank.

- *NRI banking:* This consists of —
  - NR External (NRE) Account for investment needs.
  - NR Ordinary (NRO) Account for local funds.
  - Foreign Currency NR (FCNR-B) Scheme for retaining the funds in foreign currency.
  - With IDBIs business special current account and business premium current account, the bank offers free fund transfers, free cheque collection and free inter-branch banking.

CANARA BANK

Corporate cash management services (CCMS), an innovative service offered by Canara Bank for speedy collection of cheques and other instruments, pooling of funds at designated centers, provide funds to the corporates/business houses/partnership firms etc.

Under CCMS the products of the bank are:

1. Super fast service – local cheque collection service.
2. Fast track service – Up country cheque collection service.
3. Bulk collection service – Bulk cheque collection service.

CITI BANK

CITI bank comes out with the innovative products of its bank along with the services provided by other banks like ATMs, Credit cards, Internet banking and financial services. Such products are :

1. *Woman's account*: The account for women who are either house wives or salaried or business women. Several facilities of free online banking services are assured so that they can do their shopping from their homes.
2. *Financial planning*: For the purpose of business people as a help in business financial activities for their planning and other various informative services which benefit the planning of the business persons.
3. *NRI services*: Several services are provided to NRIs also for their day-to-day activities and business purposes.
4. *Insurance*: Several types of insurance facilities are provided to their customers.

BANK OF BARODA (BOB)

BOB is 'round the clock around the globe' bank, having 61 international branches (both subsidiaries and joint ventures) spreading over 16 countries. It is the second largest bank of India spreading more than 2500 branches and 116 authorized Forex branches in India.

Services provided by the banks include general banking services with retail lending, NRI banking, foreign currency deposits, and syndication of loans of Indian corporates as well as rated multi-national corporates, correspondent banking services, trade finance, international treasury services etc.

BANK OF PUNJAB

Bank of Punjab consists of :

1. Personal banking services like current accounts, savings accounts, BOP multiplier account etc.
2. Business banking services like working capital finance, term loan, leasing, cash management etc.
3. NRI services like on-line accounts, portfolio investments for NRIs, inward remittances, outward remittances etc.
4. Forex services like international trade, foreign exchange etc.
5. Demat features like list of scrips, demat account etc.

STATE BANK OF INDIA (SBI)

SBI introduces Vishwa Yatra Card. The services provided by it are:

- Personal banking, gold banking, NRI banking, international banking, corporate banking, small business finance, rural banking, government business and other services.
- Working capital finance, for financing inventories, managing internal cash flows, supporting supply chains, funding production and marketing operations.
- Project finance which covers industrial projects, capacity expansion at existing manufacturing units, construction ventures or other infrastructure projects.
- Channel financing is an innovative finance mechanism by which the bank meets various fund necessities along the supply chain at supplier's end itself, thus helping to sustain business flow along the arteries of the enterprise.
- Equipment leasing–for arranging lease contracts for procuring expensive equipment for the project or plant. Lease contracts worth minimum of Rs.5 crores for 5-7 years are provided.
- Loan syndication: SBI leverages its vast network of relationships to arrange syndicated credit products for corporate clients and industrial projects.

HONGKONG-SHANGHAI BANKING CORPORATION (HSBC)

HSBC provides the following innovative services:

- Factoring
- Quick finance against invoices

- Instant DC advising
- E-mail DC advising for great efficiency, convenience and cost savings
- Internet banking, Phone banking, ATM network, etc.

CONCLUSION

In India, the change in the banking and financial system has accelerated due to the global market scenario that existed at times. India is able to achieve great heights in the field of banking sector and customer services. This is possible only through the latest technology that it can cultivate in its daily and routine activities in banking business competing with the rest of the world. As 'Necessity is the mother of invention', innovation has become the order of the day. However, innovative banking with new technology should not result in innovations in banking fraud. The case of Global Trust Bank is a classic example. Here, the shareholders of GTB stand to loose heavily. They may not get anything, inspite of the working of the GTB's branches under the umbrella of OBC. SEBI and RBI may think of formulating and implementing some suitable code of conduct.

2

TRENDS AND DEVELOPMENTS IN INDIAN BANKING INDUSTRY

A. B. Thapliyal*

The social banking era witnessed rapid branch expansion, tremendous growth in deposit mobilization and credit deployment, and attention to agricultural and rural credit, poverty alleviation schemes. Bank were to meet the target set for priority sector and for other schemes for weaker section. The goals for operational efficiency were like C.D. ratio, net profit maximization.

The financial sector reforms started in 1991 greatly affected the banking system. The Indian banking industry moved gradualy from a regulated environment to deregulated market. In one way the restrictons are lifted and operational freedom is granted but some other norms are evolved and prescribed for the banks. The banks tag along the prudential accounting norms, capital adequacy requirements and further global standards in efficiency and customer service.

The entry of new private and foreign banks changed the market scenario entirely. It led shift in marketing patterns in banking. The product centric approach is switched over to customer oriented approach. A range of new generation products like debit card, smart card, electronic clearing service, farmer and consumer credit card, ATM outlets entered in the banking business.

*Senior Lecturer, Deptt. of Commerce, H.N.B. Garhwal University Campus Badshashithaul (Tehri Garhwal) Uttaranchal.

The present Banking system in India was evolved to meet the financial need of trade and industry of the country. The constituents of the present Banking system in India are of varying origin and sizes. At the apex is the Reserve Bank of India (R.B.I), the Central Bank of the country, which is followed by the State Bank of India (S.B.I) which is created in July 1955 by nationalising the Imperial Bank of India. In 1959 an act of associate banks was established. In July 1969, 14 Scheduled Banks were nationalised and another six banks were also nationalised in April 1980. A Nationalished Bank (New Bank of India) was merged with P.N.B. in 1992-93. So at present there are 27 public sector Banks (1 SBI, 7 Associates of S.B.I. and 19 Nationalised Bank) are working with their branches in India and abroad. Besides these 27 Public Sector Banks (P.S.Bs.), 21 old private sector banks, 9 new private sector banks and 36 foreign banks are also working in India and abroad.

The progress of Indian Banking Industry is shown in the following table:

(Rs. in crore)

Year	*Total Branches*	*Deposits*	*Advances*	*Investment*	*Net profit*
Dec. 1950	4,163	1,002	553	389	N.A.
Dec. 1960	4,870	1,953	1,217	724	14.09
Dec. 1970	11,146	6,194	4,653	1825	13.80
Dec. 1980	34,594	43,987	27,267	13,455	N.A.
March 1990	58,914	2,02,720	1,11,274	66,832	555.33
March 2000	65,521	9,00,307	4,43,469	4,13,871	7,306.36
March 2001	N.A.	10,55,386	5,26,151	4,91,755	6,403.00
March 2002	66,355	12,02,699	6,45,743	5,88,058	11,572.00
March 2003	66,514	13,55,871	7,40,474	6,93,791	17,071.00

(Source : I.B.A. Buletin March 2001, page 19; Jan 2004 page 160, 309 and 312).

It is very clear from the above table that the progress of Indian Banking Industry from 1950 to 1970 (after independence and before nationalisation) was remarkable. Banks expanded their branches from 4163 to 11146 with a deposit growth of Rs. 5192 crore. The advance and investment figures are showning also a good progress during this period. The Banks show net profit of Rs. 13.80 crore at the end of Dec. 1970.

After the nationatisaton of Banks a banking revolution had seen in the country. Banks acted rapidly in every path of banking functions, such as branch expansion, deposit mobilisation, loan disbursements. Lead bank scheme and District credit plans had been introduced. Regional Rural Banks were established in 1975 to improve the requirements of rural areas. In the decade of 1970 to 1980, there was an expansion of 23,448 branches. Deposits, advances and investment were also increased.

After 1980, Banking Industry is functioning progressively with implementing the govt. targets and achieving the goals and aims in different parameters. Highest priorities has been given to social banking, attainment of priority sector credit, C.D. Ratio, rural and weaker sector upliftment, deposit mobilisation and achieving the net profit targets.

After comparison of the figures at the end of Dec. 1980 and March 1990 from the table mentioned above it is cleared that the progress of expansion of branches as well as deposits, advances and investments are rapidly increasing. In this decade the progress of banking industry was as under —

- Branch expansion–24,320
- Depsits increased Rs. 1,58,733 crore
- Advances increased Rs. 84,007 crore
- Investment increased Rs 53,377 crore
- Net profit was Rs. 555.33 crore at the end of March 1990

The priod of 1990 onwards can be mentioned as 'second banking revolution' for Indian Banking industry, because after 1990 many reform measures had been introduced in Banking Industry. Such as, New accounting system, capital adequacy norms, assets classification, minimum capital requirements, liberalisation measures etc. The annual growth of branch expansion during this decade was 1.1%, the annual average growth rate of deposits and advances were 16.1% and 14.8% respectively. The growth of investment was 20% and the net profit increased by Rs. 6751.03 crore during this decade. The progress of Banking Industry in India may also be seen in the beginning years of 21st centrury. It is clear that all the figures relating deposits, advances, Investment and net profit had increased. At the end of March 2003, total deposits was Rs. 13,55,871 crore, while total outstanding advances was Rs. 7,40,474 crore. Total Investment was Rs. 6,93,791 crore and Net profit was increased upto Rs 17,071 crore. Banking Industry today is intensively competitive. Regulations are much more refined now. While banks are given greater operational freedom, the quality of regulation has hightened with stringent norms prescribed in respect of capital adequacy, classification of assets, provisioning, valuation of investments etc. Regulation is evolved broadly on the emerging international developments which while promotes deregulation and liberalization at the same time prescribes stringent rules governing business operations and market developments.

Post reforms period (1990 onwards) in Indian Banking unleashed a wide range of new products and services. Driven by technology a number of new generation products such as electronic funds transfers, debit cards, smart cards, electronic clearing service, farm and consumer credit cards etc. are introduced. Retail banking has received the greatest thrust in the post-reform period. Deregulation of the insurance sector is envisaged to lead to further proliferation of the products.

While public sector continues to account for a major part of the banking, greater inroads are made by the private sector in the form of new banks allowed in the private sector, entry of a large number of foreign banks, partial divestment of the government equity in the public sector banks, allowing the public sector banks to dilute government equity upto 33 percent, allowing direct foreign investment in banking etc. Competition intensified with a larger base of players and non-banking financial institutions emerging stronger in a liberalized and deregulated environment. A code of governance in banking is yet to be evolved but the implementation of prudential norms and adoption of banking standards particularly in respect of transparency and disclosure has significant impact on the quality of governance in Indian banking.

Indian Banking is gearing up for absorbing the challenges of global finance. Starting with harmonization of the operational norms and procedures, endeavours are being made to enhance the quality and content of the efficiency parameters which is essential to withstand the impact of global competition. The ushering in the second generation reforms is envisaged to strengthen the role and performance of Indian Banking in this regard. The 21st century banking is going to be highly competitive and information technology driven. The networking of banks, remote access, ATM facilities etc, would transforms the face of banking industry.

The Indian banking industry has responded well to the challenging tasks put before them during the last 50 years and withstood the revolutionary changes by transforming dramatically, will once again prove their dynamism in meeting, with all the odds, the challenges that may arise in the years to come. In summation, banking industry in India is poised to meet the changing global environment. Significant progress has been made in India for strengthening the banking system under the financial sector reforms. However, the future would belong to those who would be able to offer excellent customer service by keeping pace with changing technology and transparent operations.

REFERENCES

1. Ammannaya K.K., Former Chairman, Varda Grameena Bank, Udubi : Indian Banking 2010, *IBA Bulletin*, Jan 2004, p. 160.
2. *IBA Special Bulletin*, January 2004, Trends and Selected Variables, 1993-94 to 2002-03. pp. 309 and 312.
3. Samual B., Chairman and MD, Allahabad Bank, Kolkata, *Indian Banking System*, March 2001, p. 19.
4. Srivastav R.M., *Management of Indian Financial Institutions*, Himalaya Publising House, New Delhi, 2000.

3

INNOVATIVE BANKING : A CHALLENGE BEFORE INDIAN BANKING

N. P. Singh*

Parmil Kumar**

The banking in our country is no longer the same as it was a couple of years before. It is neither expected to remain the same a couple of years after. The technology implementation resulted in the introduction of new products and services in the banking sector. The innovation refers to launch of new technology, products or services. The main innovations in the baking are–ATM, telebanking, remote access, CMS, Cards, Net banking mobile banking and connectivity. The innovative banking provides 24 hours service to the customers. There is a strong need for customer education in banking. It will be beneficial for bank and its clients both.

The liberalization, privatization and globalization changed the entire business environment for the banks. Earlier our banks have been in a very protected environment. Now emergence of new private and foreign banks in the market has made the survival tough and challenging. The major challenges before the banking industry are—raised expectation level of customers, reduction of transaction cost and multiplicity of products and services in the market. The innovating banking searches the solutions to the puzzles aroused in banking business.

*Reader, Commerce Department, Sahu Jain College, Najibabad, U.P.

**Lecturer, Commerce Department, Sahu Jain College, Najibabad, U.P.

Innovation is a dynamic phenomenon. Innovation refers to a process of adoption of new technology, products, services and methods. The technological innovation in banking actually began in 1950s, well before it began in most other industries, when the first automated bookkeeping machines were installed at a few U.S. Banks. Automation in banking became common in the subsequent decades as bankers quickly realized that much of their labour-intensive information handling processes could be operated on the computer. Next innovation occurred in the 1970s with the advent of Electronic Payment technology recognizing the importance of information security; the banking industry during the late 1970s and early 1980s was the first to implement Encryption Technology widely.

COMPONENTS OF INNOVATIVE BANKING

Automated Teller Machine (ATM)

It is an electronic machine, which allows the user to withdraw and lodge cash, pay bills, request statements and other banking transactions. The customer requires ATM card and ID No. to gain access to the machine. Some ATM cards are also debit cards, which can be used in shops and other markets. The purchase amount is deducted from the customers account. The banking transactions such as withdrawal of cash up to the daily limits, cash deposit, transfer of funds between accounts, check balance and request for statements, etc. can be done through the ATM. The introduction of ATM has a lot of influence on banking transactions. The job of employees has become diverse and challenging in addition to convenient service to the customer. Efforts have been made to upgrade ATM and make it user-friendly and customer-oriented. The use of ATMs is increasing day by day. The introduction of ATMs in banking is causing reduction in jobs and a reduced need for physical bank.

Para Banking

If a bank undertakes such activities as leasing, merchant banking, mutual funds, capital market activities, credit and business etc. then this is called para banking.

Telephone Banking

The banks are aiming to make themselves more accessible by introducing telephone banking. Telephone banking means dialing one telephone number using any telephone to access the account transfer funds, request statements or cheque books simply by following a recorded message and touching a key on your phone. It allows the customer to check account at a convenient time and get simple things done without visiting the bank premises. It aims at providing 24 hours service that is fast, convenient, secure for all customers.

Universal Banking

The banking system, which provides service relating to saving and loans besides investments, is called universal banking. This is most common in western countries. The idea is to have access to basic accounts of banking through post offices. In fact this is a stepping-stone to financial inclusion. In Universal banking customer will have the opportunity to use the post office for over-the-counter banking services such as internet banking, credit card accounts, basic accounts and other online banking transactions.

Linkage Banking

It is rural banking with special help groups (SHGs). It is the name given by banks to implement village development programmes by the rural branches under the direction of the urban head/district offices. Poverty alleviation programmes were also part of this. Banks adopted villages and technical cadres were recruited by commercial banks to assist in the implementation of projects of development agriculture, horticulture, rural industries to number of activities that were financed under rural development and employment generation programmes.

Virtual Banking

It is also known as remote banking. It is the banking with use of credit cards, debit cards, smart cards, interactive television, internet terminals, screen phones, normal telephones and hand held personal digital assistants.

On-line Banking

It allows customers to manage their money from any type of browser device including mobile phones, Internet-enabled television and even small hand electronic organizers. Using a PC to access your account, transfer funds, pay creditors hand check if payment has been made, is called on-line banking. It allows customers to have constant access to accounts at any time of day or night. Online banking ensures the following services:

- Checking the position of accounts
- Moving the spare cash into an intrest bearing account
- Making high value payments without risk

Internet Banking

The Internet in the form of web services will have a significant impact on banking. It is a platform to build system within the banks and between banks and their partners. Internet offers safe and convenient new ways not only for banking transactions but also web-shopping. In internet banking, accounts can be accessed 24 hours a day and financial transaction can be done conveniently. This system enhances communications with customers and is free of cost. It helps to make good choices and decisions, which avoid scams in banking.

E-Banking

It can be identified with three channels of ATM, Internet Banking and Telebanking. These channels can supplement each other in ensuring the conventional way of delivering banking service.

Electronic Cheque

Like paper cheques, E-Cheques are legally binding promises to pay. They are having the same legal treatement as paper cheques. In the place of hand written signature on a paper cheque, E-cheque uses digital signature that can be automatically verified. The digital signature gives a lot more authenticity and security than the normal hand-written signature. On the computer screen, the E-cheque looks just like the paper cheque and is filled out in the same way. It has details about the payee's name, drawer's account information, amount, date, drawee bank etc. The e-cheque is being developed by the Financial Service Technology Consortium (FSTC) of the US.

Real Time Gross Settlement (RTGS)

RTGS is a centralized system in which inter-bank payment instructions are settled. "Real time" what this means is that banks can settle their payments to one another immediately and irrevocably. Now if you want to transfer money to your friend or relative in another city, it can be done within seconds.

MERITS OF INNOVATIVE BANKING

- Innovative banking helps to provide 24 hours service to customers by bank.
- Banks are more easily and conveniently accessible due to innovative banking.
- Innovative banking helps in making high value payments without risk.
- Innovative banking enhance communications with customers and are free of cost.
- Innovative banking helps to make choices and decisions, which avoid scams in banking.
- Innovative banking helps to reduce workload on employees of banks.
- Innovative banking reduced the need for physical bank.
- Innovative banking reduced the time to complete banking transactions.

RISK MANAGEMENT FOR INNOVATIVE BANKING

Innovative banking has provided new opportunities for banks to expand their markets and to offer new products and services. The benefits include reducing the costs for banks significantly in addition to provide efficient service and convenience to consumers. The unprecedented developments of innovative banking have increased some of the traditional risks associated with banking activities.

Risk Associated with Innovative Banking

- The information security is vulnerable to internal threats as well as external threats. Innovative banking creates new security issues for banks with respect to confidentiality and integrity of data, authentication of users and access control due to hacking, sniffing, denial of service attacks.

- A bank faces the risk that the system is not well defined and may not fulfil the users expectations.
- Banks have to rely upon external service providers to develop, implement or maintain the activities associated with innovative banking. The outsourcing of activities gives rise to potential operational, legal and reputational risks.
- The absence of adequate measures to verify customer's transactions may result in financial loss to the bank.
- Reputational risk may arise when system or products do not work as expected and cause widespread negative public opinion.
- Customers who have not been adequately informed about their rights and obligaton may bring suit against a bank.
- Banks accepting foreign currencies in payment over internet are subject to Foreign Exchange Risks.

Risk Management Techniques

- Bank Officers should be continuously aware of the information security risk inherent in the activities of the bank.
- Review and approve information security policies to address information security risk inherent in bank's products, services and processes.
- Review and approve aceptable risks exposure for any change in technology, introduction of a new product or service.
- Review and approve institutions internal audit programme for appropriate scope and frequency with regard to compliance with information secuity policies.
- The information policy should be communicated to all appropriate individuals.
- Banks can use a number of methods to establish authentication including PINs, Passwords, Smart Cards, Biometrics and digital certificates.
- The system should be designed to ensure the no single person or Outsourced Agency is able to enter, authorize and complete a transaction.
- Information or data should not be altered without authorization.

- Information should remain private and customer's data should not available to any unauthorized source.
- Banks must have contingency backup system to avoid the risk arising out of deliberate attacks or happening of any contingency.

INNOVATIVE BANKING IN INDIAN CONTEXT

The adoption of innovative banking has positive effect on banking management. The nature of jobs in management has completely changed. The tasks of financial reconciliation, financial control, collection of information about branches etc. become easy for policy decision. However, there is a techno-phobia or fear of failing to grasp the new technology of banking operation by the employees. If the computer system gets crashed, then majority of employees would have very little to do as much of their work is computer based. Innovative banking has removed manual labour and replaced the old control room with one operator. However, coverage area of innovative banking is still very less in India. Innovative banking till date does not cover majority of village and towns. Customers residing in big cities reap maximum benefits of innovative banking.

There are some areas where customers can not be satisfied by innovative banking even now. One area of complaint is the fact that banks charge for the mistakes made on accounts due to lack of sufficient knowledge of technology. There is fear of fraud with increased use of telephones or computers. Customers are greatly confused with new concepts of banking. The success of innovative banking depends upon customers awareness.

CONCLUSION

To sum up the topic we can say new concepts such as online banking, Internet banking, ATM, telephone banking, Universal banking have made life easy and convenient. We can say that last two decades have really been revolutionary for banking sector as lot of innovations have come. Though in India Innovative banking is not free from shortcomings. There has been several instances of malfunctioning / disfunctioning of ATMs, breakdown of technology leading to failure of services. It can be argued that Indian banking is moving through the transformation phase and these are inevitable and it is a passing phase. Adoption of innovative banking should not be done in haste but it should be properly planned with pre-launch test and key-men training, which should be percolated down the line. There is a strong need for customer education and care. Undoubtedly innovative banking in developed countries is very familiar, successful and cover a large area but in India the picture is not as such but we can say future of Indian banking belongs to innovative banking.

4

INFRASTRUCTURE FINANCING IN INDIA: AN APPRAISAL OF SHIFTING GEARS

Manoranjan Sharma*

A poor country is poor because it is poor. Backwardness in infrastructure development makes it poorer. India knows that it will have to make an optimum use of its invaluable (but unused) resources if it ever wants to become a developed country. During last decade, Indian government has initiated various steps to develop its infrastructure by opening its doors to private sector for strengthening its state electricity boards, road network, telecommunication, water supply system etc. Golden quadrilateral and NESW corridor are ambitious plans of road construction. Banks now have very powerful role to play. They can promote investment in those sectors. They may work as financer, consultant or promoter.

Development of infrastructure will certainly help other sectors, like agriculture, industry and business. Banks may become the agent of overall development of Indian economy. This paper provides in-depth study of infrastructure financing in changing banking environment.

INFRASTRUCTURE—CATALYTIC ROLE

Infrastructure development has emerged as the core determinant of the strategy to provide the cutting edge of development the world over. The genesis of the concept of infrastructure could be traced to

*Chief Economist, Canara Bank, Head Office, Bangalore.

the 19th century in the major role played by public investment in American economic development. Infrastructure refers to all those activities and facilities, which help to generate, sustain and enhance, directly or indirectly, the growth in production and income in the rest of the economy rather than production and income generation within the infrastructure enterprises themselves because of the multiplier effects of such investment. More generally, it encompasses all institutional prerequisites of efficient working of competitive markets and expansion in production (Stiglitz, 1996).

Infrastructure development could be demand-driven (e.g., bypasses, bridges) or supply-driven (e.g. express ways). The government promoted infrastructure because of the structural weaknesses of the laissez-faire mechanism and the natural features of many of the infrastructural services, such as scale economies and high demand externalities has traditionally provided infrastructure. The dichotomy between social and private costs (and benefits) necessitates the selection of projects not justified on the basis of the conventional and extended cost-benefit techniques to avoid both the monopolistic abuses of infrastructure operations and the vagaries of the market. In India, the Finance Ministry recognises roads, new airports, ports, railways, irrigation, water supply, sanitation, sewerage system and telecommunications for several fiscal benefits. The benefits offered to these sectors are: (a) Five year tax holiday to be claimed within 12 years of operation. For the balance years, a 30 per cent exemption is available, (b) Income tax credits for investments up to Rs. 70,000, (c) Increased limit for external commercial borrowings, (d) Concessional import duties and port charges for project-related imports, (e) Exemption from Minimum Alternate Tax.

The *World Development Report* (1994) suggested a strong positive relationship between the level of GDP and infrastructure stock per capita. For, World Bank studies estimated that a one per cent growth in infrastructure development translates into a one per cent growth in the economy. India's immediate goal is to achieve an industrial growth of at least 10 per cent per annum and a sustainable GDP growth of at least 7 per cent per annum. Enhancing investment in infrastructure would be critical to attaining these objectives.

STRATEGIC PRIORITIES

In the overarching context of globalisation, the requirements of infrastructure have increased tremendously. However, the regional dimensions of infrastructure for diffusion and dispersal of industries across regions are also important. The evolving pattern of level of basic infrastructure items indicates accentuation of regional imbalances and the associated spatially uneven pattern in infrastructure across States because of deeply ingrained historical, demographic, structural and institutional factors, infusion of large and continuous investment and the divergence in priority accorded to infrastructure by different State Governments.

Historically, measures relating to strengthening of the support mechanism for financial infrastructure to stem 'infirmities' include the Industrial Estates Programme (1955), Integrated Infrastructural Development Scheme (1994), the Growth Centre Schemes (1988) and the government's creation of a Rural Infrastructure Development Fund (RIDF). Setting up of industrial areas and industrial estates, District Industry Centres (DICs), common production facilities and generation and distribution of electricity, incentives for growth of clusters—both natural and induced were also attempted. But these programmes were adversely affected by non-assessment of economic viability, tardy implementation, insufficient maintenance, misallocated investment, and unresponsiveness to users and technical inefficiencies.

There is a strong correlation between the productivity of the industrial sector and the availability of marketing infrastructure. The multiplier effects provide an impetus to the industry by slashing production and marketing costs and enhancing the competitive edge. Marketing infrastructure problems emanate from intensified competition, inadequate means of transport and communication, lack of quality certification, unorganised physical marketing infrastructure with several intermediaries, inadequate institutional arrangements, weak and ineffective distribution channels, etc. These require assistance for intangible marketing activities, such as branding, franchising, advertisements and participation in trade fairs to create and enhance brand equities. The core elements of an effective marketing strategy like business environment, emphasis on value-added products, business process re-engineering (BPR), financial restructuring, appropriate repositioning, product and process innovation, etc. need to be emphasised.

The experience across the world reveals a convergence of ICE (information and communication) technologies. These and other momentous changes have blurred geographical barriers and shrunk the world into a "global village". This is why change, reform and radicalism are not abstruse doctrinaire reference points but an immediate necessity. As 'technological evangelization' and narrowing of the 'digital gap' have become significant instruments of the growth escalation process, it is important to identify the needs of the industry in terms of aligning technology initiatives with business priorities for maximum benefit. Management of change ushered in by streamlining of infrastructure requires an attempt to overcome technological obsolescence and bring about secular dynamic change and structural transformation. These include creation of Research and Development to enrich management knowledge. Design Cell to create a new product for the market, testing facilities for introduction of latest techniques of production, prototype development for creation of viable technical base and tool room for basic tool engineering, laboratories, technology research centres, etc. Further, development of industrial clusters has been promoted through Cluster Development Programme by providing infrastructural facilities and support services including technological upgradation for strengthening of competitive position. Several companies could be tapped to spearhead cluster development projects together with firms in that cluster. Through these synergies, the clusters could serve as a common facility for transfer of know-how in key areas, such as operational efficiency, management, market development, testing and certification facilities, including development of international market.

REVIEW OF POLICIES

POWER SECTOR

Considered in a historical perspective, the Government has played an important role in providing infrastructure. Over 90 per cent of India's infrastructure is owned, controlled and managed by the public sector. Let us first briefly examine the situation in the power sector. In India, power is generated by the following entities—

- Central Utility such as NTPC, NHPC, Nuclear Power Corporation, Damodar Valley Corporation and NEEP-CO.

- State Electricity Boards, which are state-owned utilities. Some states, e.g. Orissa—OPGC/OHPC; Haryana—Haryana Vidyut Utpadan Nigam (HVUN); Andhra Pradesh—APGenco; Uttar Pradesh—UP Thermal Corporation, UP Hydel Power Corporation; Karnataka—Karnataka Power Corporation Ltd. have corporatised their SEBs.

The broad sector-wise generation mix is as under —

Sector	*Per cent*
Central Sector	34
State Sector	58.1
Private Sector	59.1
Licensees	3.9
IPPs	2.6
Others	1.4
All-India	100

The installed generating capacity of the country rose from a mere 1,352 MW in 1947 to 1,01,154 MW by end-March 2001. But the projects of the public sector suffered from 'leakage' in almost all sectors, 'pilferage' and transmission and distribution (T&D) losses in the power sector, which increased the cost of the projects, and, in the ultimate analysis, adversely affected the quality of service. The need for power sector reforms emanates from All-India energy and peaking shortages of 6.2 per cent and 12.4 per cent, respectively during 1999-2000. These shortages rose to 7.8 per cent and 13 per cent, respectively during 2000-01. The malaise is due to the inability of the government to mobilise resources for further investment in the power sector because of severe resource crunch and the fundamentally flawed organisational structure and management of the State Electricity Boards (SEBs) leading to their precarious condition. The omnipresent sickness of SEBs emanated from politicisation, low thermal plant load factor (PLF), low average tariffs with high cross-subsidisation leading to inefficient patterns of energy consumption, and even to non-recovery of their own costs, over staffing and large T&D losses. This has led to capacity shortages, poor system reliability and frequent blackouts. Out of the total energy generated only 55 per cent is billed and only 41 per cent is realised. Despite government introducing private sector investment in generation, reforms, such as unbudling of State electricity boards, privatization of generation and eventually distribution, investments in T&D sector to minimize technical losses, effective mechanism to eliminate corruption and theft, demand-side management to improve efficiency of end-use and minimize wastage, elimination of redundancies in work-force and realization of appropriate user-charges need to be pursued more vigorously. For, losses of the SEBs crossed Rs. 26,000 crore and dues to the Central PSUs stood at Rs. 40,000 crore. This necessitates greater involvement of the private sector in generation, transmission and distribution of power. The government has initiated several measures, such as development of district level distribution improvement plans/ projects for all districts, setting up district level energy committees for monitoring and resource planning, 100 per cent metering, privatisation and corporatisation of distribution, etc. But these measures need to be effectively implemented.

Looking Ahead

Presently thermal plants account for 74% of total power generation, hydroelectric plants for 24% and nuclear plants generate the remaining 2%. Approximately 85% of India's 627,000 villages have electricity and there is a nationwide network for the transfer and distribution of power to all parts of the country. The Central Government has identified a slew of initiatives to give a new thrust to the power sector. The government has agreed to set up a power trading corporation, which would be a centralized agency to trade in power. The proposed corporation could purchase power from large projects and trade in it at the inter-state level. In view of the paucity of resources and the need to bridge the gap between the rapidly growing demand and supply, the Government has undertaken a policy to encourage greater investments by private enterprises in this sector. Incentives include generation and distribution power projects of any type and size are allowed, foreign equity participation can be as high as 100%, return on equity of up to 16% is assured at 68.5% PLF for thermal power plants (with the possibility of earning higher returns for higher PLF). Similar incentives are provided for hydroelectric power projects, a renewable license period of 30 years has been set, import duty at the concessional rate of 20% has been set for import of equipment and the Government allows a 5-year tax holiday for power generating projects with an additional 5 years in which a deduction of 30% of taxable profits is allowed.

The achievement in terms of creation of fresh generation capacity during the Eighth Plan was 51 per cent. The achievement, however, did not exceed 50 per cent in the Ninth Plan necessitating a thorough streamlining of the power sector. The thrust areas for reform include rationalisation of tariff structure, reduction of T&D losses, transparency in the grant of subsidy, rural electrification and collection efficiency. Based on the 16th Electric Power Survey (EPS) Report, the Working Group on Power for the 10th Plan has also been estimated to ensure 'Power on Demand', additional generation capacity of 1,00,000 MW needs to be created. There were similar shortfalls in capacity creation in roads and ports. In view of the failure of the private sector to expand, the problem was aggravated. Consequently, total investment in infrastructure development was grossly inadequate and led to large infrastructure gaps. The economy was, however, able to achieve higher economic growth in the post-reform years because of some slack in the system. But it is abundantly clear that accelerated GDP growth of around 8 per cent in the Tenth Plan period would require industrial growth of over 10 per cent. Consequently, the energy-transport sector could emerge as a key determinant of the growth strategy by increasing domestic production together with enhanced quality of services in terms of both price and reliability. This requires a major attitudinal change in the conventional pattern of development and financing by better utilisation of power plants and machinery, reduction in technical and commercial losses in distribution, renovation and modernisation of old plants and distribution reforms. Viewed in this perspective of inadequate fulfill ment of felt needs down through the years, the ambitious target for generation capacity addition by 2012 does not seem to be too far-fetched. The key issues in enhancing power supply to lead and manage differently to build a globalised, strong India relate to:

- Incremental capacity - both fossil fuel based as well as nuclear to control the energy shortages.
- Prioritisation of hydro-based capacity addition to reduce the peaking shortages and optimise utilisation of resources.
- Focus on renovation and modernisation of old stations—a low cost and quick return option for adding capacity.
- Much greater exploitation of vast conventional energy viz. bio-gas plant, improved chulhas, biomass, solar photovoltovic, solar thermal system, wind power, small hydropower, power from municipal wastes etc.

Historically, India's initiation of the power sector reforms in the early 1990s was driven by the assumption of the deficit in generation capacity. Consequently, power reforms emphasised power generation at the cost of transmission and distribution aspects. Without reforming the distribution side, sizable investments in the generation sector by private entrepreneurs is unlikely. While an econometrically devised energy demand prognostication and a similarly prepared energy supply model may be abstruse and not even fully reliable, some of the fundamental elements of the strategy to resuscitate the energy environment in India relate to achieving a competitive market with wholesale and retail competition. Power sector reforms have to be implemented in all states so that the sector becomes viable, the citizens get better quality power and entrepreneurs invest in power generation and transmission on an increasingly larger scale. Following the Tripartite Agreement signed between the Centre, RBI and state governments, which entailed one-time-settlement of SEB dues to central power public sector units, the financial performance of central power PSUs has improved.

Changing Focus

The interests of four major players in the system viz., promoters, lenders, government and consumers should be carefully balanced for discernible improvement. It is, therefore, necessary to reevaluate the development paradigm that facilitated the fast track growth of some states, and if necessary, modify it in the light of the resource endowment and the peculiarities of the state to eradicate the poverty that stymies growth and development and foster faster growth. Reforms of the power sector, apart from improvement in SEBs, have so far attempted to focus on encouragement of facilitation of Independent Power Producers (IPPs) and promotion of mega power projects. The Union Budget 2001-02 announced a slew of measures, which fundamentally aimed at reforming and restructuring the country's power sector. These included exemption of generating companies established by captive power plants from the requirement of seeking a techno-economic approval of the Central Electricity Authority up to a capital cost of Rs. 30 billion, the introduction of the 'availability based tariff' concept for utilities initially effective for central power utilities like the National Thermal Power Corporation by the Central Electricity Regulatory Commission, etc. Under this regime, the power generator would have to operate the plant at minimum capacity of 80 per cent for qualifying for incentives. A reform linked lending mechanism has also been prescribed for use of digital signatures/ electronic records.

Seeding Future Growth

Three crucial elements of the Electricity Bill, 2001 related to permission to all consumers for a non-discriminatory access to efficient suppliers and distributors of electricity, drastic reduction of bureaucratic and political interference and the phased and graduated reduction power subsidies. The electricity Act 2003 was ostensibly enacted to achieve the anowed objectives of 'power for all' by 2012 but the act has run into rough weather. In an attempt to develop the power industry to promote competition, protect consumer's interest ensure supply to all areas, rationalise the tariff and to make the subsidy policy transparent, the act revisited laws relating to generation, transmission, distribution trading and use of electricity. These and other changes of far reaching significance imply a redefinition of the role of the Government from being a sole provider to that of a facilitator providing a credible legal, judicial, administrative and regulatory framework. This requires transcending of a simple extrapolation of past consumption caused by under-investment and grossly insufficient and inefficient infrastructure. For example, telecommunications and the information that it provides constitute significant inputs for production, economic efficiency and competitiveness (Norton, 1992). During the Union Budget 2001-02, the Government maintained the overall thrust on infrastructure through synergistic measures. Tax holiday provisions were widened to promote the development of IT infrastructure by assigning infrastructure status to Internet service providers as well as bandwidth providers. The tax holiday provisions were extended to increase the efficacy of relief to be provided to companies executing these projects. Promoters of Special Economic Zones were provided with a tax holiday.

Power is a concurrent subject under the Indian Constitution. The states thus have equal or even greater share of generation and transmission, and almost the entire distribution is under their control. This makes the reform process that much more difficult as all the states are not equally forward looking in implementing reforms. Naturally, the Central Government has adopted a carrot-and-stick policy to make the state governments veer round to its point of view. Consequently, in the post reforms phase, the state governments became proactive and even competitive in attracting investments into their respective states. These projects usually involved high costs and several of them were even abandoned later. With the Union government permitting private participation in the private sector including foreign investment, the state governments relied increasingly on the private sector for its power requirements because of the problem of severe resource crunch. A study conducted by *The Economic Times* revealed that between 1994-95 and 2001-02, the share of aggregate expenditure on energy in the state budgets declined sharply from 4.58 per cent to 3.98 per cent. What is particularly galling is that at the individual level, some of the states, particularly the Eastern and the North-Eastern ones witnessed an even sharper fall. In West Bengal, the share of energy in the state's total expenditure declined from 3.56 per cent to 1.11 per cent, while in Bihar, it declined from 5.18 per cent to a paltry 0.02 per cent. The same pattern of decline is discernible even in industrially prosperous states like Maharashtra, Tamil Nadu or Andhra Pradesh. In Maharashtra, it declined from 8.65 per cent in 1994-95 to 1.92 per cent in 2001-02 and in Andhra Pradesh from 7.99 per cent to 7 per cent. In the case of Gujarat, however, the share of energy in the state's total budget rose sharply from 7.58 per cent in 1994-95 to 10.37 per cent in 2001-02. The share of transport and communications in the state's aggregate expenditure also declined. Further, the decline was considerably sharper in prosperous states like Maharashtra, Tamil Nadu or Andhra Pradesh. The decline in the share of infrastructure in total public investment adversely affected not only the industrial sector but also the economy as a whole because of its multiplier effects. It could, therefore, be maintained that the Accelerated Power Development Programme (APDP) introduced in the Ninth Plan needs to be greatly expanded to enable states to undertake power sector reforms.

AIRPORTS

India currently has 5 international and 88 domestic airports with passenger traffic being concentrated at Bangalore, Calcutta, Chennai, Delhi and Mumbai. The Airports Authority of India operates all these airports. The Air Corporation Act, 1953, repealed on March 1, 1994, ended the monopoly of Indian Airlines and Air India over scheduled air transport services. Despite some improvement caused by the entry of the private players in the sector, India's airports sorely need modernization of equipment and services, terminal technologies and transport facilities to bring existing facilities up to international standards and to handle the expected increase in passengers and cargo. Specific investment opportunities include expansion of import and export wings at international airports, building of new integrated cargo and airfreight terminals, building of common user domestic terminals at all international airports, introduction of elevating transfer vehicles with stacker systems and introduction of electronic data interchange at all airports to enable handling of international cargo. During 2003-04, the Lok Sabha passed the Airports Authority of India (Amendment) Bill, 2003 to provide greater operational and managerial independence to private operators. The Union Cabinet has approved the plan for privatisation and modernisation of Delhi and Mumbai airports. These two airports along with Bangalore and Hyderabad are to be developed through the joint venture route with 74 per cent participation by private parties and 26 per cent by Airports Authority of India. Concession period is expected to be 30 years for all these projects.

PORTS

Indian ports, which handle over 90 per cent of India's volume of foreign trade, are notorious for long ship turnaround times of three to five days on an average, dock congestion due to inadequate equipment, lack of Electronic Data Interchange facility, higher freight handling costs because of obsolete technical equipment systems and staff-related inefficiencies. Given this scenario, productivity is extremely low by international standards and necessitates a perceptible increase in the productivity and capacity of ports. India has 11 major ports (overseen by the Ministry for Surface Transport) accounting for over 90 percent of the country's port traffic apart from 143 minor working ports (under state jurisdiction) along the coastline of 5,550 km. To decongest the ports, the Ninth Plan drew an outlay of Rs. 17,000 crores. Private and foreign investment in ports is being encouraged by the government, particularly since October 1996 to meet the huge gap between demand and availability of port capacity. The central government has adopted broad policy measures to open ports to private investors and operators. Some maritime states are also attracting private investments. The central government is seeking private investment in captive and other facilities and state governments are seeking private investment, largely in new sites. Key issues relate to separating statutory and operational roles at the major ports, continuing to transfer operational roles to the private sector, enhancing competition between ports to provide greater choice for consumers and improving the sector's institutional structure, particularly the distinction between major and minor ports.

The privatisation of pilot and tug services at the ports was widely thought to be risky because of heightened risk perception. The privatisation of ports, however, received an impetus through an amendment to the Major Ports Trust Act of 1996, which permitted major ports to enter into joint ventures (JVs) with minor ports, foreign ports and domestic or foreign companies. The amended Act sought to overcome the major problems associated with Indian ports by bringing in private sector participation. The success of National Highways Development Project (NHDP) encouraged the launch of some mega infrastructure projects including the gigantic maritime infrastructure development programme, Sagar Mala. The project is to be implemented over the next 10 years at a cost of Rs 80,000 to Rs. 1 lakh crore. Finding financing on such a large scale will undoubtedly be a challenging task.

RAILWAYS

Indian Railways is the second largest system in the world under a single management, with an extensive network of about 65,000 kilometers, nearly 25 per cent of which is electrified. Indian Railways operates an extensive network. It ranks second in the world (after China) in terms of freight intensity, track to land ratio, wagons to track ratios, passengers and cargo. Indian Railways' program to reduce terminal delays and turnaround time of its rolling stock aims at increasing freight carrying capacity by 50 per cent through continual usage of wagons. Railways' share of total freight transported, however, declined from over 80 per cent to 50 per cent in the last three decades because of low wagon turnaround times, primitive facilities for loading and unloading at the stations, poor security and endemic corruption. Indian Railways is soliciting private sector participation in freight movement through a Build-Own-Operate-Transfer (BOOT) scheme and Own-Your-Wagon-Scheme (OYWS). Thrust areas identified for improvements and expansion include replacement and renewal of over-aged assets, augmentation of terminal and rolling stock capacities, gauge conversion and electrification, and introduction of new routes and long distance special parcel services.

RAKESH MOHAN COMMITTEE

The Ministry of Railways (Railway Board) had constituted an Expert Group (with Rakesh Mohan as Chairman) on 31 December 1998 to study the railway sector in order to estimate the financing requirements of an expansion and upgrading programme for the Indian Railways; to identify sources of funding of estimated investments over 15-year period; to study models of structure and ownership of rail transport facilities in developed countries and to recommend suitable regulatory arrangements that would facilitate orderly expansion of the system, promote desired degree of competition and protect users' right to quality service.

The Expert Group found that increase in real wages have far exceeded the increase in productivity and that is the root cause of the financial problem confronting the Railways. Consequently it recommended:

1. Achievement of high growth through expansion of capacity and modernization and upgradation of facilities and yet to explore avenues to economize costs.
2. Rationalisation of freight structure and tariff rebalancing with a view to removing distortion.
3. Increase in speed of freight trains, expansion of capacity for upper classes, upgradation of rolling stock, improvement of signalling and communication system.
4. The Indian Railways should be reorganized. The government of India should be only incharge of setting policy direction. The Indian railways must ultimately be corporatized into the Indian Railways Corporation. Indian Railways Regulatory Authority should be set up to regulate tariffs.

ROADS

India's road networking covers 2.9 million kilometers, the third largest in the world, with only 34,298 km of National Highways suitable for speedy transportation. Though it constitutes less than 2% of the total road network, road traffic accounts for 87% and 65% of passenger and goods traffic, respectively. The Government is promoting both private investment and foreign to build national highways and their maintenance through budgetary allocation to the National Highway Authority of India (NHAI), permission to private parties to recover their investment by way of collection of tolls for specified periods, considerable liberalization of provisions relating to foreign investment in the road sector, including automatic approval for foreign equity participation up to 74% in the construction of roads and bridges, automatic approval for foreign equity participation up to 51% in land transport support services, such as operation of highway bridges, toll roads and vehicles, land required for construction and operation of facilities, duty-free imports of road-building machinery, etc. Banks and FIs have started a draft model concession agreement for road projects, which incorporates project-specific traffic guarantees. It also envisages safeguards for both investors and the National Highway Authority of India (NHAI). The government has decided to offer sovereign guarantees on all new multilateral loans in the road sector routed through NHAI. Key issues for central and state governments include identifying and preparing financially viable projects, factoring how tolls fit into the overall funding of road projects, both public and private and providing for the contingent liabilities that privately financed projects imply for the public sector.

TELECOMMUNICATIONS

India operates one of the largest telecom networks in Asia with over 25,000 telephone exchanges with a capacity of about 25 million lines. Recent spectacular growth witnessed was facilitated by the entry of the private sector, leading to greater competition. The tele density has risen from 2.8 in March 2000 to 7.2 in March 2004, the mobile subscriber base grew by about 160 per cent and reached a figure of 3.6 million in March 2004, falling prices in long distance and mobile services and levy of adequate user charges for the financing of investments and for operation and maintenance. India has not lagged behind in attracting foreign direct investment in telecommunications. This can be substantiated by the fact that groups, such as Hutchison and AT&T as well as Tata and Reliance are building rapidly growing businesses with their local partners.

Many villages, however, still lack telephone service and long-distance service. With the deregulation of the economy in July 1991, the entire telecom equipment manufacturing industry was de-licensed and de-reserved. The National Telecom Policy of 1994 opened up basic telephone services to private sector participation. In August 1995, the Lok Sabha passed a bill amending the Indian Telegraph Act, 1885, paving the way for setting up a Telecom Regulatory Authority of India with well defined functions, responsibilities and powers. The Telecom Policy (March 1999) provided a platform for further development and liberalization of the sector. Key issues here relate to defining relationships among the regulatory agency, policymakers, and the current service provider, establishing an efficient interconnection regime to spur competition and continuing to rebalance prices within a more competitive environment. Specific Government reforms include value-added services (VAS), including cellular mobile telephones, radio paging, electronic mail, voice mail/audiotex services, videotex services, data services, video-conference and credit card authorization services, were opened for private sector participation in 1992.

URBAN WATER AND MUNICIPAL SERVICES

Historically, Central, state, and city governments have been providing and regulating urban water and municipal services. While the 74th Constitution Amendment attempted to move towards municipal management of urban water services, the process is yet to make substantial headway. The efficiency of existing networks could be stepped up by introduction of private operators and measures to provide an adequate revenue stream. This necessitates that municipal governments must be stronger and have sound finances, private sector management is needed to improve efficiency and pricing reform made a strategic priority.

PROMOTING GROWTH OF PRIVATE SECTOR

In view of the changed paradigm, the extent of the fiscal crisis and the urgency of keeping it at bay at various levels of government together with the relative reduction of current and capital expenditures on infrastructure and social sectors in the last few years, a more holistic approach in streamlining infrastructure with substantial private sector financing in a competitive environment to improve quality and enhance coverage is needed. While there has been growing recognition that the State should not occupy the commanding heights, there is insufficient recognition that the State should not occupy the demanding heights either. Extensive empirical examination on the performance of major segments of infrastructure demonstrates that heavy reliance on the public sector led to shortfalls in outlays and capacity utilisation. Inside the rhetoric, there are clear indications of a thaw all-around that success in these spheres is a function of the resolution of the issues of 'privatisation and depoliticisation, unbundling and project structuring, project appraisal, financial engineering and project implementation' of the infrastructure sector (Ahluwalia,1998; Raghuram, *et al*, 1999). Privatisation helps to relax capital constraints, enhance efficiency and increase investments. This is attributable to the facts that (a) the placement of both residual control rights and residual cash flow rights in the hands of private shareholders (Boycko, Shleifer and Vishny, 1992, 1993; Sappington and Stiglitz, 1987; Shapiro and Willig, 1990) and (b) privatisation is a way for the government to credibly itself the private information concerning enterprise costs that would be necessary for easy intervention and subsidisation (Schmidt, 1996; Shirley and Walsh, 2000). 'Unbundling' refers to separation of activities in which economies of scale are not important and hence can be provided competitively, e.g. separation of electricity generation from transmission and distribution, in telecommunications, the operation of value-added services (e.g., radio-based services) are typically separated from basic telephone services. Establishment of appropriate and transparent regulatory structure requires streamlining of the Indian Railways Act and Acts relating to ports, roads, etc. Project structuring requires structuring of project small enough to make them both investment-friendly "commercially" viable. Project appraisal and financing deals with appraisal of the project against future cash flows rather than an asset base or collateral security. Various forms of revenue, control over revenue, risk guarantees and the availability of vital banking infrastructure also figure in the appraisal.

INNOVATIVE STRATEGIES: BROADENING DEVELOPMENT PARTNERSHIPS

While the financing of the Plans was always beset with difficulties, the resource crunch exacerbated in recent years. The Seventh Plan underscored severe macro-economic constraints and the dampening effect of the resource crunch, which limited the capacity to mobilise funds for expansion and modernisation of infrastructural projects:

"This would obviously require restructuring of the present pattern of development financing so as to rectify emerging imbalances and maintain sound financial planning to achieve the desired goals... the process of resource erosion would have to be immediately checked and also reversed in due course, if development is to be protected. In essence, the Indian fiscal system would have to accomplish the delicate task of raising the resources in a non-inflationary manner, besides providing enough incentives for savings and growth in production".

SEVENTH FIVE-YEAR PLAN, PARAGRAPH 4.18

With further worsening of the overall resource constraint in the economic landscape of liberalisation, privatisation, globalisation and the 'right-sizing' of the government, the growth theoretic formulation of the Eighth Plan strongly emphasised the development of infrastructure. The Ninth Plan carried this pro-active approach much further when it cogently argued that in order to achieve 6.5 per cent annual rate of growth in the economy with the targetted growth rate for agriculture sector at 3.9 per cent per annum and that for industrial sector, including construction at 7.6 per cent per annum and

> "to accelerate it in the perspective period, matching infrastructure will need to be created to meet the requirement of different sectors of the economy. The demand for power, petroleum products, roads, ports, urban transport, telecommunication services, etc. is likely to increase rapidly and so will the investment requirements for creating these facilities... New ways and means of financing these projects will have to be explored, greater competition will have to be encouraged and the performance of the constituent sectors should be bench marked against the rest of the world."

NINTH FIVE-YEAR PLAN, VOL. I, PARAGRAPH 2.131

Evidently, the grim challenge of steering India to higher growth requires an effective and transparent state, one that plays a catalytic, facilitating role, increasing and complementing the activities of private businesses and individuals. A World Bank Report designed to improve the environment for private sector involvement in infrastructure emphasized that the full potential of the private sector to meet the pressing infrastructure needs is largely untapped. The Report pointed out that the private sector had built new infrastructure, such as, independent power projects and new port sites and established companies that compete with public operators, especially in the telecommunications sector. The productivity and efficiency improvements that private management and ownership could bring to bear on the existing public sector providers, under a suitable regulatory arrangement and with competition when possible, would help relieve some of the infrastructural constraints. The key issues identified included increasing demand for long-term debt instruments through pensions and insurance reforms and making the debt market work by simplifying taxes to reduce distortions, regulating the private placement market, supporting securitisation and simplifying and harmonising debt option procedures. The key policy recommendations of the Report included: (i) improving efficiency and transparency in contracting infrastructure projects to the private sector, (ii) reporting and valuing contingent liabilities and (iii) auditing public support to private infrastructure projects. Restructuring a public-sector entity before privatising it would be ineffective. A private-sector company that takes over a public-sector company would anyway conduct 'change therapy' with 'due diligence'. The experience of private investors in power and telecommunications suggests the need for determination of tariffs on the basis of competitive bidding, mitigation of fuel supply risk, easy assignability in case of debt service default by original licensee and a revenue-sharing arrangement to protect against the downside of market risk (Ahluwalia, 1999). This is not an isolated or a stray case in relation to India but in fact is the norm all over the world (Baker and Schafer, 1995). All this strongly suggests that at least for the present Government presence in the infrastructure is indispensable as the infrastructure industry has few characteristics of a free market. However, this must go together with a comprehensive restructuring package, of which privatisation has to be an essential element.

Of late, there have been momentous changes reflected in the end of cold war, shift in the global balance of power, globalisation of trade and production, changing patterns of finance and new ideological currents. While different regions responded differently, the development context has undoubtedly altered significantly. Against this backdrop of the process of intermeshing of the national economy into the global system, the meeting of infrastructural needs of various industries can be an important instrument of building a competitive, vibrant and integrated economy. With India's infrastructure investments requirements estimated at US $ 115-130 billion during the period 1996-97 to 2000-01 and US $ 215 billion in the period 2000-01 to 2005-06, a significantly increased role of banks and FIs is imperative. The *India Infrastructure Report* (Table -1) assessed the infrastructural requirements of the country as follows:

Table 1: Financing Requirements for Infrastructure Projects

Assuming an average 10 to 12 per cent annum industrial growth and a 15 per cent aggregate growth rate for exports for the next decade, the estimated investments required in the infrastructure sector were estimated as under:

	1996-97 to 2000-01	*20001 -01 to 2005-06*
Total Investment Requirement in Infrastructure	Rs. 4,000 billion-4500 billion US $ 115 billion-130 billion	Rs. 7500 billion billion (US$ 215 billion)

Sourcing : It is estimated that 40 per cent of external capital inflows could flow into infrastructure. This suggests that about 15 per cent of total capital requirements will be externally financed. The rest, nearly 85 per cent, will have to be domestically financed.

	1996-97 to 2000-01	***2000 -01 to 2005-06***
• Annual Level of Investments in Infrastructure		
As % of GDP	5.5% to 7%	7% to 8%
Absolute value	Rs. 600 billion - Rs. 1,100 billion	Rs. 1,800 billion
• Sourcing		
Public	Rs. 480 billion (80%)	Rs. 1,000 billion (55%)
Private	Rs. 120 billion (20%)	Rs. 800 billion (45%)
• Public		
Internal	Rs. 200 billion	Rs. 500 billion
Market	Rs.100 billion	Rs. 200 billion
Financial Institutions	Rs. 140 billion	Rs. 185 billion
Foreign	Rs. 40 billion	Rs. 115 billion
Total	Rs. 480 billion	Rs. 1000 billion

• Public		
Internal	Rs. 10 billion	Rs. 265 billion
Market	Rs. 75 billion	Rs. 240 billion
Financial Institutions	Rs. 25 billion	Rs. 200 billion
Foreign	Rs. 10 billion	Rs. 95 billion
Total	Rs. 120 billion	Rs. 800 billion
• Demand on domestic capital markets		
Public and Private Sector Infrastructure Entities	Rs. 260 billion	Rs. 440 billion
Financial Intermediaries and Government	160 billion	280 billion
Total	Rs. 420 billion	Rs. 720 billion

Sector-wise financial requirement for the 10–year period were estimated as under:

Power	Rs. 5,000 billion
Telecommunications	Rs. 1,000 billion
Roads	Rs. 1,150 billion
Ports	Rs. 255 billion
Urban Infrastructure	Rs. 2,800 billion
Railways	Rs. 2,000 billion

Source: India Infrastructure Report.

This approach, which manifests a clear commitment to change and transformation, provides a holistic long-term objective of strengthening the crucial link between the growth of infrastructure, flow of investments and their role in influencing the development process of the economy. But there are differences about the collaborative strategy to be adopted for spawning, nurturing and sustaining innovations. Increased private sector participation within a competitive framework could reduce cost to the economy and enhance complementarity between public investment and private capital in developing and maintaining critical infrastructure. Montek S. Ahluwalia (1998) succinctly summed up the prerequisites for creation of an enabling environment for development of infrastructure in conformity with the rapidly growing present needs and requirements as follows:

> "public recognition of the need for private investment in infrastructure (which helps to reduce perceptions of political risk), a

structure of tariff's which can assure remunerative return for investors, clarity of government policy and transparency of procedures governing the interface between private investors and various public authorities to reduce uncertainty and finally, establishment of independent regulatory agencies charged with ensuring fair treatment for private investors".

With the world shifting towards the identification of "production spaces", which offer the least-cost, highest-value possibilities for infrastructure, the significance of logistics infrastructure has increased greatly. While ports and airways are crucial terminal "gateway" infrastructure, roads, railways, pipelines, telecommunications, power and water are essential "network" infrastructure. Private participation in infrastructure development is basically influenced by risk profile of the projects and source and modalities of finance, besides, the question of public guarantee and legalities. Despite broad consensus on the salubrious impact of the private sector on infrastructure financing, the modalities for working out long-term pricing mechanisms for natural monopolies, such as, water supply, transport, power and irrigation without compromising on social and equity goals have yet to be worked out. The requirements of different infrastructure sub-sectors require to be speedily addressed to in different ways to reconcile various conflicting objectives. Success comes down to a four-part paradox: (a) creating incentives for productive efficiency and providing sufficient comfort to investors to ensure implementation of desirable projects and (b) promoting allocative efficiency in the face of distortionary, anti-competitive and non-transparent effects of cross-subsidisation and avoiding heavy burden on the users, particularly the vulnerable sections of the society —all at once.

The need for calibrating the pace and character of integration with the world economy requires higher investment in the non-tradable sector, i.e. economic infrastructure in the broadest possible sense and a marked improvement both in the quality and the quantity of infrastructure services by ensuring realistic prices for infrastructural facilities through elimination or reduction of subsidies and a more active involvement of the private sector, including public-private participation in ownership of assets and provision of services. This constellation of factors arguably requires the creation of a coherent policy, regulatory and legal framework to logically address the concerns of both the government and the private sector in a synchronised manner to strengthen linkages and competitive advantage in this era of globalisation (Klein, So and Shin, 1996, Fishbein and Babbar, 1996; Sharma, 2000). While the primary objectives of creating an incentive framework should be to benefit consumers, secondary objectives could relate to reduction in national debt, stimulation of domestic capital markets, reduction in capital and operating subsidies, increased range and improved quality of services, etc. The pace and sequence of transfer of infrastructure components to the private sector depend on the complexity of infrastructure sector, rate of growth in demand and the competitiveness of marketing options for unbundling by function or geography, legal regime regarding ownership of land and other critical assets and capacity for economic regulation (ADB, 2001).

Knowledge infrastructure, characterised by high R & D components and intangible cost structure, project life cycle, scaling up, early stage financing, substantive intellectual capital, test marketing etc., is also fast emerging as an integral element of the framework of future infrastructure. In view of the long period involved in research and development of knowledge industries, investments in such infrastructural knowledge industries customarily have a long gestation period and therefore need continued government support for innovation and incubation. The Compact Oxford Reference Dictionary (2003) defines Incubator as "a heated enclosed apparatus in which premature babies can be cared for" or "an apparatus used to hatch eggs or grow micro-organisms". "Innovation" customarily implies bringing about new methods of doing things. While the rapidity of change has brought into focus the need for constant innovation, "innovation" itself needs nursing and a support system to make a perceptible difference in the long term.

Indian entrepreneurs primarily in the knowledge-based sectors like Information Technology (IT) have already demonstrated how a judicious combination of ideas, knowledge, entrepreneurship and technology can create unprecedented wealth. However, most of such success stories have come from the "Land of opportunities" because of adequate infrastructural and other support available in Silicon Valley prior to launching of venture capital. In India, such facilities are not so readily available, despite several Government schemes for funding of R & D projects. The situation, however, improved as seen by CMIE's comprehensive field survey between May and October 2001.

The survey received responses from 304 investment projects (165 owned by private Indian groups, 61 by foreign entities and 78 by government) covering industrial and services sectors under various levels of implementation. Projects from power, telecom and irrigation sectors were excluded, because factors influencing the progress of implementation of these projects were considered to be significantly different from those affecting the rest. Respondents were required to indicate the degree of problems faced in the implementation of their projects in relation to government clearances, availability and cost of finance, infrastructure and demand. The salient features of the survey were as follows:

- Infrastructure was perceived by those surveyed as the least important of the problems.
- Only 19 per cent of the respondents considered government clearances to be a problem because of the fall in the lending rates over the past five years.
- Over capacity, or lack of sufficient demand was the most serious problem faced by the investment projects surveyed.
- FDI investments were concentrated more in the manufacturing sectors in value terms.

ROLE OF BANKS AND FINANCIAL INSTITUTIONS

The vision and long-term direction of infrastructure financing in contemporary Indian lexicon reveals a marked trend towards privatisation. While banks have a major role to play, the crux of the issue lies in reforms in several other areas, e.g. public investment, levy of appropriate user charges, etc. Effective long-term resource mobilization is also indispensable and banking system may have to access market to raise such resources by way of taxable/tax free bonds.

The move towards a markedly different orientation requires direct involvement of the private sector in designing, building, financing and operating public services to provide the cutting edge of development. Parties involved in triggering the process of integration and development of the macro-economic variables of the economy through private infrastructure financing are the following:

- **Sponsors** (owners) who provide equity and are driving force behind a project
- **Contractors** - Construct or operate the assets; sometimes form part of the sponsor group, e.g. the engineering, procurement

and construction (EPC) contractor, the operation and maintenance (O and M) contractor, the feedstock and equipment suppliers.

- **Financiers** - Banks and financial institutions that lend money to the project. Investors may also provide passive equity. Multilateral agencies like the World Bank group - IBRD, IFC and regional agencies, including the ADB, play an important role in infrastructural financing.
- **Customers** : Could be single customer (e.g., power supplied by IPP to an SEB) or by many users (e.g., toll road).
- **Government** : The involvement ranges from public-private partnerships, where governments participate directly to private deals, where government acts as regulator. Preparing a project involves *inter alia* dealing with government agencies, the regulatory framework, environmental permits, land, imports and access to foreign exchange.
- **Facilitators** : Assessing a project and designing legal and financial structure to suit all parties requires lawyers, financial analysts, engineers and the credit rating institutions.

As the major financing requirements in infrastructure are in terms of volume and maturity, debt constrains the development of infrastructural projects. Given the recalcitrance of a single bank/ financial institution in meeting all the credit requirements of a large project, syndication of lenders could justifiably be resorted to for larger coverage because of the multiple impacts generated by infrastructural projects. The need for securing synergies in technology and infrastructure also provided an impetus to the rapid move to convergence. This is why the emerging macro-economic scenario has brought into focus the possibility of All India Development Banks (AIDBs), such as, IDBI, IFCI, ICICI, SIDBI and IIBI transforming themselves from being financiers and intermediaries in chanelling domestic private savings to infrastructure and other investments into more pro-active facilitators to not only salubriously impact the bottomline of AIDBs but also positively influence the long-term growth potential of the economy. Moreover, the Infrastructure Development Finance Company (IDFC) is a specialised financial institution set up in 1997 to provide credit enhancement to infrastructure projects and to extend long term loans and guarantees that existing institutions may not be able to provide. The Asian

Development Bank and the International Finance Corporation are stake-holders in the IDFC. The IDFC and Power Finance Corporation (PFC) have developed a comprehensive funding package. At the state level, the PFC is primarily focused on public sector projects, while the IDFC concentrates on the private sector.

The Annual Policy Statement of RBI (May 18, 2004) broadened the definition of infrastructure (a) lending by including construction related projects involving agro-processing and supply of inputs to agriculture (b) construction for preservation and storage of processed agro-products, perishable goods such as fruits, vegetables and flowers including testing facilities for quality and (c) construction of educational institutions and hospitals. Further, banks have been allowed to raise long-term bonds with a minimum maturity of 5 years to the extent of their exposure of residual maturity of more than 5 years to the infrastructure sector. Outstanding industry-wise deployment of gross bank credit in various infrastructural segments, such as, power, telecom, road and ports as on March 21, 2003 stood at Rs. 10,752 crore, Rs. 4,110 crore and Rs. 5,171crore, respectively. While there has been a substantial increase in credit flow to the infrastructure industries, viz., roads and ports, power and telecommunications, much more needs to be done to adequately meet the infrastructure requirements of the country.

The attempt of the Centre to boost infrastructure through greater involvement of the private sector is indicated by its decision to establish an Infrastructure Development Fund to catalyse Rs 40,000 crore over the next three years. Finance Minister Mr. P. Chidambaram, in his Union Budget for 2004-05, gave an accent on infrastructure through higher allocations and innovative financial arrangements, including setting up a fund for project financing. Mr. Chidambaram directed the Inter-Institutional Group (IIG) formed by IDBI, IDFC, ICICI Bank, SBI, LIC, BoB and PNB to ensure speedy conclusion of loan agreements and implementation of infrastructure projects. But the crux of the issue lies in a sound policy framework, which emphasises effective enforcement of user charges, transparency and high quality regulation.

SBI has project finance as a strategic business unit (SBU). During FY 2004, the SBU sanctioned 18 projects involving a total amount of Rs 2,640.68 crore (fund-based limits of Rs 1,574.30 crore and non-fund based limits of Rs 1,066.38 crore) and made an operating profit of Rs 134 crore. SBI has also played an advisory role to the Centre through various committees, particularly in the power sector. Insurance behemoth LIC, with over Rs 3,40,000 crore of assets, has budgeted a total investment plan of Rs 1,00,000 crore for 2004-05. Almost 70 per cent of the entire investible resources of the life insurance behemoth would be deployed in different segments like G-Sec and infrastructure.

SLOW AND DIFFICULT REFORMS BUT THERE IS NO ALTERNATIVE

The setting up of an infrastructure project has several positive spin-offs, e.g. demand is created for steel, cement, capital goods, engineering equipment, etc. Besides generating employment, the local economy, where the project comes up, also gets a boost. Hence, the quest for solutions to the intractable problems of the millennium agenda not only envisages increased role of the AIDBs in orchestrating the flow of production cycle across a wide spectrum but also attempts to provide an impetus to the growth process through increased private sector investment in infrastructure to broaden growth horizons. This can also be substantiated by the findings of a cross-country study (Mody, 1996,1997). The study vindicated that banks worked as active conduits of mobilisation of savings in Thailand, Indonesia, etc. However, in view of the heterogeneity and multi-dimensional nature of the infrastructural projects, a uniform approach to the development of the infrastructural projects would not suffice. Hence, the policy frame for development of infrastructure in India has to be constantly fine-tuned in the light of the past experience and learning from the experiential initiatives of the Government by bringing about restructuring and positioning, reducing lead times and uncertainties, measurement and monitoring of customer service needs, etc. This would provide the all-important road map for translating the vision of accelerated development into action.

Maintenance–predictive, preventive and breakdown–of infrastructural facilities all along the line necessitates planning for maintenance by design in the building of every asset and its constant monitoring and evaluation to optimise the use of scarce investible resources. The efficacy of the infrastructure sector as an engine of growth in the emerging milieu is hampered by allocative inefficiency, unresponsiveness to users and widespread inefficiencies and wastages, both in investment and delivery services. Consequently, management of infrastructure like a business, introduction of competition, a strong voice and real responsibility to users and other stakeholders, cross-subsidy and public-private partnership in financing and continuing, *albeit* changed role in infrastructure for government, resolution of regulatory issues is sorely needed (World Bank, 1994; *RBI's Report on Currency and Finance, 2001-02)*.

Universal availability, building competitive strengths, eminent affordability, contestability, enforceable contracts, development of markets for long-term debt instruments, efficiency and responsive delivery of infrastructural services through realistic pricing and transparent and nondiscriminatory rules constitute integral elements of the strategy to surmount emerging obstacles and achieve high growth in India. In view thereof, the RBI introduced new guidelines relating to the financing of infrastructure projects such as the criteria for infrastructure financing, the types of financing, the appraisal, the regulatory structure, the administrative arrangements, the inter-institutional guarantees, etc. to accelerate credit to infrastructure in April 1999 for accelerating the flow of resources to the identified projects. It raised the group exposure limit for financing infrastructural projects for financial institutions from 50 per cent to 60 per cent of the capital funds and relaxed the debt-equity norms up to 4:1 in exceptional cases to provide a major fillip to the infrastructure projects. These norms applied only to projects in roads, ports, power and telecommunications. Other features of the scheme were: (a) loans sanctioned should be within the prudential exposure norms prescribed by RBI, (b) the forms of financing include funds raised through subordinated debt and take-out financing with Infrastructure Development Finance Company (IDFC) and other FIs, (c) the credit risk of the project would be borne by the bank and not IDFC and (d) the amount refinanced would depend upon IDFC's risk perception. Some of these conditions relating to regulatory and prudential aspects were further relaxed subsequently to substantially step up credit to infrastructure. These measures, *inter-alia,* included: (i) enhancing the scope of infrastructure lending, (ii) relaxing the prudential single borrower exposure limit from 15 per cent to 20 per cent of capital funds in respect of infrastructure companies, (iii) assigning a concessional risk weight of 50 per cent on investment in securitised paper satisfying certain conditions pertaining to an infrastructure facility, (iv) permitting lending to special purpose vehicles (SPVs) in the private sector, registered under Companies Act for directly undertaking viable infrastructure projects subject to certain conditions and (v) lending to promoters, with certain safeguards and where appropriate, for acquiring a controlling stake in existing infrastructure companies.

In accordance with RBI guidelines, which are effective from April 1, 2002,. the credit exposure norms to be followed in respect of infrastructure projects (including under IID Scheme), has been suitably modified by banks and FIs. These guidelines stressed: (i) overall exposure under the infrastructure portfolio shall not exceed 15 per cent of the total portfolio, (ii) exposure to individual borrowing unit shall not exceed 15 per cent of capital funds as per last audited accounts, (iii) assistance to infrastructure projects in a State shall not exceed 50 per cent of capital funds as per last audited accounts and (iv) generally restricting financing to the extent of 50 per cent of the total loan requirement in case of infrastructure projects costing more than Rs. 100 crore.

The discussion clearly brings out that India's decade-old economic reform effort is arguably at crossroads. While there is broad consensus among planners and policy-makers of the need to implement second-generation economic reforms speedily, infrastructural bottlenecks have constrained the development process. An important way of overcoming development constraints could be the thrust on the role of banks and FIs in infrastructure financing. With the changing profile of infrastructural projects, the diverse modalities of infrastructure financing consistent with the market-oriented economy has brought to the fore the need for strategic interventions for revitalisation and growth. It is in this context that the issue of internal resource generation by infrastructural projects can no longer be swept under the rug or an ostrich like attitude adopted.

HERE TODAY, WHERE TOMORROW?

The incentives need to be enhanced through commercial management, competition and stake-holder involvement by the two approaches of the Concession and the Structured Financing Option (SFO) to planning, development, management and financing of infrastructure projects in a futuristic perspective. A concession, which involves several legal and economic issues, including the organisation of government entities responsible for concession programmes and the adequacy of the broader legal and regulatory environment, is a legal arrangement in which a firm obtains from the Government the right to provide a particular service, which can be subsequently transferred to the Government in the case of longer-lived assets like roads, highways, airports, bridges, etc. (Michael Kerf, *et al*, 1998). The Concession Approach, where the concessionaire builds the project and is granted a franchise period during which the cost and return can be recovered, is thus well suited to projects that can charge users and leaves the Government with the option of imposing a tariff subsequent to the transfer. Concession schemes of the Build-Operate-Transfer (BOT) type for the development of infrastructure projects by the private sector attempt to meet the shortage in public resources and widespread disenchantment with the performance of state-owned utilities. However, such schemes are of limited applicability, where the required investment is relatively large in relation to the importance of the net cash flows generated by the infrastructure, after maintenance and operating costs. They also refer to projects, whose revenues have a high degree of uncertainty. Trujillo, Jose A., Remy Cohen, Xavier Freixas and Sheehy Robert (1997) have strongly contended that BOT schemes, defined by the concentration of all responsibilities (building, management and financing) in a unique private agent (or a joint venture of private agents) are inefficient in the case of projects characterised by high relative investment and high uncertainty. More specifically, there are efficiency gains if financing is made through a neutral special purpose vehicle (SPV) sponsored by the public sector on behalf of the infrastructure users and payers. Such a risk-return mechanism allows the mitigation of the consequences of the uncertainty that typically characterizes both revenue flow (demand) and financial cost (interest rates and exchange rates). Further, the mechanism allows a better treatment of subjective risks of a political and regulatory nature. Apart from the reduction of the overall cost, the unbundled mechanism provides the sponsor with a higher degree of flexibility, particularly the characteristics of the operating and maintenance contracts and pricing policy. Moreover, the SPV is the appropriate means to channel all public subsidies and guarantees, including those of the multilateral agencies (MLA).

FAST-TRACK TREATMENT

The Government adopted new bidding norms for the 23 short-listed BOT projects for four-laning of 3000 km of National Highways. About 3,000 km length of National Highways are proposed to be taken up during 2003-2004 for widening to 4-lanes on Build-Operate and Transfer (BOT) basis. The civil works cost varies from Rs. 3 to 4 crore per km. The successful bidders are given the assignment of design, construction, operation and maintenance of the highway stretches. The Feasibility Study is to be carried out separately. Variants of the BOT approach of "project financing" to attract private participation in financing, construction and operation of infrastructure, where the value of efficiency gain from private participation can outweigh the extra cost of borrowing include (i) Build-Operate-Transfer (BOT) used in the context of a country's highway network, energy, utility and port sectors provides private consortium with a concession to finance, build, operate and maintain a facility. Investors levy user-charges to compensate for costs of construction, debt servicing and operations during the life of the concession. However, the facility reverts to the public authority on completion of the concession. While the concept is constrained by the problem of non-excludability of users, the Government of India amended the National Highway Act in 1995 to permit private sector financing of highway projects under BOT Scheme. (ii) Design-Build-Finance-Operate (DBFO) basis, where the private operator has the flexibility to design the project to minimise the maintenance costs which could be 1 per cent of the total project cost per annum. The cost is recovered by the annuity method, i.e. a fixed annual return accrues to the project operator in a pre-determined manner, irrespective of various other considerations; (iii) Build-Own-Operate-Transfer (BOOT) is broadly similar to BOT but ownership of project assets is more explicit and may also encompass underlying infrastructure. The project reverts to the government on completion of the stipulated period; (iv) Build-Transfer-Lease-Operate (BTLO) scheme, where the government provides the right-of-way on which the highways build and agreements require the promoter to pay a nominal rent or payment for use of the land; (v) Build-Operate-Lease-Transfer (BOLT) wherein the asset is owned by the creator and is subsequently leased. During the lease period, the owner receives lease rentals. Other similar mechanisms include (a) Build-Own-Operate-Sell (BOOS), where the Government buys the infrastructure from the franchisee after the end of the franchisee period and Lease-Refurbish-Operate-Transfer (LROT).

In sum, all these variants of the basic approach stress the role of the government as a limited regulator in respect of safety, security, environment, etc. with flexibility to developers in respect of fixation and collection of tariff, framing of suitable manpower policies, planning of area development, operation and marketing of its facilities and finalisation of means of finance and structure of the project finance. While there is a high degree of viability in ports, power and telecommunications, the element of risk could be high in road building unless BOT is properly structured. Structured Financing Option (SFO) basically implies non-recourse project specific financing. Securitization, which is an off-balance sheet financing technique, involves the removal of the lending institutions assets from the balance sheet and its funding by investors, who purchase a negotiable financial instrument evidencing this indebtedness without recourse to the original lender. This requires securing of debt instrument by cash flows of the collateral value for the specified asset financed by the instrument to optimise total outlays. It thus enables AIFIs to avoid holding assets to maturity and leverage a given corpus into larger volumes of debt-financed periods over a period of time. In view of the enormity of required investments, no single body—the Government, financial institutions or the private sector corporate have resources to invest entirely on one project. We need, therefore, to look at innovative restructuring and creative solutions to issues that have defied conventional approaches. The litmus test of effective infrastructure necessitates joint participation of all agencies of government—either state or central, reduction of deficit or dissavings, allocation of more funds to infrastructure projects, etc. to reduce real and worrisome fault lines. Corporate and public savings could be used with appropriate instruments and pension funds set up for inducing investment in long-term instruments.

The banks and financial institutions need to mobilize domestic savings with innovative instruments—with differentiation in price-period-hedge against inflation, legal statutory relaxation, exit options and deepening of secondary market to provide momentum to the growth process. The broad parameters of a wide raft of reforms relate to public acceptability of a infrastructure project and acceptability of cost recovery together with acceptability of private sector involvement, private sector entities with credibility, reinforcing the confidence in quality of service of the public and willingness to pay for such service. Residual needs of infrastructure could be addressed to by involving social aspect requiring special skills for appraisal of the projects, funding of the project and monitoring of the implementation of the projects to curtail leakage, wastage and for ensuring quality of construction, pricing of tariff, and revenue management, proper coordination of various agencies. Loss of coordination would lead to mismatch, e.g. power generated by private sector entity agreed to be transmitted by public sector entity; but delay in laying transmission lines and inability to lift the power, etc. This, however, necessitates the tapping of capital market through a innovative credit rating system, launching of innovative borrowing instruments, development of an active secondary market in such securitised assets, as also of greater rigour and market-oriented lending activities by these institutions.

COMMERCIALISATION OF INFRASTRUCTURE

While infrastructure continues to be largely in the domain of the public sector, private participation is growing and a greater role for private-public partnership is on the anvil. In view of the peculiarities inherent in the infrastructural projects, the banks' usual instruments for evaluating business proposals on a corporate financing basis—essentially balance sheet analysis—are not very meaningful because the project SPVs (Special Purpose Vehicles) balance sheet does not reveal much except projections for the future. The increasing popularity of SPV is, however, reflected in the execution of the projects like the Moradabad bypass and the Ahmedabad-Vadodara Expressway. The Ministry has also worked out a novel mechanism to leverage NHAI funds to set up SPVs, wherein the NHAI puts in a certain amount of equity into the SPV with or without a partner and uses this equity to raise money from the market. The money is to be paid back from the future toll revenues.

In sum, there are three ways of moving ahead in infrastructure—privatisation, commercialisation and private financing of public infrastructure (PFPI). Privatisation involves sale of assets under conditions, which bring about investments from the private sector and improved quality of services. Commercialisation attempts to sweat assets already created through enhanced investments and improved service. PFPI leads to contraction a structure in a way that enables the public sector to buy services for citizens, which cannot be easily charged for through user charges. In line with the impeccable nature of facts marshalled in support of streamlining of infrastructure finance, IDFC has created the framework conditions for the privatisation of Indian ports as well as for creating the first PFPI in India for annuity-financed roads. Both frameworks are in use and the process paradigm has also been created for ports and roads so that appropriate investment can fructify. Nine such roads have been contracted out, well below benchmark pricing resulting in real value for money for public investments. IDFC is also creating similar frameworks and process paradigms in the area of power distribution, agri-infrastructure and thus on driving the whole framework for PFPI in India.

The *Expert Group* stressed the significance of commercialisation of infrastructural projects 'through a system of user charges, which bear a direct relation to the special benefits that the facility provides to the user'. The infrastructure projects are characterised by risks of development, construction, operating, demand, financial, market and political and the problematic involved in the operational process. To meet acceptable risks in alternative decision-making models, the *Expert Group* recommended credit enhancement of borrowing entities by institutional innovations such as upgradation of appraisal institutions, bond insurance, provision of guarantees, credit rating of infrastructure projects and companies, funding of pre-feasibility and feasibility studies and securitisation of fixed assets to make them quickly and easily transferable. As flow of private investment in infrastructure is hampered by attendant risks, attempts to check these risks would facilitate greater investment and reduce the cost of services. The accepted rate of return for a project in a developing country is likely to be higher than the acceptable minimum anywhere else in the developed world. Government action in terms of minimising red-tape, providing a fair and timely transparent bidding process, assurance of foreign remittances, proper supportive legal and political framework ensuring no interference after the implementation of the project will reduce risk premium and induce investors to accept lower returns.

The policy level significance of this approach stems from grossly inadequate internal resources of public infrastructure entities, dwindling Plan outlay for infrastructure and even shortfall in public investment *vis-a-vis* the target. The response of the private sector has been woefully inadequate in offsetting the declining public sector investment. The failure of the private sector in this sphere is usually attributed to thc levy of inadequate user charges, difficulty in assessing the long-term risks in financing by the private sector, non-transparency in project outsourcing processes and numerous time consuming clearances.

While infrastructural development has largely been driven by fiscal constraints, it has also been motivated by concerns about the effectiveness of infrastructure. The statistics are revealing: freight traffic increase of almost 85 times and passenger traffic increase of over 75 times as against a measly increase of just over 8 times in the road network starkly reflects the need to ensure efficient, responsive delivery of infrastructure for inducing the desired level of private investment and facilitating all-round accelerated growth in the context of tectonic changes brought about by the Structural Adjustment Programme (SAP). Elements of the second-generation reforms germane to the infrastructure sector include emphasis on streamlining existing facilities, tariff reform for cost rationalisation, removal of subsidy and simultaneous action at the level of central and states to recover appropriate user charges in a wide range of infrastructural services to encourage private investment. These could provide the substance, parameters, direction and strategy for scripting a new road map in the future—a future in which the per capita income is doubled in the next ten years.

The Approach Paper to the Tenth Five-Year Plan aimed at an intermediate indicative target of 8.0 per cent. A growth rate of this magnitude—a growth rate well above Professor's Raj Krishna's 'Hindu rate of growth'—requires initiation of innovative and proactive efforts in respect of infrastructure. While the main catalyst for the progress is the establishment of the Road Development Fund, private sector participation continues to remain sketchy with most of the investments are coming from government bodies. Most private sector investments are towards bypasses, bridges and the like. However, the actual investments on national highways or any major project is marginal. Road is the only sector on which budgetary support is set to rise. Actual spending as per revised estimates increased by 56.8 per cent in 1999-2000 and budgetary support for 2000-01 increased by 25.5 per cent. The National Highway Development Programme (NHDP) is expected to see substantial spending in future. The major sources of financing include Petrol Cess, NHAI Bonds, Multilateral Funding, etc. The NHDP envisages strengthening and 4/6-laning of high density roads, which includes:

- Golden Quadrilateral, which is a 5952 kms stretch connecting Delhi, Calcutta, Chennai and Mumbai.
- North-East-South-West Corridor, a 7300 kms distance connecting Kashmir to Kanyakumari and Silchar to Porbandar.

According to the 208th Flash Report issued by the Ministry of Statistics and Programme Implementation for February 2004, spillage in implementing the major infrastructure projects, costing over Rs. 100 crore, in sectors like roads, railways and power, resulted in cost overruns of Rs. 18,644.25 crore. The steps initiated by the Government to fine tune the monitoring mechanism to ensure timely completion of projects include adoption of two-stage clearance system and stricter appraisal of project reports before investment approval; taking up of projects for implementation only after funds have been fully tied up; in-depth review of projects on monthly as well as quarterly basis by the Government; setting up of an Empowered Committee in the administrative ministries for review of departmentally executed projects; setting up of Standing Committees in the Ministries/ Departments to fix responsibility for time and cost overruns; appointment of nodal officers for each project with continuity of tenure and issue of guidelines on standard bidding documents for adoption.

DEVELOPMENT OF PROJECTS ON DIFFERENT METHODS OF TOLLING

In view of the operational problems involved in normal tolling in many regions (e.g. the Coimbatore bypass constructed by L&T) and the uncertainty regarding the viability of such projects, different innovative methods are being explored to provide a stimulus to industrial growth. Some of them are: The annuity based tolling was tried in the 65 km. Panagar-Palset stretch in Delhi-Calcutta part of Quadrilateral, where IDFC advised the government. Under annuity-based tolling certain annual / semi-annual payments are made to the concessionaire, which cover the fixed and variable costs and profit element. Projects are awarded to the developer bidding for lowest annuity payment. Under Shadow Tolling, the concessionaire receives toll on the basis of assumed load. IDFC advises GoI on shadow tolling used in the

Tuni-Ankapally stretch between Calcutta and Chennai. Under Direct Tolling, the concessionaire collects the toll directly from user. User resentment for direct tolling is very high in India as a result of which it may not be very successful. A modification of direct tolling whereby toll is based on actual entry and exit point is expected to cause less resentment. This method is being tried in the Bangalore-Mysore expressway corridor. The toll collected will be on the basis of distance travelled, which will be monitored at multiple entry / exit points. The project promoted by the Kalyani group, VHB International and SAB International is estimated to cost Rs. 40 billion and includes an outer peripheral road, 121 km expressway, 5 self-sustaining townships which can house 1 lac residents in each township, 400 MW of power generation, telecom, water supply, sewerage treatment, theme parks, amusement and recreational facilities. As far as state projects are concerned substantial progress has been made in 3 states—AP, Punjab and Maharashtra. Important road projects in various states include MSRDC flyovers, Mumbai-Pune Expressway, Bandra-Worli Link, APSRDC projects, Punjab State government projects, etc.

India's most ambitious infrastructure project since independence christened the National Highways Development Project (NHDP) led the way with timely completion of projects through prompt decision-making and faster payments to suppliers, better quality and cost of infrastructure, adequate quantity and reliability of roads through high quality work specification and the use of state-of-the-art equipment, lean officer-trained organisation tapping private sector efficiency by consolidating its sourcing and supply-chain efficiencies in terms of work supervision and maintenance. A report by Morgan Stanley Dean Witter asserts, "the current pace of execution of the Golden Quadrilateral (GQ) shows a degree of commitment not normally associated with government projects." The attempt to provide permanently recurring benefits and enhance the quality of life of the people requires that a top-of-the line infrastructural system is in conformity with implementation schedules to prevent time and cost overruns. This requires time bound clearances at different stages and effective inter-agency co-ordination together with streamlining of monitoring and evaluation systems. The multiplicity of special economic regulatory agencies overseeing important infrastructural segments as power, telecommunications and ports in India complicate matters considerably. Hence, issues, such as, effective delineation of the responsibilities of regulators and policymakers and placing the creation of an independent regulator within a broader restructuring of the sector require to be resolved quickly.

A FUTURISTIC POLICY FRAMEWORK

The process of economic liberalisation requires fulfillment of the unswerving objectives of intensification and consolidation of the ongoing thrust on competitiveness, productivity and efficiency. While building on the past, we must invest in the future; while strengthening our core competencies, we must explore new vistas of development and seed options for future growth. The emergence of the new paradigm of high growth with moderate inflation on the strength of ever increasing productivity rests on the technological renaissance, the smoothening of the business cycle, supply side management, etc. These aspects can be decisively influenced by infrastructure. Adequate development of infrastructure in the present-day non-linear world cannot, however, be effectively addressed without a focused, long-term strategy implemented nationwide with adaptations to suit regional conditions to help achieve economies of scale and cost. The success of the infrastructural system requires coordinated and concerted action from the government, the private sector, the industry, finance, banks, technology institutions, the users and stakeholders urgently to transform the economy. .

The challenge of leading change in these turbulent times points to evolving considerations and indeed a paradigm shift in the approach of banks and FIs with support of the Government. This support can take the forms of direct financial contributions, exemption from / reduction of taxes, royalties, complementary investments, a period of exclusivity, etc. (Freshfields, 1995). This is necessary to meet the exponentially increasing requirements of infrastructure financing for enhancing the country's competitive edge in a wide range of activities. These include enhancing power availability and streamlining its transmission and distribution system, setting up of Technology Parks, creation of new planned cities and upgradation of civic infrastructure.

While this process of change and transformation could lead to a win-win situation all around, the promise will be dissipated unless there is a conscious direction of the process. We need, therefore, to implement the "priority agenda"—a work programme with defined milestones with concerned ministries and a facilitating mechanism. Thus cognisance of the totality of situation leads us to a renewed focus on infrastructure as an effective instrument of taking the country to new and greater heights—heights, which might not even have been foreseen in the not too distant past.

REFERENCES

1. Ahluwalia, Montek S (1999): "India's Economic Reforms: An Appraisal", in *India in the Era of Economic Reforms*, (Eds.) Jeffrey D. Sachs, Ashutosh Varshney, Nirupam Bajpai, Oxford University Press, New Delhi.
2. Asian Development Bank (2001): "Private Participation in Infrastructure: Best Practices from ADB", Reprinted in *Indian Infrastructure*, Volume 4, No. 4, November.
3. Baker, Dean and Todd Schafer (1995): *The Case for Public Investment,* Washington, D.C.: Economic Policy Institute.
4. Boycko, Maxim, Andrei Shleifer and Robert W. Vishny (1992): "Property Rights, Soft Budget Constraints and Privatisation" in Harvard University and University of Chicago. Processed.
5. Expert Group on Commercialisation of Infrastructure (1996): *The India Infrastructure Report: Policy Imperatives for Growth and Welfare*, Ministry of Finance, Government of India, New Delhi, Volumes I-III.
6. Fishbein, Gregory and Suman Babbar (1996): "Private Financing of Toll Roads", Resource Mobilization and Cofinancing (RMC), *Discussion Paper Series 117*, The World Bank, Washington, D.C.
7. Government of India: *Seventh, Eighth, Ninth and Tenth Five Year Plans*, Planning Commission, New Delhi, various years.
8. Gramlich, E M (1994):"Infrastructure Investment: A Review Essay", *Journal of Economic Literature*, 32.
9. Kerf Michael, R. David Gray, Timothy Irwin, Celine Levesque, Robert Taylor (1998): *Concessions for Infrastructure: A Guide to Their Design and Award*, The World Bank, Washington, D.C.
10. Klein, Michael, Jae So and Ben Shin (1996): "Transaction Costs in Private Infrastructure Projects - Are They Too High?" *Viewpoint 95.* World Bank Finance and Private Sector Development Department, Washington.
11. Mody, A. (1996, 1997): "Infrastructure Strategies in East Asia", *EDI*, World Bank.
12. Sappington, David E.M. and Joseph E. Stiglitz (1987): "Privatisation, Information and Incentives", *Journal of Policy Analysis and Management 6.*

13. Schmidt, Klaus M. (1996): "The Costs and Benefits of Privatisation: An Incomplete Contracts Approach, Information and Incentives", *Journal of Law, Economics and Organisation 12(1).*
14. Shapiro, Carl and Robert D. Willig (1990): "Economic Rationales for the Scope of Privatisation", in *The Political Economy Reforms of Public Sector Reforms and Privatisation*, (Eds.) E. Saleiman and J. Waterbury, Boulder: Westview Press.
15. Sharma, Manoranjan (2000): "Sustainable Agricultural and Rural Development: The Case for Infrastructure", *Rural Prosperity and Agriculture: Policies and Strategies — Infrastructure and Institutional Support* (ed.) R.C. Choudhary and R.P. Singh, National Institute of Rural Development (NIRD), Hyderabad.
16. Shirley, Mary and Patrick Walsh (2000): "Public versus Private Ownership: The Current State of the Debate", World Bank, *Policy Research Working Paper 2420,* Washington, DC.
17. Stiglitz, Joseph E. (1996): "The Role of Government in Economic Development", in *Annual World Bank Conference on Development Economics*, (Eds.) Michael Burno and Boris Pleskovik, Washington, D.C., The World Bank.
18. Trujillo, Jose A., Remy Cohen, Xavier Freixas and Sheehy Robert: *(1997)*: "Infrastructure Financing with Unbundled Mechanisms". Paper at Conference: *Alternatives to Traditional BOTs for Financing Infrastructure Projects,* sponsored by the Infrastructure and Financial Market Division of the Inter-American Development Bank, Washington, D.C.

5

RISKS IN BANKING: AN OVERVIEW

M.C. Pande*

On July 26, 2004–the RBI announced amalgamation of Global Trust Bank (GTB) with Oriental Bank of Commerce (OBC). GTB's non-performing assets (NPAs) mounted and its net worth turned negative. Fall of this bank has once again raised the issue of risk management in banks. Asset Liability Management (ALM) is gaining importance day by day. ALM is called a comprehensive and dynamic framework for measuring, monitoring and managing the market risk (i.e. liquidity, interest rate and exchange rate risk) of a bank. This article is an attempt of giving a wide view of various types of risk in banking sector.

Risk is defined as probability of loss. It can also be defined as uncertainty in the profit. Risk is strictly attached with the business. Risk taking is entrepreneurship. None of the business can be run without the risk of profit. Proverb 'No risk no gain' proves true in business. An entrepreneur tries to minimize the risk in business but he cannot overcome them completely. Grace Happer has rightly said, "A ship in port is safe but this is not what ships are built for." In the field of economics, profit is considered as the return of entrepreneurship (risk taking). So an enterprise is not an act of removing the risk, but of managing them tactfully.

*Faculty of Commerce, Govt. P.G. College, Rudrapur (Uttaranchal).

RISK IN BANKS

Risk is inherent in banking and is unavoidable. Main functions of banks are borrowing money (accepting deposits) and lending it to the prospective customers. All the activities of the banks are monetary in nature and bear risk at every step. Banks earn most of their profits in the form of interest on lending. For this they invest their money in different loan accounts. They analyze the repayment capacity of the client and provide them money.

Right decisions at right point of the time can pave the path of success. On the contrary a wrong or delayed decision may ruin the institution. A bank has to take the risk of repayment. Bank can earn profit in the form of interest or may loose the principal itself. Risk is necessary part of banking but sometimes high-risk becomes cause of trouble. Following cases are noteworthy:

1. Marrill Lynch lost $377 million through trading mortgage-backed securities in an innovative form in 1987.
2. Midland Bank lost a reported pound sterling 116 million by guessing wrong on interest rates movement in 1989.
3. Bank of New England made massive bad debt provision, suffering a ruin on deposit and had to be supported by government to the time of some $ 2 billion in 1991.
4. In the year1996 the major Japanese banks wrote off a total of some Japanese Yen 6000 billion of bad debt accumulated from the preceding boom years.
5. In the year 2003, RBI's inspection report revealed the net worth of Global Trust Bank as eroded and capital adequacy ratio at zero. This bank amalgamated with Oriental Bank of Commerce on July 26th, 2004.

KINDS OF RISK IN BANKING BUSINESS

During the mid-term review of the monetary and credit policy for 1998-99, the governor of RBI has stated on October 30th 1998- "Banks are advised to introduce effective risk management system to cover credit risk, market risk and operational risk on priority basis. To this end a comprehensive risk management approach should be adopted and a detailed structure of operating limits, guidelines and other parameters should be put in place. Banks have also been advised recently to address market risks in structured manner by adopting a more comprehensive asset-liability management practices with effect from April 1, 1999.

Risk manifest themselves in many ways and the risk in banking are a result of many diverse activities, executed from many locations, and by numerous people. Based on the origin and their nature risks are classified into various categories:

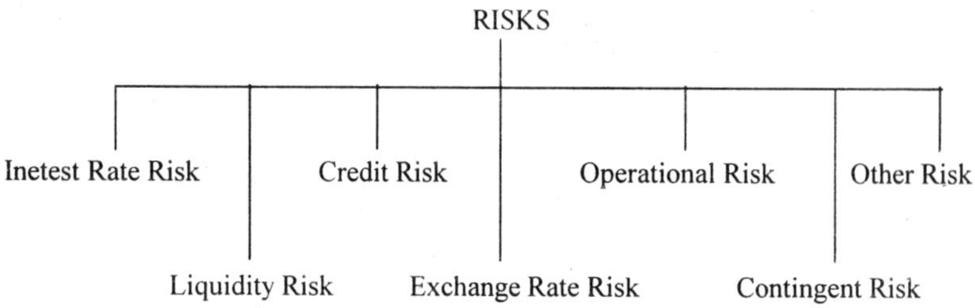

INTEREST RATE RISK

Interest rate risk is the risk where changes in market interest rate might adversely affect a bank's financial condition. It is felt when changes in the interest rate structure put pressure on the net interest margin of the bank.

Interest rate risk arises by the variability of return caused by changes in interest rates that affects expected earnings on financial transactions.

Interest rate risk may occur in the following ways:

(a) *Restructuring Risk* : Sometimes banks have to restructure the interest rate levels either due to market condition or due to regulatory intervention of the Reserve Bank of India. RBI announces changes in rate of interest by the banks.

This may effect decisions regarding the type and the mix of asset and liabilities and their maturity periods. The effect will be seen on all the existing assets but on only new deposits. This will lower the marginal cost of funds. In other words the loss of interest received on loans will be higher than the gain due to reduction in interest on deposits.

(b) *Volatility Risk* : Sometimes short-term fluctuation in market may create risk for banks. If there is a sudden shortfall in supply of cash, people may approach to banks to withdraw money from bank and to invest directly in open market. They also try to take maximum loan from the banks so that they may get higher returns. This may cause default in maintenance in CRR or borrowing funds at high rates. This adversely affects the profits of the banks.

(c) *Prepayment Risk* : Banks prepare their policies according to the prevailing market conditions. They fix the asset liability mix as per those policies. In case of reduction in interest rates, bank may suffer losses on prepayment of loans by its customers because bank will have to reinvest it on lower rates of interest on deposit as per previous rates. This will narrow the gap of interest on deposits and advances and will cause losses to the banks.

(d) *Call/Put Risk* : The issue of bond and securities by the banks may include call /put option. In call option a bank may redeem the bonds before maturity while in put option the investor may seek premature payment of bonds. In increasing interest rate trend investor exercises put options and bank have to bear high replacement cost.

(e) *Reinvestment Risk* : The fluctuation in the return from reinvestment due to change in interest rates is called the reinvestment risk. The risk can be associated to the intermediate cash flows arising due to the payment of interest, installments of loans etc. These intermediate cash inflows arising from a security/loan are usually reinvested and the income from such reinvestments will depend on the prevailing rates of interest at the time of the reinvestment and the reinvestment strategy. Due to uncertainty in the market, reinvested cash flows may give lower returns.

(f) *Bases Risk* : When the changes in interest rates on deposits and advances are not uniform, it will affect the spread of interest. Bank may suffer losses due to unfavorable changes in interest rates. For example, if a bond provides 9% interest on its deposits and charges 14% on the advances. Suddenly rates on deposits are slashed by 1% on deposits and 0.5% on advances resulting new rates on deposits and advances as 8% and 13.5% respectively. This will result the increase in spread from 5% (14-9%) to 5.5% (13.5-8%). On the other side spread may be narrowed.

LIQUIDITY RISK

Liquidity means keeping the fund readily available for payment of bank's current liabilities. Measuring and managing the liquidity needs is very important for effective operation of commercial banks. Banks accept deposits and the amount so received are mostly invested in advances. A part of it is kept at bank for liabilities payable on demand or at very short notice. Liquidity risk is the possibility of not having adequate cash and hence a deficit situation. Liquidity risk management represents the ability to deal with shortage or surplus of fund. On one hand surplus funds causes danger to profitability, on the other hand shortage of funds places the bank in hard waters.

Liquidity crises may occur for any of following reasons-

1. When a large amount is received as short-term deposits and invested into long-term investment.
2. When short-term payment requirement is not assessed properly and money is not kept in liquid form.
3. When due to unexpected change in volatile market, political or other reasons or due to any rumor customers withdraw their funds for investing in more profitable investment.
4. Faulty appraisal of NPAs, inefficient recovery efforts, recession in market are few other reasons which may cause the crisis of liquidity before a bank.

CREDIT RISK

The credit or default risk is the function of the borrower's probability of default. The primary danger of granting credit is the chance that the borrower will not repay the loan. This uncertainty is known as credit or default risk. Lending money is one of the basic functions of a bank and also the main source of its revenue. They (banks) must earn higher yields on assets to maintain positive spread and suitable net interest income.

A credit risk begins from the time of disbursement of loan continuously throughout the payment period and ends only with the full and final payment of loan. Credit risk also has an intricate linkage with interest rate risk and liquidity risk, which makes it more critical to the bank.

EXCHANGE RATE RISK

When a bank is involved in multi-currency operations, it is exposed to foreign exchange risk. Generally banks undertake transactions in foreign exchange like accepting deposits making loan and advances and quoting prices for foreign exchange transactions. In these transactions the amount of currency that have to be delivered in exchange for another currencies will depend on the exchange rate. This rate keeps on changing depending upon the value of currency, which is influenced by various factors, including demand and supply, balance of payments, trade deficit, government borrowing, inflation, interest rates and political stability. Change in exchange rate affects banks' assets and liabilities. If the liabilities on one currency exceed the level of assets in the same currency then the currency mismatch can add value or erode value depending upon the currency movements.

Exchange rate risk can arise in two forms, viz. translation risk and transaction risk. Transaction risk occurs when change in price of a currency causes loss in any particular transaction. On the other hand translation risk is exposed when the balancesheet of the bank is converted in home currency and due to change in exchange rate bank's level of investments or borrowings in foreign currency is adversely affected.

OPERATIONAL RISK

Operational risk arises due to failure of operating system in a bank because of certain reasons like fraudulent activities, natural disaster, human error or omission or sabotage etc. Internal check system is essential for minimizing the operational risk. In this system the work of a level voluntarily checked by the work of another level. Therefore in the internal check system the probability of fraud and omission reduces to the minimum level.

With the introduction of new products like credit cards, debit cards, smart cards etc. the risk of frauds has increased manifolds. According to an estimate, card fraud is likely to claim the lions share of frauds being experienced in general, and could will dominate average operation losses as a whole. The greatest cause of losses occurred due to loss or steal of plastic cards. The second largest source and the fastest growing reason for loss is use of counterfeit cards. Emergence of E-Commerce and Internet Banking is also a matter of concern.

CONTINGENT RISK

Contingent risk arises due to off balancesheet items such as guarantees, letters of credit, underwriting, commitments etc. Bank extends guarantee for payment and underwrites on obligation to a third party in case of its client defaults. Therefore, in this case only default of the client will trigger a loss or result in it acquiring a sub-standard assets. In case of foreign exchange agreements, the risk arises when the client company is unable to exercise its obligation and creates a binding agreement. Contingent liabilities, therefore are referred to as off balance sheet items.

OTHER RISKS

Apart from interest rate risk, liquidity risk, credit risk, exchange rate risk, contingent risk and operational risk, there are some other risks in banking which are given below —

- Few political activities and decisions arise as political risk in banking.
- Labour unrest, dispute among top executives, lack of motivation, inadequate skills and en-mass resignation by competent executives lead to human risk.
- Change in technology and obsolescence of old one cause technological risk. Adoption of computers and frequently change in its various versions have burdened the bank.
- Legal changes threat from customers is known as legal risk. Popularity of consumer courts / forums has also increased this up to a great extent.
- When failure of a system creates problem for other systems as a chain reaction, systemic risk arises. Rise of credit risk may adversely affect solvency, profitability and liquidity position of the banks.
- Price risk arises due to change in market prices of assets, liabilities etc. This results in strain on the profitability of the bank. Sudden fall in stock exchange rates may cause huge losses to a bank. It may even collapse a bank.
- Apart from above mentioned risks many other risks also cause harm to the banking. These are liability risk, compliance risk, tax risk, crime risk, funding risk, market risk etc.

MANAGEMENT OF RISKS

Risks in banking are complex in nature. Exposure of one risk can lead to exposure to another risk. In 1980, American commercial banks had been eager to lend to developing countries like Brazil and Mexico, but they hoped to escape exposure to currency, interest and credit risk. An instrument known as syndicated Eurodollar loan seemed to provide the perfect answer. It was denominated in dollars (no currency risk), was payable on a floating rate basis (no interest rate risk) and was made to governments (which were unlikely to go out of business). But, after US interest rates sky rocked in the early1980s, countries like Mexico and Brazil went into default. They were unable to make the interest payments on their loans and the general credit assumption that government do not default proved to be wrong.

Market risk may give birth to credit risk, default risk and others. Some times curing of one risk may give birth to other risk. Risk management is an exercise that makes a bank ready for achieving the targets. It works as balancing act between risk levels and profit needs of the bank. It can be compared to the mock exercises that army has to undertake so that it may remain prepared for eventual war. Stress and other tests to assess the load bearing capacity that have to be performed by an architect before he allows construction of a building, a quality control check before releasing of goods to market or repeated rehearsals that a theatre group has to conduct before performance. Indian banks, under guidance and control of Reserve Bank of India, are managing their business risks with the help of Asset Liability Management, that is a uniform effort of banks for measuring, monitoring and managing the risks. In fact, all these risks have always been the part and parcel of banking business and banks are well aware of all them. Sometimes it is said that risk management practices are like fresh cup of tea blending Assam tea with Darjeeling tea. But, it is very clear that this blending is the need of time because globalization has placed tough competition before our banks and such tea is in good demand.

REFERENCES

1. *Business Today*, August29, 2004.
2. Bagchi, S.K. (October 2003), Credit Risk Management- A Panacea or Conundrum, *SBI Monthly Review* (Mumbai).

3. Deep Chandra (2000), "Asset Liability Management in Commercial Banks" – An unpublished project report - IGNOU.
4. Khurana, S.K. (1999), *Security Analysis and Investment Management*, Skylark Publication, New Delhi.
5. Ravi Kumar, T. (2000), *Asset Liability Management*,Vision Books, New Delhi.
6. RBI (1999), Circular BP. BC 8/21.040098/99 dt.10-02-1999.
7. Sabnani Prahlad (July 2002), *IBA Bulletin* (Mumbai).
8. Subrahmanyam, Dr. Ganti (June 1993) *SBI Monthly Review* (Bombay).

6

BANKING SECTOR REFORMS: RETROSPECT AND PROSPECT

B.K. Agrawal* & Subodh Kumar**

The liberalization of market, privatization of ownership and globalisation of economy was initiated in 1991 in the light of recommendations of Narasimham Committee. Other important changes in the banking sector were deregulation of interest rate, reduction in SLR and CRR, operational freedom to the commercial banks and recapitalization of weak public sector banks.

The first phase of India's financial reforms were 'curative' as they were for cleansing of balancesheet of banks and putting them on a recovery path. The second generation reforms will be 'preventive' aimed at building a strong and robust banking system which can withstand the pressures of globalisation.

Indian banks move gradually towards universal banking where bank is financial service provider and it is one-stop financial super market with range of services, such as commercial, merchant, investment banking and even insurance. Thus, banking system is getting redefined. The public sector banks have come across the multi facet competition that involves cost reduction and production diversification along with technological advancement.

The process of strengthening the banking system has to be viewed as continuing one. There is no finite end to improving the levels of efficiency and profitability. The banks have to cope constantly with changes occurring in the business environment.

*Reader and Head, Dept. of Economics, HNB Garhwal Univ. Campus, Badshahi Thaul Distt. Tehri Garhwal, Uttaranchal.

**Senior Lecturer, Dept. of Commerce, HNB Garhwal Univ. Campus, Badshahi Thaul, Distt. Tehri Garhwal, Uttaranchal.

India's economic policy has a triangular base of democratic compulsions, fundamental issues along with globalised environment of economic reforms. The banking sector has been in the centre of economic policy as it occupies predominant position in Indian Financial System. We have earned an experience of a decade in implementing the reform process. The public sector banks dominate our banking system. They contribute for more than 85 percent share in total banking business. They practiced the set of norms during the period for improvement of their health and better future in global market. Some of the measures were implemented very successfully and for others they are struggling like NPA management.

Main reform measures in the banking industry have been:

- Prudential accounting norms
- Capital adequacy ratio
- Entry of private sector banks
- Gradual reduction in CRR and SLR
- Phased deregulation in interest rates
- Directed credit and rural finance
- Financial supervision system
- Risk management
- Rationalisation of manpower in public sector banks

PRUDENTIAL ACCOUNTING NORMS

Before reform process, the banks were booking incomes on accrual basis and to the extent banks were booking incomes, which were unrealizable, their balancesheet was overstated. Therefore, the initial reform measures were centered on cleansing of the balancesheet of banks. The prudential accounting norms were implemented. These norms are internationally followed in the banking business wherein assets are classified into four categories—standard, sub-standard, doubtful and loss. The income recognition is done on realized bases instead of accrual basis. Other than standard assets, the rest are named as non-performing assets (NPA) and no interest is taken into account from these assets. Necessary provision from 10 to 100 percent is required for NPA. Initially, the norms were liberal but by now they have become stringent. From the financial year 1999-2000 the banks are making a general provision of 0.25 percent in respect of even standard assets. For NPA recognition the period of 180 days or proposed to be changed as 90 days which is the norm of international banking.

An uninterrupted declining trend in quantum of NPA is observed over the period from 1994 to 2003. Further throughout increasing trend in standard assets is seen. The share of sub-standard assets and doubtful assets in the total advances is considerably reduced as compared with the position of 1994. The gross NPA of public sector banks at the end of March 2001 were estimated at over Rs. 54,700 crore that is 13 per cent of gross advances. The percentage of net NPA to net advances of total nationalized banks was as 7.8 per cent in March 2000, which came down to 4.77 per cent in March 2003 (Table 1).

Table 1: NPA in Public Sector Banks

Sr. No.	*Bank*	*Net NPA to Net Advances (%)*			
		1999-2000	*2000-2001*	*2001-2002*	*2002-2003*
1.	Allahabad Bank	12.24	11.23	10.57	7.08
2.	Andhra Bank	3.47	2.96	2.45	1.79
3.	Bank of Baroda	6.95	6.77	5.06	3.72
4.	Bank of India	8.61	6.72	6.02	5.59
5.	Bank of Maharashtra	6.97	7.41	5.81	4.82
6.	Canara Bank	5.28	4.84	3.89	3.59
7.	Central Bank of India	9.84	9.72	7.98	6.74
8.	Corporation Bank	1.92	1.98	2.31	1.65
9.	Dena Bank	13.47	18.37	16.31	11.63
10.	Indian Bank	16.18	10.06	8.28	6.15
11.	Indian Overseas Bank	7.65	7.01	6.32	5.23
12.	Oriental Bank of Commerce	3.80	3.60	3.20	1.4
13.	Punjab & Sind Bank	8.52	6.69	5.32	10.89
14.	Punjab National Bank	9.39	12.27	11.70	3.86
15.	Syndicate Bank	3.17	4.05	4.52	4.29
16.	UCO Bank	8.75	6.35	5.45	4.36
17.	Union Bank of India	7.97	6.87	6.26	4.91
18.	United Bank of India	12.70	10.50	7.90	5.52
19.	Vijaya Bank	6.65	6.23	6.02	2.8
Total of Nationalised Banks		7.80	7.01	6.01	4.77

There has been lack of means for quick recovery of dues from non-performing loans. The Govt. has established 22 Debt Recovery Tribunals but effectiveness of DRTs has been quite insufficient. They settled only about 4 per cent of cases out of 47,000 by March 2001. For improvement in this direction Settlement Advisory Committees (SAC) have been introduced which were further extended to OTS scheme. The Public sector banks succeeded in recovering more than 2000 crore of their dues. But the scheme was closed in June 2001 for the possibilities of encouraging moral hazard in financial character. The scheme was for defaulting borrowers of up to Rs. 5 crore.

For solving the NPA problem in banks, Corporate Restructuring (CDR) system is proposed on the basis of 'London Approach' where CDR is evolved voluntarily to minimize losses to banks and others. It has been successful in Malaysia, Thailand and Korea.

CAPITAL ADEQUACY RATIO

The capital acts as a cushion against losses and provides as incentive to owners to manage their banks efficiently. Thus, it was felt imperative that banks should be capitalized adequately. As per the Narasimham committee recommendation a system of capital adequacy was implemented and banks were required to attain a capital to risk asset ratio of 8 per cent, which was later enhanced to 9 per cent to be achieved by March 2000. As regards the capital adequacy position of our public sector banks, out of 27 banks all the 19 banks have acquired the prescribed standard by March 2003. Among the nationalized banks Dena Bank was at the lowest of 9.33 per cent capital adequacy ratio and Corporation Bank was at highest of 18.5 percent capital adequacy ratio in March 2003 (Table 2).

For filling the gap created after prudential norms, the Government provided Rs 20,774 crore for recapitalization up to March 2000. Recently a package of Rs. 2550 crore is expected to support the three banks. The financially sound banks are asked to raise funds from market to strengthen their capital base. Some of the banks have raised long-term resources from market to supplement their capital base. The Government holds not less than 51 per cent of paid up capital but it has been decided to rduce the holding to 33 per cent but public sector character will be unchanged.

Table 2: Capital Adequacy in Public Sector Banks

Sr. No.	*Bank*	*Capital Adequacy Ratio (%)*		
		2000-2001	2001-2002	2002-2003
1.	Allahabad Bank	10.50	10.62	11.15
2.	Andhra Bank	13.42	12.59	13.62
3.	Bank of Baroda	12.80	11.32	12.65
4.	Bank of India	12.23	10.68	12.02
5.	Bank of Maharashtra	10.64	11.16	11.76
6.	Canara Bank	9.84	11.88	12.50
7.	Central Bank of India	10.02	9.58	10.51
8.	Corporation Bank	13.03	17.90	18.50
9.	Dena Bank	7.73	7.64	9.33
10.	Indian Bank	Neg.	1.70	10.85
11.	Indian Overseas Bank	10.24	10.82	11.30
12.	Oriental Bank of Commerce	11.81	10.99	14.04
13.	Punjab & Sind Bank	10.24	10.70	10.43
14.	Punjab National Bank	11.42	10.70	12.02
15.	Syndicate Bank	11.72	12.12	11.03
16.	UCO Bank	9.05	9.64	10.04
17.	Union Bank of India	10.86	11.07	12.41
18.	United Bank of India	10.40	12.02	15.17
19.	Vijaya Bank	11.50	12.25	12.66

ENTRY OF PRIVATE SECTOR BANKS

The norms of entry of private sector banks were declared in Jan. 93. The minimum capital for these banks is 100 crore right at beginning and they are also required to follow prudential accounting norms. Nine such private banks were established. Presently these banks are in metropolitan areas and serving corporate and high alue clients besides forex operations.

GRADUAL REDUCTION IN CRR AND SLR

As one of the reform measures, the RBI gradually reduced the SLR and CRR to the level of 25 per cent and 4.5 per cent by March 2003. The SLR level of 25 per cent is minimum as per the provisions of Bank Regulation Act. The objective of the lowering the SLR and CRR is to free more resources for profitable investment by banks. In 1991, these two ratios put together reached at 63.5 per cent, which could lower to 29.5 per cent. Now, the Govt. moved to market for resources at market interest rates.

The interest rate is to be deregulated totally but it is carried out in phased manner. The important reform in this direction was deregulation of lending rates for loans above Rs. 2 lac. The predominant portion of bank loan is of this category; hence banks have enough liberty to fix the interest rates. Banks are required to declare their PLR and maximum spread over PLR. Now, the RBI has activated bank rate with an objective of its linking to interest rate. The bank rate has been lowered to 6 per cent in March 2003. Banks have lowered their PLR over the period considerably.

In respect of deposit rates the interest on saving deposit has not been deregulated but interest rates on term deposits have been deregulated and banks can fix their own rate for term deposits of different time span.

DIRECTED CREDIT AND RURAL FINANCE

The multi agency approach is continued in respect of rural credit. The bank credit to rural sector mainly comes under Priority sector that includes agriculture and allied activities, small-scale industries, weaker section advances. The target for Priority sector advances is 40 per cent of total bank credit. In the year 2000-01 advances in respect of priority sector were Rs. 1,47,478 crore, which was 43.2 per cent of net bank credit. For making the opportunities equal for all, foreign banks are also required to finance priority sector as other private banks do.

FINANCIAL SUPERVISION SYSTEM

The Board for Financial Supervision has been set up, as it was one of the recommendations of Narasimham Committee. A process of rating the banks on CAMELS (Capital Adequacy, Management, Earning, Liquidity and Systems) has been introduced. For off site supervision system, there is a set of 12 returns on capital adequacy, asset quality, credit concentration, connected lending, risk exposure etc.

The RBI has evolved the system of Prompt Corrective Action (PCA) on the pattern of model practiced in USA. The review is mainly on three yard sticks - capital adequacy, NPA position and assets quality. The mandatory and discretionary measures as well are prescribed for different stages. Through PCA the problem can be diagnosed at initial stage and cured in time.

RISK MANAGEMENT

The system of Asset Liability Management (ALM) has been started which is aimed at tackling the interest rate risk and exchange rate risk. The RBI has issued guidelines for handling default risk and portfolio risk. Suggestions for development of credit rating tool, credit scoring models, preventive monitoring system, loan audit, operational risk like computer failure have also been given. As an internal control measure, banks have constituted Asset Liability Management Committee and Credit Risk Management Committee (CRMC).

RATIONALISATION OF MANPOWER IN PUBLIC SECTOR BANKS

The public sector banks have implemented VRS (voluntary retirement scheme). It was one of the recommendations of Narasimham Committee. Nearly about 1 lac employees have accepted the offer. Thus, banks succeeded in reducing their staff by 11 per cent of total strength but its cost disturbed the profit position in balancesheet of the banks. For this purpose, banks are allowed to spread the expenditure on VRS over the period of five years. Other challenge is to manage post - VRS situation, as it will need mass transfers, promotions, abolition of posts etc.

CHALLENGES AHEAD

Indian banks gradually move towards universal banking where bank is financial service provider and it is one stop financial super market with a range of services such as commercial banking, merchant banking, investment banking and even insurance. Thus, banking business is getting redefined. Banks have come into insurance business also.

The higher capital adequacy standards may result in consolidation with public sector banks through mergers. There has been a recommendation of Narasimham Committee 1991 for having 3 to 4 large banks with international presence and 8 to 10 with national presence is again relevant. The mergers will fetch advantages of size and higher capitalization as well.

The human resource strategy will have to deal with career path, provision of incentives for better performance, training for areas like management, technology and marketing.

The public sector banks have to make a lot of efforts in the field of electronic banking for bank services at retail level. It could be through card based mechanisms like Stored value products (Smart Cards), Internet based banking and telebanking. This will cause innovative technology based products and services.

Nine privates banks have come into existence but it has not led to competition but competition forces are expected to become powerful in coming period. The public sector banks will come across the multi-facet competition, i.e. competition in cost-reduction, competition in technology adoption, competition in customer relations management, competition of varied product range, competition in services diversification. Now, they are to prepare themselves for the time to come. They will have to undertake business process reengineering, redefine their strategy and align their organizational structure.

REFERENCES

1. Jakhatiya GP 1995, Economic reformation of a democratic developing country-India as a case study, *SBI Monthly Review* 34(10), 495-513.
2. RBI 2003, *Report on trend and progress of banking 1999-2003,* Bombay, Reserve Bank of India.
3. Radhakrishnan R, 2001, A decade of financial sector reforms. *PNB Monthly Review* 23 (7): 5-25.
4. Singh ON, 2001, Indian banking-emerging challenges and strategies. *IBA Bulletin* 23 (3): 44-46.

7

MERGER OF ICICI WITH ICICI BANK: ITS IMPACT ON THE VALUE OF SHAREHOLDERS

P.C. Kavidayal*

Merger and acquisition are common terms in the banking world. Earlier some strong banks undertook comparatively poor banks, but Merger of ICICI and ICICI Bank looks to be a strange incidence where parental bank merged with its young one.

This paper is an attempt to visualize the impact of merger of ICICI with ICICI Bank on shereholders' value on the date of merger. Impact of the said merger on the value of shareholders of both enitities after two years of merger is also discussed in the paper.

Business combinations, which may take forms of mergers, acquisitions, amalgamation and takeovers are important features of corporate structural changes. The trend towards globalisation of all national and regional economies has increased the intensity of mergers, in a bid to create more focused, competitive, viable, large players, in each industry. The recent liberalization of the earlier state controlled, sluggish Indian economy has made mergers more necessary and acceptable. The globalisation may entail redundancies and closures of inefficient units as a consequence of technological upgradation and modernization. The working units below average efficiency and in public sector, which were hitherto enjoying the protection, are likely to face retrenchment and closure of the inefficient units.

---

*Reader, Faculty of Commerce S.S.J. Compus Almora, Uttaranchal.

Now the Indian industry is finding itself in an "excel or exit environment". If an industrial unit wants to survive, it has to excel and compete successfully both with domestic and multinational competitors in internal as well as in external markets. If one cannot do it the market forces would show such inefficient units the exit door of the industrial arena. All the Indian companies have started realising that they have to play skillfully dice which are heavily loaded in favour of multinational companies with vast resources, advanced technology and available managerial skills.

DEFINING MERGERS AND ACQUISITIONS

One plus one makes three: this equation is the special alchemy of a merger or acquisition. The key principle behind buying a company is to create shareholder value over and above that of the sum of the two companies. Two companies together are more valuable than two separate companies, at least, that's the reasoning behind the mergers and acquisitions. The rationale is particularly alluring to companies when times are tough. Strong companies will act to buy other companies to create a more competitive, cost-efficient company. The companies will come together hoping to gain a greater market share or achieve greater efficiency. Because of these potential benefits, target companies will often agree to be purchased when they know they cannot survive alone.

DISTINCTION BETWEEN MERGERS AND ACQUISITIONS

Although they are often uttered in the same breath and used as though they are synonymous, the terms "merger" and "acquisition" mean slightly different things.

When a company takes over another one and clearly becomes the new owner, the purchase is called an acquisition. From a legal point of view, the target company ceases to exist and the buyer "swallows" the business, and stock of the buyer continues to be traded. A merger happens when two firms, often about the same size, agree to go forward as a new single company rather than remain separately owned and operated. In practice, however, actual mergers of equals do not happen very often.

A purchase deal will also be called a merger when both CEOs agree that joining together in business is in the best interests of both their companies. But when the deal is unfriendly, that is when the target company does not want to be purchased it is always regarded as an acquisition. Therefore, whether a purchase is considered a merger or an acquisition really depends on whether the purchase is friendly or hostile and how it is announced. In other words, the real difference lies in how the purchase is communicated to and received by the target company's board of directors, employees and shareholders.

FACTORS DRIVING MERGERS AND ACQUISITIONS

Mergers and acquisitions of companies are implicit in free enterprise system because of their obvious advantage-infusion of better management, consolidating capacities to economic level by forward and backward linkages and healthy growth of capital market and finally enhancing the value of stakeholders. A number of benefits of mergers are claimed. All of them are not real benefits. Based on the empirical evidence and the experiences of certain companies, the most common motives and advantages of mergers and acquisitions are as below:

- Maintaining or accelerating a company's growth, particularly when the internal growth is constrained due to paucity of resources;
- Enhancing profitability, through cost reduction resulting from economies of scale, operating efficiency and synergy;
- Diversifying the risk of the company, particularly when it acquires business whose income streams are not correlated;
- Reducing tax liability because of the provision of setting off accumulated losses and unabsorbed depreciation of one company against the profits of another;
- Limiting the severity of competition by increasing the company's market power.

When a company wants to acquire another company, its shareholders must pay a consideration to shareholders of acquired company. This consideration is the value of the acquired company's assets or shares transferred to the acquiring company. In a competitive market situation the current market value is a correct estimate of the acquired company's value. In a normal course, the acquired company would not accept any value less than its current market value. Premium may be paid because of shares of the target company may be under-valued. It may also be given as an incentive to shareholders of the acquired company to be willing to sell their shares so that the acquiring company is able to obtain controlling voting rights of the target company.

CREATING SHAREHOLDER VALUE

Increasing shareholders value is generally held to be paramount objective of most Mergers and Acquisitions today. At its most basic, creating shareholders value means that the market favours firms that increase the productive use of their assets by increasing turnover ratios margins and profitability. Increasing sales growth adds shareholders' value as long as reinvestment earns returns that exceed the firm's cost of capital. Conversely, firms without such opportunities destroy shareholder value by reinvesting and should return the money to shareholders through dividend increases or share buy-backs. These are largely motherhood statements in finance, but are often not reflected either in managerial policies or corporate culture.

The basic argument that M & As increase shareholders value through exploitation of synergies is based on the assumption that the combined organization can be operated in a way that generates greater value than would be the sum of the value generated by the "stand-alone" companies (the 2+2 > 4 equation). Potentially, synergies may be extracted from cross-selling products, increasing economies of scale, elimination of duplicated functions and premises and greater market capitalization and therefore lower financing costs.[1]

At least in theory, mergers create synergies and economies of scale, expanding operations and cutting costs. Investors can take comfort in the idea that a merger will deliver enhanced shareholder value.

The success of a merger is measured whether the value of the shareholders is enhanced by the action. In this paper an attempt has been made to visualize or what could be the impact of merger of ICICI with ICICI Bank on shareholders value on the date of merger, i.e. 31.03.02. An attempt has also been made to analyze the impact of the said merger on the value of shareholders of both entities after two years of merger as we have got post-merger operating results of the acquiring entity. In order to make the study meaningful 5 years (which include pre-merger and post-merger) financial results have been

[1]Financial times, 10 August 1998.

analyzed. Let the prospective shareholders have a better idea of whether they should cheer or weep when a company they own buys or gets bought by other companies.

MERGER OF ICICI WITH ICICI BANK

In the past four or five years, the Indian banking sector has seen consolidating as both local banks and international banks doing business in India have undergone mergers and acquisitions. The RBI has encouraged consolidation in the hope that it will create a more robust banking sector.[2] ICICI, originally called the Industrial Credit and Investment Corporation of India, is the second largest bank in India, and the largest in the private sector with total assets values at approximately Rs 1.25 trillion. The bank was initially set up to fund industrial development in India and has evolved into a major player in the Indian financial services community, serving both consumer and corporate clients. ICICI took advantage of the decision in April 2000 of the Central Bank of India, the RBI, to allow development financial institutions to become commercial banks.[3] ICICI was one of four DFIs (the others are IDBI, IFCI and HDFC) and this move by the RBI allowed it to transform itself into a diversified financial institution.

In May 2002, the merger of ICICI with ICICI Bank was realized, creating what is now referred to simply as ICICI. The merger of ICICI and its subsidiaries with ICICI Bank created a combined entity "with complimentary strengths and products and similar processes and operating architecture. The merger has combined the large capital base of ICICI with the strong deposit raising capability of ICICI Bank, giving ICICI Bank improved ability to increase its market share in banking fees and commissions, while lowering the overall cost of funding through access to lower-cost retail deposits.

ICICI Bank would now be able to fully leverage the strong corporate relationships that ICICI has built, seamlessly providing the whole range of financial products and services to corporate clients. The merger has also resulted in the integration of the retail finance operations of ICICI, and its two merging subsidiaries, and ICICI Bank into one entity,

---

[2] Dasgupta, Saibal. March 2001, "India's Banks Start Paring Off," Asiamoney 12.2, 77-78.

[3] Dasgupta, Saibal July/ August 2000, " How ICICI wants to reinvent itself," Asiamoney 11.6, 39-41.

creating an optimal structure for the retail business and allowing the full range of asset and liability products to be offered to all retail customers."[4] The merger joined India's largest financial institutions with the country's largest private sector bank. The new entity has been structured to be responsible to the needs of the new combined firm, to be able to support the needs of a company of significant size while remaining nimble enough to respond quickly to market demands. The organization structure of ICICI is divided into five principal groups:

1. Retail banking
2. Wholesale banking
3. Project finance and special asset management
4. International business
5. Corporate centre

The share exchange ratio approved for the merger was one fully paid up equity share of ICICI Bank for two fully paid up equity shares of ICICI. This was determined on the basis of a comprehensive valuation process incorporating international best practices, carried out by two separate financial advisors and an independent accounting firm. With the merger taking effect, the paid up share capital of the bank has increased to Rs 6.13 billion comprising 613 million shares of Rs 10 each.

The merger was approved by the shareholders of both companies in January 2002, by the High Court of Gujarat at Ahmedabad in March 2002, and by the High Court of Judicature at Mumbai and the RBI in April 2002. The challenge of mobilization of resources for compliance with statutory reserve requirements applicable to banks, on ICICI's outstanding liabilities on merger, was met successfully within the target date of March 30, 2002. While the merger became effective on May 3, 2002, in accordance with the provisions of the scheme of amalgamation and the terms of approval of RBI, the appointed date for merger was March 30, 2002.

FINANCING THE MERGER: EXCHANGE OF SHARES

Just before the news of merger of ICICI with ICICI Bank, the market value of ICICI share was Rs 80 and that of ICICI Bank Rs 120.

[4]. ICICI annual report, FY 2001-2002, p. 48.

According to market value the share exchange ratio was:

$$\frac{\text{Share price of the acquired firm}}{\text{Share price of the acquiring firm}}$$

i.e, $\frac{80}{120} = 0.67$

But the share exchange ratio fixed by experts was .5:1.

In terms of the MV per share of the combined firm after the merger, the position of ICICI Ltd. shareholder would not remain the same, i.e. their per share value would be

$$120 \times .5 = \text{Rs}.\,60$$

Number of share offered to ICICI Ltd. = SER × Number of shares

i.e. $0.5 \times 78.5 = 39.25$ crore.

Total number of shares of the bank after the merger would be 61.25 crore.

Combined earning (PAT) would be Rs. 1670.42 crore. (Rs. 257.42 crore + Rs. 1413 crore).

Post-merger combined EPS = Rs.1670.42 /61.25 = Rs. 27.27

EPS of ICICI Bank would increase from Rs.11.7 to Rs. 27.27

EPS of ICICI would decrease from Rs.18 to Rs.13.6

The effect of P/E ratio on the wealth of shareholders of the individual company is given in Table 7.1.

Table 1: Effect of P/E ratio on Shareholders Value

P/E ratio	*EPS After Merger*	*Combined Firm's MV after Merger*	*MV of ICICI Bank*		*MV of ICICI*	
			Before Merger	*After Merger*	*Before Merger*	*After Merger*
4.44	27.27	121	120	121	80	61 (4.44 × 13.64)
10.26	27.27	280	120	280	80	140 (10.26 × 13.64)
5.34	27.27	146	120	146	80	73 (5.34 × 13.64)

Combined P/E = pre merger P/E of ICICI Bank × pre merger PAT of ICICI bank / post-merger combined PAT i.e.

$$10.26 \times 257.42/1670.42 + 4.44 \times 1413/1670.42 = 1.58 + 3.76 = 5.34$$

After merger the shareholders of ICICI Bank would gain and the shareholders of ICICI Ltd. would loose.

The acquiring company would loose in value if post-merger P/E ratio is less than the weighted P/E Ratio. Any P/E ratio above the weighted ratio would benefit both the acquiring and acquired company in value terms.

An acquiring company would always be able to improve its EPS after the merger whenever it acquires company with a P/E ratio lower than its own P/E ratio. The higher EPS need not necessarily increase the share price. It is the quality of EPS rather than the quantity, which would influence the price. ICICI Bank would lose in value if its post-merger P/E ratio would be less than the weighted P/E ratio. Any P/E ratio above the weighted P/E ratio would benefit both the companies in value terms. When the post-merger P/E ratio is 10.34 ICICI Bank gains 135% and ICICI gains 76% in their respective share prices (but the net gain to the shareholders of ICICI would be only 17.25% as the SER is .5:1). If the acquiring company takes over another company by exchanging a P/E ratio, higher than its P/E ratio, its EPS will fall and that of the acquired company would increase after the merger.

At the time of merger ICICI Bank had a higher P/E ratio, which was an indication of the investor's expectation of high future growth. At a share exchange ratio of .5, ICICI Bank's EPS after merger would be Rs. 27.27. The earnings per share of ICICI bank over the last three-years, i.e. from fiscal year 2000 to fiscal year 2002 has been growing at a rate of more than 27% and the EPS of ICICI has not shown a constant growth rate, rather it has been volatile for the last 6 years, i.e. from 1997 to 2002.

Table 2: ICICI Bank

	Fiscal 2000	*Fiscal 2001*	*Fiscal 2002*
No. of Share (in crore)	19.6	19.6	22
EPS (in Rs.)	6.38	8.13	11.7
M.V. per share	100	173	120
P/E (in times)	15.67	2L.28	10.26

Table 3: ICICI

	Fiscal 1997	*Fiscal 1998*	*Fiscal 1999*	*Fiscal 2000*	*Fiscal 2001*	*Fiscal 2002*
No. of Share (in crore)	44	48	48	78.5	78.5	78.5
EPS (in Rs.)	16	21.1	18.2	14	17	18
M.V. Per share	100	110	50	164	98	80
P/E (in times)	6.29	5.19	2.75	11.71	5.76	4.44

Data taken from ICICI website

On the basis of past years earnings we assume that earnings of ICICI Bank are expected to grow at 25% and ICICI at 12% for the next couple of years and visualize it's impact on shareholders earnings.

Table 4: ICICI Bank EPS with and without merger

Years	*Without Merger 25%*	*With Merger 14%**
0	11.70	27.27
1	14.63	31.09
2	18.29	35.44
3	22.86	40.40
4	28.58	46.06
5	35.73	52.51
6	44.66	59.86
7	55.83	68.24
8	69.79	77.79
9	87.24	88.68
10	109.05	101.10
11	136.31	115.25
12	170.39	131.39
13	212.99	149.78
14	266.24	170.75

$$* 25 \times \frac{257.42}{1670.42} + 12 \times \frac{1413.00}{1670.42}$$

$$= 0.4 + .10 = 0.14 \text{ or } 14\%$$

It may be observed from Table 4 that merger would help the acquiring company, i.e. ICICI Bank to grow rapidly (than without merger) for ten years after merger. After ten years, the position would be reversed. Thus, the company would either acquire other companies with lower P/E ratios; or improve its operating efficiency and continue growing. ICICI Bank would also stand to benefit, if the P/E ratio of this company stays at 10.26 times. The Market price per share of ICICI Bank after the acquisition, all other things held constant, would be:

Total earning (Rs. crore)	1670.42
Number of Share (crore)	61.25
EPS (Rs.)	27.27
P/E ratio (times)	10.26
Market price per share (Rs.)	280.00.

As a result, an acquiring company is able to show a steady growth in EPS if it acquires a sufficient number of companies over time in this manner.

What would be the impact of merger on the value of ICICI shareholders? On the basis of the estimated growth rate of the acquiring entity and the target company the following situation emerges:

Table 5: ICICI EPS with and without merger

Years	*Without Merger 12%*	*With Merger 14 %*	*EPS per share of ICICI (.5 of with merger EPS)*
0	18	27.27	13.64
1	20.16	31.09	15.54
2	22.58	35.44	17.72
3	25.29	40.40	20.20
4	28.32	46.06	23.03
5	31.72	52.51	26.25
6	35.53	59.86	29.93
7	39.79	68.24	34.12
8	44.56	77.79	38.90
9	49.91	88.68	44.34
10	55.90	101.10	50.55
11	62.61	115.25	57.63
12	70.12	131.39	65.70
13	78.53	149.78	74.89
14	87.95	170.75	85.38
15	98.50	194.66	97.33
16	110.32	221.91	101.96

From Table 5 we observe that the shareholders of ICICI would not cheer up the merger, as they would not be benefited from the merger (in terms of the EPS). The shareholders value would get increased only if:

1. ICICI Bank would be able to maintain its pre-merger P/E., i.e. 10.26 times.
2. ICICI Bank posts explosive growth after merger.
3. Merger increases the market share of ICICI Bank, the increased concentration or market share improves the profitability of the firm due to economies of scale.
4. The shares of ICICI bank are not fairly valued in the market at the time of merger considering the growth prospects of the bank.

IMPACT ON SHAREHOLDER's VALUE AFTER MERGER

A merger benefits shareholders when a company's post-merger share price increases by the value of potential synergy. By merging, the companies hope to benefit from the following:

1. Staff reductions
2. Economies of scale
3. Acquiring new technology
4. Improved market reach and industry visibility

ICICI pre-merger EPS is Rs. 18 and the SER is .5 : 1. Since the P/E ratio exchanged is less than ICICI Bank P/E ratio of 10 : 26, its EPS after merger increases.

Table 6: Impact on EPS, Market value and P/E ratio

	ICICI Bank before merger	*ICICI*	*After Merger*
Profit after Tax (Rs. crore)	257.42	1413	1670.42
No. Of shares (crore)	22.00	78.5	61.30
EPS (Rs.)	11.7	18.00	27.25
M.V. per share (Rs.)	120	80	120.00
P/E ratio (times)	10.26	4.44	4.40
Total market capitalization (Rs. crore)	2640	4716	7356

We may observe that for ICICI (the acquired company) pre-merger EPS of Rs. 18, the price paid is Rs. 120 × 0.5 = Rs. 60. Thus, the P/E ratio paid to ICICI is: 60/18 = 3.33 times. Since the P/E ratio exchanged is less than ICICI Bank (acquiring company) P/E ratio of 10.26, its EPS after merger increases. The post-merger P/E ratio falls to: 120 / 27.25 = 4.4 times. We also observe that after merger the market value per share is Rs. 120 and total capitalization decreases to Rs. 7356 crore, less by Rs. 1564 crore of the sum of the capitalization of individual firms (Rs. 120 × 22 crore plus Rs. 80 × 78.5 crore) = 2640 crore +6280 crore = Rs. 8920 crore. There is value erosion for ICICI shareholders.

Total capitalization of ICICI share. holders before merger (Rs. crore)	6280
Total capitalization of ICICI share. Holders after merger (Rs. crore)	4716
Net loss (Rs crore)	1564

Table 7: Impact of EPS, Market Value and P/E ratio after two years of merger

	ICICI Bank
Profit after tax (Rs crore)	1637.11
Number of shares (crore)	61.30
EPS (Rs)	26.66
M.V. per share (Rs)	280.00
P/E ratio (times)	10.5
Total market capitalization (Rs crore)	17164

We can notice from the above table that after two years from the date of merger the market value per share of ICICI Bank has increased to Rs. 280, an appreciation of 133.33%, on the back of the growth prospects of the company. Consequently the market capitalization increases to Rs. 17164 crore, more by Rs 9808 crore of the capitalization as on March 31, 2002. This increased value has created wealth for both the companies' shareholders. The shareholders of ICICI have been benefited more than 75% in terms of market value (Rs. 280 – (Rs. 80 × 2) = 120/160). The gain to ICICI Bank shareholder is more than 133% in terms of market value.

High P/E ratio after merger is an indication of the expectation of impressive growth, which creates value to both the companies (acquirer and acquired) shareholders. Analysis that follows shall justify the high market value of its shares.

ICICI FINANCIALS

ICICI Bank has been very successful in transforming itself into a truly universal financial services firm. A look at the firm's financials illustrates the success that the ICICI has experienced. Between FY 1996 and financial year FY 2000 total income rose 291% to Rs. 84.6 billion. PAT rose 276% and total assets climbed 280% to Rs. 653.9 bn. During the same period, disbursements grew 363% to Rs. 258.36 bn. ICICI Bank's total assets increased to Rs. 1252.28 bn at March 31, 2004 compared to Rs. 197.37 bn at March 31, 2001. Total deposits increased 315.86% to Rs. 681.09 bn at March 31, 2004 from Rs. 163.78 bn at March 31, 2001. In addition, savings account deposits increased 345.08% to Rs. 83.72 bn in Fiscal 2004 from Rs. 18.81 bn in Fiscal 2001.

ICICI Bank's capital adequacy at December 31, 2003 was 11.32% (including tier–1 capital adequacy of 7.18%), well above RBI's requirement of 9%. The Table 8 sets forth, for the periods indicated, the summarized balance sheet of ICICI bank.

During the year that ended March 31, 2004 there was 35.74 % rise in PAT and 32% increase in net interest income. Notably, these figures are better than those of two other former DFIs, IDBI and IFCI. ICICI bank's operating profits increased 718% to Rs. 23.72 bn in Fiscal 2004 as compared to Rs. 2.9 bn in fiscal 2001. The Profit and Loss account for fiscal 2002 included the results of the operations of ICICI, ICICI PFS and ICICI capital for March 30 and 31, 2002, i.e. two days only. The results for Fiscal 2003 are, therefore, not comparable with the results for Fiscal 2002. The operating profits increased 71.88% to Rs. 23.72 bn in Fiscal 2004 as compared to Rs. 13.8 bn in Fiscal 2003. The bank's deposits increased 41.39% to Rs. 681.09 bn at March 31, 2004 from Rs. 481.7 bn at March 31, 2003, compared to the banking system's deposit growth of about 9% during the same period.

During this period, the bank repaid Rs. 60 bn of erstwhile ICICI's liabilities as they fell due in accordance with their terms of repayment. At March 31, 2004 deposits constituted 64% of the banks funding compared to 48% at December 31, 2002. The bank's average cost of deposits for the quarter 4 FY 2004 was 5.3% as compared to 6.7% for quarter 3 FY 2003.

Table 8: Financial Position of ICICI Bank

Rs. billion

	March 31, 2001	*March 31, 2002*	*March 31, 2003*	*March31, 2004*
Assets:				
Cash balances banks and SLR	77.06	355.80	320.72	383.89
Cash and balances with RBI and				
Banks	35.94	127.87	64.89	84.71
SLR Investments	41.12	227.93	255.83	299.18
Advances	70.32	470.35	532.79	620.96
Debenture and Bonds	30.70	64.38	56.90	55.49
Other investments	10.05	66.62	41.93	72.76
Fixed assets	3.84	42.39	40.61	40.56
Other assets	5.40	41.56	75.17	78.63
Total assets	197.37	1041.10	1068.12	1252.29
Liabilities:				
Equity capital and reserves	13.13	62.49	69.34	80.10
Equity capital	2.20	6.13	6.13	6.15
Reserves	10.93	56.36	63.21	73.94
Preference capital	-	3.5	3.5	3.5
Deposits	163.78	320.85	481.69	681.09
Savings Deposits	18.81	24.97	37.93	83.73
Current Deposits	26.22	27.36	36.89	72.59
Term Deposits	118.75	268.52	406.87	524.78
Borrowings	12.01	589.70	440.52	398.46
Of which: subordinated debt	1.68	97.51	97.50	91.06
Other liabilities	8.45	64.56	73.07	86.13
Total Liabilities	197.37	1041.10	1068.12	1252.29

Data taken from ICICI's Annual Reports.

Table 9: Operating Results Data

	Fiscal 2001	*Fiscal 2002*	*Fiscal 2003*	*Fiscal 2004*
Interest income	12.42	21.52	93.68	88.94
Interest Expenditure	8.38	15.59	79.43	70.15
Net Interest Income	4.04	5.93	14.25	18.97
Non Interest Income	2.20	5.75	19.68	30.65
Fee Income	1.71	2.83	9.01	11.98
Trading Gains	.49	2.92	10.68	18.67
Operating Income	6.24	11.68	33.92	49.43
Operating Expenditure	3.34	6.23	20.12	25.71
Operating Profit	2.90	5.45	13.80	23.72
Provision For NPA	.63	2.68	9.11	3.10
Wright Back of Depreciation on Investments	.06	.16	3.09	.09
Other Provisions	.07	.03	—	1.71
Profit Before Tax	2.26	2.90	16.34	19.00
Provision For Tax	.65	.32	(4.28)	2.63
Net Profit	1.61	2.58	12.06	16.37

Data taken from ICICI's Annual Report.

ICICI's INNOVATIONS

Growth in Retail Business: Retail banking is at the heart of ICICI's growth strategy and one of the main reasons behind the firm's impressive results. ICICI sells itself as a firm that is highly focused on the customer, defying the traditional behaviour patterns associated with banking in India. The demographic changes in India are at the core of ICICI's decision to focus on offering strong retail banking. As more Indians enter the higher income brackets there is an increased need for financial services, and a demand for high level service and attentiveness to customer needs. ICICI is positioning itself to capitalize on the needs of this upwardly mobile group and is seeking to establish a strong competitive advantage through its innovative products, wide distribution, strong credit controls and customers service standards. ICICI is investing in all of its retail areas so as to achieve economies of scale and further increase its advantage. The retail finance business as a proportion of total assets size has grown from six per cent in FY 2002 to 18% in FY 2003 to 29% at the end of Fiscal 2004. Retail assets have been growing constantly adding around 30 bn every quarter, constituting 49% of total loan portfolio.

Use of technology: The bank is way ahead in technology as compared to its peers. This provides it with first mover advantage in the industry. Technology is in such an advance stage that it provides some opportunities to the bank where it scales business with low incremental cost. As more as transactions are switched to IVR, transaction cost of the bank will come down.

Table 7.10

Channel	*March 2001*	*March 2002*	*December 2003*
Retail Customer account (mn)	1.9	3	9.8
Internet customer (mn)	.5	1.1	5.5
ATM Transactions (mn/day)	.1	.2	.5
Call centre contacts (mn/day)	.02	.05	.12

Data taken from ICICI website.

ICICI Bank uses the most advanced technology at the call centre, i.e. bleeding–edge voice–over Internet protocol technology and the most advanced desktop applications, to cross-sell products from its various subsidiaries and to facilitate the customers' banking experience. It offers fully comprehensive on line trading services at **www.icici.direct.com**. ICICI Bank was the first Indian company to list on the NYSE in September 1999. As of March 31, 2004, foreign institutional investors owned 46.85% of ICICI's share.

INCREASE IN PAID UP CAPITAL THROUGH PUBLIC ISSUE

ICICI Bank has increased its equity base by Rs. 30.5 bn through raising equity shares in market for the following purposes:

1. **Exploiting opportunities derived from industrial revival:** In order to exploit opportunities from industry revival, ICICI Bank needs to expand its business and geographical reach. To execute its plans successfully, the bank requires adequate capital. Thus, the bank decided to raise capital through public issue.
2. **Supporting global activity:** The bank has tapped almost 25% of incremental market share of total global business in financial year 2003 on back of strong growth in NRI deposits. The bank plans to grow its international business to new heights and lead in performance as compared to peers. The bank plans to deploy part of its raised funds in expanding global business.

3. **Capital support to subsidiary:** ICICI Bank believes that insurance market in India is small as compared to other countries. The bank visions to grow its insurance business by aggressively marketing and properly channeling its insurance products. This effort will require considerable amount of investment cost, a part of which the bank expects to accomplish through present public issue. After the latest public issue in April 2004 the shareholding pattern will be as below (Table 11):

Table 11: Distribution of Shareholding ICICI Bank Ltd.

	As on 31.03.2003		*As on 31.03.2004*		*As on 30.06.2004*	
	No. of share held (in crore)	*%*	*No. of share held (in crore)*	*%*	*No. of share held (in crore)*	*%*
Institutional investors:						
M.F.	2.9	4.74	.021	.03	.048	.65
Bank, FI and Insurance companies	10.13	16.52	9.39	15.24	12.4	16.90
FIIs and NRIs	23.66	38.6	28.88	46.85	35.24	48.02
Sub Total	36.69	59.86	38.29	62.12	47.69	65.57
Others:						
Private corporate bodies	3.03	4.94	2.62	4.25	3.31	4.51
Indian public	5.58	9.10	4.56	7.39	5.97	8.13
Any other:						
Duetsche Bank Trust Co. Americas (depository for ADR holders)	16	26.10	15.99	25.94	15.99	21.79
Sub Total	24.61	40.14	27.17	37.58	25.27	34.43
Grand Total	61.9	100	61.46	100	72.96	100

Data taken from annual reports of ICICI Banks.

ICICI Bank has made considerable progress in realising the benefits of merger. It has strengthened its leadership position in all segments of the market, leveraging strong distribution capabilities backed by credit and analytical skills and technology. It has also achieved rapid growth in its deposit base and continued to replace ICICI's high cost borrowings with lower cost deposits. With retail loans constituting over 50% of its loan portfolio and deposits constituting over 60% of its funding it has diversified its balance sheet significantly. This process of structural change and diversification has resulted in improvement in its interest margins. It has also achieved steady growth in fee income, reflecting the growing range and scale of operations in fee-based products and services for both retail and corporate customers. In view of the prospects for growth in various areas of business—like infrastructure projects, rural lending, life insurance business and on line trading it has strengthened its capital base substantially by raising additional equity capital of Rs. 30.5 bn. It has demonstrated capabilities across products, customer segments and markets in order to achieve its aspirations and creating value to shareholders.

The bank has got certain challenges in order to create value to its shareholders. Some of them may be as follows —

1. **Interest rate movements:** The banks are exposed to interest rate risks, which is guided on the lines of RBI. The bank is required to follow the investment norms issued by RBI time to time. This will affect the earnings of the bank depending upon the norms.
2. **Concentration of loans to certain customers and sectors:** ICICI bank has high concentrations of loans to certain customers and certain sectors. If a substantial portion of these loans were to become non-performing, the quality of loan portfolio could be adversely affected.
3. **Highly regulated industry:** Banking industry is a heavily regulated industry and material changes in the regulations, which govern banks, could cause the bank's business to suffer and the prices of the equity shares may go down.
4. **Volatility in the capital markets:** The Indian capital market has witnessed a lot of volatility during the past couple of years. The markets are undergoing major structural reforms that may lead to poor sentiments among the investors and investors may loose in terms of market capitalization.
5. **In the world of stock market it is the future that counts and not the past.** The price of a share is largely determined not by what the company has earned, or is earning, but by what it is expected to earn in the future. Thus, earnings in the years to come will decide the value to its shareholders.

Experience from most M & As of advanced countries in the mid-1980s is not very encouraging. At that time many newly merged banks and insurance companies found their cost structures increased, resulting in duplication of structures and costs rather than predicted savings. The much slower growth levels in the 1990s and the high premiums usually paid to shareholders of target companies, mean that the restructuring needed to achieve satisfactory cost savings from mergers can only be obtained with much deeper cost cutting imperiling the ability of merged companies to achieve the higher levels of sales revenue required to repay merger-related debt and increase shareholders value.

BIBLIOGRAPHY

1. Bailey, Rasul. July 9, 2002. "India acts to clean up Bad loans — Aim Is to Resell Debt; Will Faster Foreclosure Tempt Foreign Investors ?" *Wall Street Journal*: A12.
2. Dasgupta, Saibal. July / August 2000. "How ICICI Wants to Reinvent Itself," *Asiamoney* 11.6:39-41.
3. Dasgupta, Saibal. 3 February 2001. "ICICI Buy Continues Indian Merger Fervour," *Asiamoney* 12.1:12
4. Dasgupta, Saibal. 3 March 2001. "India's Bank start Pairing off," *Asiamoney* 12.2: 77-78.
5. Annual Reports of ICICI and ICICI Bank.
6. September 25,1999. "Finance and Economics: Hybrid," The *Economist*: 91.
7. January 6, 2001. " Finance and Economics: Living Dead," *The Economist:* 68.
8. October, 1999. "ICICI Makes Marks as First Indian company to list on NYSE," *Asiamoney* 10.8:10.
9. Narain, Aditya. January 31,2003. "*ICICI Bank*". Salomon Smith Barney Equity Research.
10. Narain, Aditya. 3 November 14,2002. "*ICICI Bank: NPA Nervousness; Cutting Estimates And Target Price*,". Salomon Smith Barney.
11. Rajpal, Amit. December 16, 2002 "*ICICI Bank: Time Out*". JM Morgan Stanley Equity Research.
12. Varma, Rajeev. Febuary 3, 2003. "*ICICI Bank Ltd.: Changing Shape*," Merrill Lynch Equity Research.
13. Varma, Rajeev. January 31, 2003. "*ICICI Bank Ltd.: Greater Visibility of the Future*," Merrill Lynch Equity Research.
14. I.M. Pande, *Financial Management*, Vikas Publishing House Pvt. Ltd. New Delhi.

8

BANCASSURANCE—AN INNOVATIVE STEP

M.N. Mishra*

The bancassurance refers to the selling of insurance products by a bank, of its own subsidiary or any other insurance company. The concept has evolved following the merger of banks and insurance companies in Europe. A bank's involvement in the insurance business can either be restricted to distribution and selling or be extended to policy administration and underwriting.

The insurance business offers an opportunity for banks to increase fee-based business for improving their profits and make utilization of their branch network and customer base optimally. Insurance is an appropriate option since banks fulfill three major requirements for a successful insurance business, i.e. asset management and investment skill, distribution channel and capital adequacy. There is ample scope of life insurance business because our population is either uninsured or under insured. Hence, there are tremendous possibilities for bancassurance in Indian market.

Insurance and Banking are coexisting financial institutions while complementing and supplementing each other. The Insurance Regulatory and Development Authority Act, 1999 have created more opportunities to Banks for expansion of their markets. They can serve the society in a very effective manner. Banking Institutions have got the opportunities to enter in insurance business while insurance institutions have already under the autonomy of starting their banking business. Many non-banking institutions have been opened, acquired funds and dissolved with public money at their stakes. Since they

*Professor of Corporate Studies, Faculty of Commerce, Banaras Hindu University, Varanasi, U.P, India.

were totally in the hands of private persons, the Government control became ineffective. Banking institutions in India are mainly under the control of Reserve Bank of India. People need insurance but they prefer investment over risk coverage although latter is more important. Indian mentality for insurance is very bleak. People do not feel need of insurance although they have dire-necessity for that. Insurance institutions in India have not considered forced insurance. The voluntary-purchasing of insurance policies is rare phenomena. They prefer to go to bank-offices rather than going to insurance offices for getting risk coverage. The insurance institutions procure the business through their agents who are the main link between people and the company. Agents' attitude and environment may work against the free-will environment of insurance. The IRDA, Act is expected to mobilise insurance coverage and resources for investment in the economy. The government has assured that there would not be any disinvestment in the LIC, GIC and their subsidiaries. Insurance Act, 1938 has not been sufficient to regulate the insurance business in India. Foreign companies would not be allowed to hike their equity in the country through their Indian subsidiaries. It has opened a great opportunnity for the banking and insurance institutions. They can perform both the functions.

INSURANCE AS BANKING INSTITUTE

The Life Insurance and General Insurance Corporations are performing their respective functions with the help of banks. LIC and GIC have opened their accounts with banks. Policy holders have to approach the banks for realisation of cheques. Indirectly banks have to intervene in their business. If the insurance companies perform the business of banking institutions, they get benefits of business in financial transactions. Policy holders are also benefited as they have not to run from pillar to post. The claims amounts will be deposited in insurance banks. The account holders get all the benefits and facilities of banks. It can be analysed under premium collection, claims payment, pension plans, funds, investment consultant and employment opportunities.

PREMIUM COLLECTION

Insurance as bank will facilitate deposit of premium. The burden on cash-counter is lessened or the cash transaction is shifted to insurance bank. The premium amount is regularly collected without any pressure on other activities of insurance. Insurance business is expanded with extra zeal and effort as people working in the marketing areas develop specialisation. They devote with additional knowledge and equipment for the expansion of insurance business on the other hand. Management of premium collection becomes easy as the insurance bank has diversified its activities. New bank customer get information about insurance. They collect, analyse and reinforce the available information at insurance-bank counter, from the fellow depositors of premiums and receivers of claims amount. Insurance policy is accepted by its realisation of actual benefits towards which Indian population is a pathetic. The premium amount is regularly collected as the customers visit often the insurance-bank for their daily transactions. They are reminded of premium-deposits. The premium collected are deposited in a commercial bank who uses the money for their transaction and investment. If so much money is retained by insurance-bank, it would be utilised by them for getting some profit on the money.

Table 1: Premium Collected

(Rs. in crores)

Years	*Life Insurance Corporation of India*	*General Insurance Industries*	*Total*	*Growth Index*
1990-91	5600	2742	8342	100
1991-92	6960	3450	10410	125
1992-93	7987	3868	11855	142
1993-94	9735	4427	14162	170
1994-95	11527	4879	16406	197
1995-96	14182	5956	20138	241
1996-97	16240	6734	22974	275
1997-98	19252	7357	26609	319

Table 1 reveals that the total premium collected by insurance industry has gone from Rs. 8342 crore in 1990-91 to Rs. 26609 crores in 1997-98 by 3.19 times during the period of seven years. If this much of money is retained by insurance industry; they would earn enough profit margins. But, at present insurance industry operates their financial functions through commercial banks. The functions of commercial banks should be performed by the insurance industry itself. There are many other income than the premium income which are also deposited in banks.

Table 2: Total Income

(Rs. in crores)

Years	*Life Insurance Corporation of India*	*General Insurance Industries*	*Total*	*Growth Index*
1990-91	8518	3308	11826	100
1991-92	10691	4202	14893	126
1992-93	12244	4727	16971	144
1993-94	15212	5384	20596	174
1994-95	18102	6029	24131	204
1995-96	22047	7431	29478	249
1996-97	25821	8431	34252	290
1997-98	30732	9335	40067	339

The public is accustomed to get insurance and banking services at a place. Insurance industry will work like a multiple shop store wherein all the financial functions would be performed by them. The investor would also come to the insurance offices for getting all the information and services fulfilled. However, the insurance-bank should not have to confine only on insurance-investment but should have widen its horizon to help all types of people seeking financial suggestions.

Payment of premium would be easy and prompt if the policyholder has opened account with the insurance-bank. It would be like salary saving scheme wherein no policyholder would bother for monthly remittance of premium. Merely accounting transaction in the insurance-bank facilitate the payments. The account holder would be reminded of the minimum balance in the account for payment of premium. The insurance-bank becomes total bank of people as it takes care of all financial transactions. Payment of electricity bill, income tax and business-invoices would be easy by insurance-bank.

Total income received by insurance industries comes through banks. In other words, banks maintain their total income which increased from Rs. 11826 crore in 1990-91 to Rs. 40067 crore in 1997-98 by 3.39 times during the period of seven years. If this amount is not deposited or transacted through commercial banks, all these money is used by insurance industries as bank too. Therefore, it is advisable for the insurance industry to start its own bank wherein public is also invited to transact as bank-customer. Thus, the deposit of insurance industry in a year would exceed Rupees 50 thousand crore at the minimum. Bank certainly gets some benefit on the amount deposited by insurance. They maintain their liquidity level and invest rest of the money received from insurance. This earning would be earned by insurance companies as commercial banks if they transact business of a commercial bank.

CLAIMS PAYMENT

The claims-amount paid by the insurance industry is not immediately used by the clients. It is deposited in the banks from whereby they withdraw their amount from time to time leaving a sufficient amount with the bank for their investment as per rule. If this amount is retained by the insurance-bank, the money would be utilised for further investment. The client's account in the insurance-bank is immediately credited with the amount of claim from which they withdraw amount from time to time. Such types of facilities of premium-deposits and claim-settlement by banks motivate public to deal with the insurance bank wherein they would prefer to deposit their other savings. Old-age people get monthly withdrawal of the amount. They would not suffer any more by making que in commercial banks. The technological development where in phone and computer facilities would serve their clients at their home. Employment opportunities would increase as expert people would have been appointed to meet the clients at the residence who would pay cash at the time of need. Only telephone facilities would do all the jobs as automation-services would be completed on computers. If the client has personal computer, it would be more useful and efficient services to them. The claims amount of insurance industry reveals the bulk of banking business based only on it.

Table 3: Claim-Amount

(Rs. in crores)

Years	*Life Insurance*	*General Insurance*	*Total*
1990-91	1951	1898	3849
1991-92	2422	2303	4725
1992-93	3580	2839	6419
1993-94	3845	3050	6895
1994-95	4666	4289	8955
1995-96	5353	4427	9780
1996-97	6599	5105	11704
1997-98	7823	6525	13448

The claim amount of insurance industry has increased from Rs. 3849 crore in 1990-91 to Rs. 13448 crore in 1997-98 by 3.49 times during seven years. It reveals that amount Rs. 13 thousand crore money would have been with the insurance-bank for a time-being as is put in commercial banks. The commercial banks collect too much of funds from insurance industry. They credit the amount with the accounts of their depositors who do not withdraw all the amount at a time. They gradually withdraw it leaving a major portion with the bank. Similarly a major portion of claim amount remain in float, i.e. date of writing the cheque to the date of realisation in account. This float would be abolished if the insurance-bank is opened as it would do all the payments merely passing certain entries. It is thus clear that insurance bank would use a major portion of claims-payment for its transactions which are used by commercial banks. The insured can get the amount of claims in pension form which would again help insurance-expansion. The clients would get pension regularly from the insurance bank which can start door to door financial services. There exists a large potential of business of financial nature in adopting insurance-banking systems.

PENSION PLANS

People are investment-oriented. Risk of life is universal truth but people by their nature are least concerned with life insurance coverage. If insurance-bank is opened, people will enjoy the benefits of pension plans by depositing the saving, claim-amount and purchasing pension-plans.

Table 4: Group Superannuation Schemes

(in crores of Rs.)

Years	*Number of Members in lakhs*	*Amount of Annuities per annum*
1990-91	2.43	253.12
1991-92	2.54	301.77
1992-93	2.69	358.93
1993-94	3.14	403.51
1994-95	3.54	427.66
1995-96	4.19	483.05
1996-97	5.54	545.59
1997-98	6.71	682.84

The number of persons insured under group-superannuation schemes has increased from 2.43 lakhs in 1990-91 to 6.71 lakh in 1997-98 and the amount of annuities increased from Rs. 253.12 crore to Rs. 682.84 crore in the corresponding year by the same proportion. The rising trend reveals that LIC can manage a significant amount by its insurance-bank. All the money is not immediately paid. A certain portion is paid at different interval. The rest of amount is managed as bank-money for credit and investing in the growing economy of India. Insurance-bank would perform better than the commercial bank. The claim-amount would also be deposited with the insurance-bank from where a new pension-plan can be purchased. The total claim-amount is usually converted into pension-plans. People would be benefited by such schemes. They are given option either to take all the money at the time of claim or convert some of them or all of them into pension-plan. This facility would benefit a large number of policy-holder who would enjoy it and the LIC would get sufficient amount for financial transactions. The employment opportunities would increase and the contribution to economic development would be appreciable.

FUNDS

The insurance fund is significant contribution to national income as it is invested for economic development. The amount of fund available with LIC would increase further as saving in from premium income, claim amount and other out go would also enhance as a result of establishment of insurance-bank.

Table 5: Life Insurance Fund (LIC)

(in crores of Rs.)

Years	*Total income*	*Outgo*	*Excess of income over outgo added to Fund*	*Total fund*
1990-91	8517	3588	4929	28400
1991-92	10690	4400	6290	34691
1992-93	12244	5937	6306	40998
1993-94	15212	6544	8667	49665
1994-95	18102	7789	10313	59978
1995-96	22047	9245	12801	74780
1996-97	25821	10841	14979	87760
1997-98	30732	12659	18072	105832

Table 6: Expected Investible Funds of LIC

(Rs. in crores)

Years	*Total Life Insurance Fund*	*50% of the outgo*	*50% of Premium Income*	*Total Insurance Bank Funds for investment*	*% Increase over Life*
1990-91	28400	1794	2800	32994	116
1991-92	34691	2200	3480	40371	116
1992-93	40998	2968	3993	47959	116
1993-94	49665	3272	4867	57804	116
1994-95	59978	3894	9763	69635	116
1995-96	72780	4622	7091	84493	116
1996-97	87760	5420	8120	101300	(115)
1997-98	105832	6329	9626	121787	(115)

The investible funds for LIC has been Rs. 105832 crore in 1997-98 as compared to Rs. 28400 crore in 1990-91, an increase of 372.6 per cent. It is a welcome step. If LIC starts its banking business, the life insurance functions only will enhance the investible fund by more than 15 per cent of the total life Fund. It is clear from Table 8.6 that the investible bank fund would have been Rs. 14787 crore in 1997-98 if insurance had started its banking business because about 50 per cent of outgo will remain in the bank for gradual withdrawal and the premium income would increase by 50 per cent as a result of banking operation. The total bank investible fund was expected to be Rs. 32994 crore in 1990-91 an increase of 369 per cent over the period of seven year.

Table 7: Cash at Bank (Life business)

(in crores of Rs.)

Years	*Deposit A/C*	*Call short Notice Deposit A/C*	*Current A/C*	*Remittance in Transit*	*Total*
1990-91	31.67	631.35	174.93	51.42	889.39
1991-92	80.84	761.06	157.39	77.61	1076.91
1992-93	88.70	314.28	416.61	118.91	938.50
1993-94	111.91	121.12	418.31	314.21	965.56
1994-95	38.71	653.59	519.27	258.46	1570.04
1995-96	55.64	230.53	559.17	638.70	1484.04
1996-97	284.97	272.84	563.76	539.88	1661.47
1997-98	715.95	789.24	728.53	485.02	2718.74

The deposits at banks have revealed that Rs. 2718 crore was lying with commercial banks in 1997-98 which was Rs. 889 crore in 1990-91. The banks are not bothering for the remittance in transit which was Rs. 485 crore in 1997-98. On current account LIC is earning nothing which accounted Rs. 728 crore in 1997-98. The deposit account would have been properly utilised by LIC. Thus, it is clear that LIC would have earned sufficient income if it has opened its own bank.

INVESTMENT CONSULTANT

The Life Insurance business as well as allied business would have been increased if LIC starts investment consultancy. People should approach to the offices of LIC for expert advises on investment. The present position is that LIC agents approach to people for procuring insurance business. But the people are investment-oriented. They go to take expert advises for investment to their relatives or private investment agents. The share-brokers and others are charging exorbitant fees from the investors. Their money is not properly invested. If LIC starts consultancy services, it would benefit a large number of investors.

EMPLOYMENT OPPORTUNITIES

Employment opportunities would increase if insurance bank starts functioning along with insurance-business. In foreign countries, insurance and banking business are co-existent. They perform better than pure insurance or banking business. Direct and indirect employment generation is possible if insurance-bank starts functioning. The LIC Act, 1956 and GIC Act, 1972 would have to be amended sufficiently to permit LIC and GIC to start their banking business.

BANK AS INSURANCE INSTITUTE

The IRDA Act, 1999 has opened wide challenges to financial institutions. Now banks can also enter in insurance business. The insurance is the basic need of life. Uncertainty of life and death is reducing the working capacities of people because of tension involved. Once it is secured, person feels happy to perform his job effectively. In a bank where he has his bank account, if he gets facilities of insurance; he would certainly purchase insurance policies. Insurance link deposit would be more attractive to the account holders. With payment of slightly a higher amount at the time of deposit, he can secure term insurance. Term insurance would be the most appropriate form of life insurance to be sold by banks. Health schemes and accident-benefits can be lucrative business for a bank. The banks should chalk out at the earliest to start new business of life as well as general insurance. In Canada, many banks have been successfully doing this job.

COORDINATION

The banking and insurance institutions would be working as competitive units but they are working in the same environment of India. Their coordination would strengthen their businesscs. Plans formulation, strategies implementation, socio-economic development and technological upgrading are coordinately achieved by both the institutions although Insurance Regulation and Development Authority is there is guide them. Their own thinking and mutual discussion would benefit them. The age is competition but survival is possible with coordination. It is hope that both institutions would interchange experienced employees for their development.

MARKET EXPANSION

People are aware of the product when there are a number of seller. They go to the market where selective bargaining is present for purchasing a desirable article. People want to purchase a insurance policy, e.g. health and accident which is not available. People do not want to purchase money back which are sold by LIC. These are mere examples. If people can find products of their choice in a market that is full of good sellers, they remain in the market. Ultimately insurance business would increase. A firm propagates his own product but at the same time propagates indirectly others product of the same line. If banks are telling about insurance benefits, LIC and GIC are also benefited. If insurance industry is telling banking facilities, the banks are also indirectly benefited. Market expansion is inevitable in insurance area.

MERGING OF WEAK BANKS WITH LIC OR GIC

Several banks are unable to maintain their profitability on account of non-performing assets and non-circulation of investible funds. They should merge with LIC or GIC who should be starting banking business too, for their development to achieve leadership competence in view of incoming tough competitors from outside country. Once banks have merged with LIC or GIC, they would perform better under their guidance who would need basic infrastructure for expansion of insurance banks. The banks would be performing a fresh. The employees would get a chance of revival. They would get proper training and motivation. The productivity and performance would boost their morale. Highly motivated employees would share more responsibility of insurance and banks. The educated people would get opportunities to demonstrate their capabilities. Indian economy would get sufficient funds from insurance and banking institutions. Resource mobilisation would help development of people's health, economic conditions and entrepreneurship. India will emerge a powerful nation.

9

ENTERING OF BANKING INDUSTRY IN THE INFORMATION AGE

Krishna Kumar Varma*

Internet is the foundation on which e-commerce and e-business models are built. Due to explosion of information and communication technology (ICT) in 1990s and emergence of computer networks, e-commerce has become a buzzword, which includes e-banking, e-shopping, e-marketing, e-chatting, e-brokerage, e-store etc. The e-banking allows its customer to do the work for 365 days and 24 hours, to transcend the barriers of time, distance and geography; and provides on line purchases and payments instant transactions and services at low cost.

The author deals in e-banking and internet banking well in the paper. The problems in the way of e-banking like inadequate computer literacy, heavy cost of infrastructure, lack of sufficient cyber law, non-acceptability of e-cash have been identified and solutions there to have been suggested.

Introduction of Internet System has reduced the boundaries of business line and connected different places. It facilitates transmission of business messages (information) or lives business activities within a fraction of minute to a distant place. It is the foundation on which e-commerce and e-business models are built. Due to explosion of information and communication technology in 1990s and emergence

*Lecturer, Dept. of Commerce, HNB Garhwal University Campus, Badshahi Thaul, Tehri Garhwal, Uttaranchal.

of computer networks, e-commerce has become a buzzword, which include e-banking, e-shopping, e-marketing, e-chatting, e-brokerage, e-storage etc. Here we are taking only e-banking or Internet banking.

E-Banking, i.e. electronic banking or internet banking involves use of internet for delivery of banking products and services. E-banking is more prevalent in technologically advanced countries like U.S.A., Japan, Australia and other countries of Europe. E-banking does not involve any physical exchange of money, it is all done electronically from one account to another through internet, WAP or Telephone. The transactions are paperless and on real time basis. Here the quality of goods and services is better while its costs are cutting. E-banking covers both retail and business banking. In 2 to 3 years E-banking would become the heart of Indian Banking Service. The product mix of which are offered by E-banking includes: (1) A.T.M. (Automated Teller Machine) - ATM Card holders can withdraw or deposit funds and check statement information 8760 hours a year, (2) SPNS (Shared Payment Network System)—It is a network of ATMs which facilitates electronic funds transfer among the participating banks, bank payments, balance enquiry, printing of statement of accounts, cheque deposit, request of cheque book and point of sale facilities. (3) EFT (Electronic Funds Transfer)– It is devised by RBI, can be used for transfer of funds between bank accounts of same or different banks in same or different cities. (4) PC/SC (Plastic Card/Smart Card)–It is a standard magnetic card that consists of a microprocessor and a storage unit carrying whole of information regarding the card holder. It can be of two types, i.e. debit card and credit card (5) POS Terminal (Point of Sale Terminal) – It consists of two components a computer terminal and a plastic card. The computer terminal is connected to online computerized customer file in a bank. The plastic card enables the cardholder for identification and transaction of money to retailer account for the amount of purchase. (6) ECCS (Electronic Credit Clearing Service) – For bulk and repetitive payment transactions as salaries and dividends by companies and government departments it is a simple, reliable and cost-effective solution. These institutions prepare credit instruction on the magnetic media and submit the same to RBI through their bankers. After possessing the data, the RBI prepares report and provides it to the bank to facilitate fast payment to the beneficiaries. (7) EDCS (Electronic Debit Clearing Service) – This service is for making the small payments like telephone bill, electricity bill, etc. by the customer. Under this scheme, if the customer is satisfied with his bill, he authorises the banker to transfer the same amount from his account to utility providing company's account (8) Tele banking (9) Tele Computer Banking and (10) EDI (Electronic Data Interchange).

METHODOLOGY OF E-BANKING

It works on the concept of e-commerce. Customers need not go to the branches of bank because they can do all banking works through internet. In other words customers are offered open access to their accounts from the global market place. A password is given to log on to on-line banking. The on-line personal and business banking products and other information relating to an account on the banks different products are offered on the internet. When the customer accesses his account, he gets his transaction on the monitor. A customer who wants to open an account or obtain a loan can apply on the internet or can download related documents at anytime and from any part of the world via WWW a convenience unknown a short time ago. Thus the presence of bank's Internet has transformed from 'Brouchreware' status to 'E-Banking'.

ADVANTAGES OF E–BANKING

E-Banking or Internet banking is ready to work for 365 days a year, twenty-four hours a day and seven days a week in easy on line applications for all accounts including personal loans and mortgages also. Due to its unimaginable benefits, as per W.T.O. report, 300 million internet users in India nearly 4.2 lakh people are estimated to be registered online with banks. This number is expected to reach at least 41.73 lakh by December 2002.

1. E–Banking allows the customers to transcend the barriers of time, distance and geography and to take the advantages of global financial market place. Thus, customers get—any time and anywhere banking.
2. E–Banking is also known as reduced cost banking because it provides global reach, transfer of funds from an a/c to another a/c, instant transactions and services at low cost without any monthly fees, free bill payment and rebates on ATM.

3. It provides online purchases and payments of utility bills, e.g. telephone and electricity bills. It also provides novel facilities like payment of children's school fees and Income tax on Internet by using the plastic card/smart cards, master card and e-cash.
4. Banks themselves get the advantages of e-banking reduction in human intervention, inter-branch and inter-bank access by using EFT and SPNS, web promotion and customised services, etc.

HOME BANKING CONCEPT

The concept of Home Banking is supported by e-banking. Here the customers of bank need not stand in long queues at the bank for any type of transaction. Now they can do all transactions from their homes, offices or even from a remote location across the world. Home banking provides services like new deposit combinations, electronic fund transfer within twenty-one seconds, on line investment, ordering a draft or pay order, interactive banking including details of transactions and access to account. Home banking allows its customers to access information on banks treasury operations and cash management services through Internet.

E-BANKING IN INDIAN SCENARIO

The Banking industry in India is facing a cut throat competition with the non-traditional banking institutions as foreign banks and private banks, which provide their services on the Internet. The internet banking or e-banking in India, market is in the initial stages of development and about sixty banks are providing some kind of e-banking services. The Internet web sites of their banks offer only the most basic service. Near about 50% websites of these banks which are in entry level, are offering little more than company information and basic marketing materials and about 10% web sites are providing the advanced services as on line funds transfer, transaction and cash management services, etc. These banks have restricted their services within a limited area like opening of accounts, transfer of account, request for stopping payment, providing information about interest rate, and DD charges. There is a potential threat from hackers who try to gain access to secrete area of the accounts and get the details of customer accounts for which bank is expected to maintain confidentiality by breaking into the web site. Due to this constraint Indian Banks have not entered in e-banking system. On the other hand the foreign and private banks are far ahead in terms of the number of web sites and their level of development. It is expected that by the year 2003 in India there will be a large sophisticated any highly competitive e-banking market. It is also expected that entry level web sites will fall from 50 to 10% and advanced web sites would increase from 10 to 40% throughout the country.

OBSTACLES IN DEVELOPMENT OF E-BANKING IN INDIA

In spite of huge potential for development and growth in e-banking, there are some obstacles in Indian Scenario. These are:

1. Internet facility is not available to the common man of India due to inadequate computer literacy and net education.
2. Due to heavy cost of infrastructure and technology, bank and customers are not adopting the e-banking.
3. There are no clear-cut cyber laws and regulations applicable to e-banking in order to protect the public interest in India.
4. Due to heavy presence of cash component in our economy, the e-money is not accepted for any kind of transaction.
5. There is also a fear that globalization of money may have serious implications for Indian economy and data may be lost/ unauthorizedly accessed due to hackers and computer virus.

EPILOGUE

According to Mr. K.V. Kamath, the M.D. and C.E.O of ICICI, "Technology today particularly via the internet is creating a platform, independent low cost communication infrastructure permiting all sector of economy." He further says that as the base for communication shifts to the electronic world there would be a gradual decline in the use of paper too. In a business transaction just at the click of mouse millions of rupees can be transferred from one account to another. Mr. P.C. Narain then Executive Vice-President of Global Trust Bank Ltd. opines that paper currency could not disappear entirely, but what is certain to happen is that payment will get increasingly electronic. Narain continues that there would be more and more buying and selling activities around the world over internet where payment of physical money will not be necessary or will perhaps go out of fashion.

International Community has already accepted that e-banking is a vehicle to boost up banking system. Globalization has increased the access of companies in the world market. Customer too has a variety of options to select where he is not actually the king. In coming years e-banking will get metamorphosed from buzz word to reality because of availability of information and communication networks such as INFINET (Indian Financial Network) using V-SAT (satellite technology) and optical fibre and other terrestrial lines, dedicated to the Indian Financial Sector and increased net working options by up-coming basic telecom service providers in India. In spite of being so much, the technologies relating to e-banking in India are in infancy stage where the challenges are more severe. We have to face these challenges and our banks should tune themselves to capitalize on the benefits of e-banking for ensuring survival in this century otherwise would start counting their days.

10

MANAGEMENT INFORMATION SYSTEM IN COMMERCIAL BANKS

S.K. SHARMA*

The poor strategic Management Information System (MIS) has been one of the major weaknesses of our banks. Earlier the management considered the expenditure on MIS as unproductive one. Later the management realized that an effective MIS is inevitable for better control over branches and further for higher efficiency level. The MIS involves – data input system, data analysis and feedback system. The MIS is developed at three levels – operational level, tactical level for short term plans and strategic level for long term perspective.

The author traces the shortcomings of banks' MIS and also brings up some practical suggestions thereto. Banks need an integrated costing and financial reportig system so that managerial decision-making may lead to high profits and low costs.

INTRODUCTION

The complexities of modern business organization demand new dimensions of modern management. The Management Information System (MIS) has now become a facilitating system for developing decision in planning, organizing, controlling and initiating. A well developed system is the sine quo non of the successful management of an enterprise. Management information system has been widely used in business section for a long time for managing finance, human

*Reader, Faculty of Commerce, HNB Garhwal University Campus. Badshahithaul Distt. Tehri Garhwal, U.A. India.

resource, materials, production and marketing. This tool is found its uses in other sectors including many private and public organizations (Singla, 1992). It is used in transport corporations, construction companies, urban planning (Patkar, 1985). The paper describes general concept of the MIS and guidelines for its design and development. Management information system in Commercial Banks in India is discussed widely. It also provides some suggestions.

The objective of an Management Information System is to provide relevant and timely information to the management on resources, activities and outcomes of an organization for planning, organizing and controlling. An MIS is usually an user machine system that utilizes computer hardware and software, manual procedure, models for analysis and a data base (Jayshanker, 1991). It can make use of manual or computer procedures. The advantages of computer are helpful in handling voluminous amount of data. An MIS does not just deal with collection of information from different sources. It involves gathering of information during actual implementation, comparing outcomes with target and corrective measures in case of deviation between the actual performance and standards. The main objective of an MIS is to refine and improve the performance of the organization or system year after year based on the feedback obtained.

An MIS enhances the information processing of the organization in the following ways:

- Compact storage of data and speedy and reliable processing of raw data into information,
- Avoidance of redundancy and reduction of work loads and
- Efficient communication and information support for managerial decision making during planning implementation and evaluation.

COMPONENTS OF MANAGEMENT INFORMATION SYSTEM

Management Information System has the following components (Fig. 1).

- Data Input System
- Data Base Management System
- Data Analysis system
- Evaluation and Feedback system

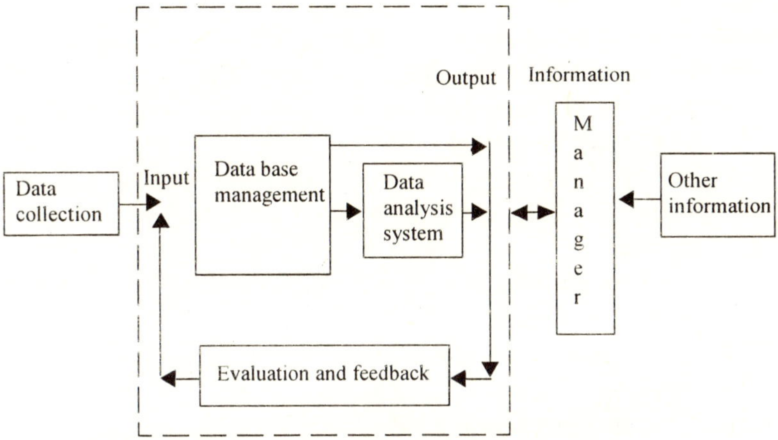

Fig. 1: Management Information System (MIS).

An MIS can be described as a pyramidal structure representing different levels of management in a organization or system (Fig. 2). In this pyramid, the bottom layer consists of information for transaction processing and status inquiries. The next higher level consists of information in support of day-to-day operations and control. The third level consists of information system resources to aid in tactical planning and decision-making for management control. The top level consists of information to support strategic planning and policy-making by higher level of management. Hence, an MIS can be developed at operation, tactical and strategic levels in any organization according to its need.

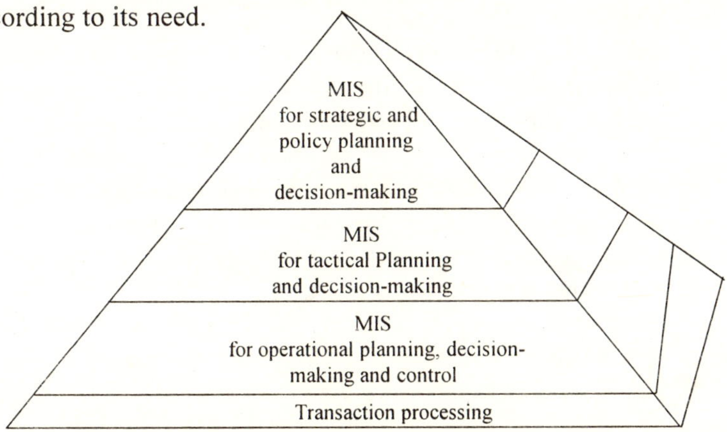

Fig. 2: The Pyramidal Structure of MIS (Head, 1967).

GUIDELINES FOR DEVELOPING MANAGEMENT INFORMATION SYSTEM

Horton *et al.* (1993) have provided guidelines for developing and implementing an MIS in an organization. They are:

(a) Focus on key management and accountability needs of an organization or system.
(b) Think of MIS as a process that integrates decision-making, planning and implementation, not a service of disconnected activities.
(c) Introduce the MIS in a gradual fashion starting from a small and simple scale.
(d) Plan on an MIS system that fits the organization's resource and needs.
(e) Use simple, practical methods of minimized time, cost and paper work.

CONSIDERATION IN DESIGNING OF AN MIS

There are different kinds of approaches in design of an MIS based on:

1. The organizational function for which the MIS is used such as production, marketing, finance, and accounting and logistics.
2. The managerial levels/activities for which MIS is used. An MIS can be developed at different levels of management according to the requirements of an organization as indicated by the pyramidal structure. Operational level MIS deals with day to day operations and control (lower mangement). Tactical level MIS deals with short-term planning, control and decision-making over six months to one year (middle level management). Strategic level MIS deals with long-term policy planning, resource allocation and decision-making over five to ten years (top level management). Information requirements of the various levels of management must be considered in the design of MIS. Generally the information for operational control are based largely within an organization while the information sources for strategic planning are from outside the organization, whereas sources for management control are more evenly distributed among internal and external origins as shown in Fig. 3.

Characteristics of Information	*Operational control (First level)*	*Management control (Top and middle level)*	*Strategic planning (Top level)*
Source	Largely internal	◄────────►	External
Scope	Well defined narrow	◄────────►	Very wide
Level of aggregation	Detailed	◄────────►	Aggregate
Time Horizon	Historical	◄────────►	Future
Currency	Highly current	◄────────►	Quite old
Required Accuracy	High	◄────────►	Low
Frequency of use	Very frequent	◄────────►	Infrequent

Fig. 3

3. Similarly, MIS can also be developed for managing different resources of an organization like Human Resource Information System (HRIS), Financial Information System (FIS) and Material Management Information System (MMIS).

INFORMATION NEEDS OF COMMERCIAL BANKS

Information is the key for reducing transaction cost. Deposits, advances, economic development, financial, personnel and external data on consumers/customers and markets are vital to the successful operation of most modern banks. Before designing suitable information system for commercial banks it will be pertinent to ascertain information needs of different levels of management in the bank. A branch/regional manager requires information about current operating performance in respect of his deposits level as well as their mix and advances level as well as their mix pertaining to various business segments. The data relating to deposits and advances, both are very important. Thus operating managers need the information for operational control purpose and for attaining predetermined operational results.

The executive management is more concerned about trends in operations vis-à-vis the norms set for the budget year so that necessary tactical as well as strategic action for rectification of any adverse results. They require information about the cost of funds received, average earnings, credit deposit ratio, levels of recovery, liquidity and other matters which determine the effectiveness and efficiency of banks operations over a period of time.

The successful implementation of performance budget depends primarily on a effective information system. The desired informations are presented in most cases by way of relating the actual current performance to the budgeted performance.

The chief executive and his team, who constitute the top echelon of bank management, play the role of an entrepreneur and innovator, architect of strategy, administrator and controller.

As an entrepreneur and innovator, they determine the destiny of the institution. They define corporate purpose and mission and long term objective so that they can serve as reference points for operations. As an architect of strategy they have to choose best course of action keeping in view the environmental opportunities and the bank's resources and communicate it to the executive and operating managers.

As an administrator, they have to formulate operational (e.g., in relation to deposits, advances, international operation, banking services, etc) and financial (e.g. personnel, inspection, planning accounting, investments, security, etc.) strategies, policies and procedures which will lead to achieve the desired targets.

As a controller they have to see that actual performance of banker which confirms the targets set earlier and take measures to correct the shortfalls. Their information requirements would pertain to the following:

- The trends in effectiveness of the banks operations in terms of productivity, adherence to policies, procedures and norms.
- Plans relating to future expansion particularly branch expansion and progress of such plans.
- Trends in sources and uses of funds.
- Summarized organizational performance report.

On the basis of above discussion it is crystal clear that commercial banks require informations for external as well as for internal purposes. Further information requirements of different levels of management in the bank vary.

On the basis of information the top management of commercial banks would be able to recognize trends in advance, initiate policy and tactical changes, shift their strategies and guide their organization to the attainment of the bank's overall objectives and goals.

In any information system, there must be a free and uninterrupted flow of information from bottom to the top and vice-versa and the transmission of information must be adequate, timely and meaningful so that the top level management may be in a position to take suitable and corrective action. The computer can analyse by permuting and combining data stored and present information in different facets and formats.

PRESENT INFORMATION SYSTEM IN COMMERCIAL BANKS

The absence of an effective/well designed management information system has been one of the major organizational weaknesses of commercial banks in India. In the beginning only some banks had set up an economic and statistics department and involved in the process. This was mainly because most of bank managements were not aware of the utility of a properly devised management information system and therefore considered the expenditure on such activity as non-productive. Now the bank managements have come to realize that without a well knit information system, it would be difficult to control branches and ensure their operational efficiency.

At present the information in Indian commercial banks falls in to two categories:

(i) Information Flow Between Reserve Bank of India and the Individual Banks

The Reserve Bank seeks information from the banks for the purposes noted earlier. It calls for certain returns from the banks, such as Scheduled Banks business in India, Return of Transactions in Foreign Exchange by Authorized Dealers, Fortnightly Return of Limits and Outstanding Amount of Unsecured Loans, Return of Demand and Time Liabilities and Cash, Gold and Unencumbered Proved securities of the Bank, Return of Asset and Liabilities of Banking Companies, Return of Advances to Agriculture, Return of Import/ Export letters of credit opened or Bank Guarantees Issued, Return of Foreign Currencies Held Abroad and Rupee Balances held in Bilateral Account Countries by Authorized Dealers, Return of Operations on Non-resident Account of Foreign Governments, Return of Partywise Credit Information, Special Return of Liabilities and Assets (as on 31 March), Survey of ownership and Investments and an Annual Statement of unclaimed Deposits, etc.

(ii) Information Flow within Individual Commercial Banks

Branch offices prepare and submit different types of statements to regional and zonal office and the head office—weekly, monthly, quarterly, six monthly and annual. There is almost total absence of feedback of processed data from the higher levels to the lower levels. Statement of assets and liabilities which contains the weekly deposits and advances of the branch is to be submitted weekly. There are two very important monthly statements, e.g. Monthly Statement of Advances, Priority Sectors excluding Agriculture and Monthly Statement of Advances to Agriculture which every branch has to prepare and submit to regional, zonal and head office. Quarterly statements are statement of Balanced Books and Statement of Irregular Accounts. Balance sheet, the profit and loss account, Basic Statistical Returns, Statements of Deposit, Insurance and the Statements of Credit Granted under Credit Guarantee Corporation, etc. are treated as half yearly statements to be furnished. Banks have to submit the branch profile to regional, zonal and head office annually.

Information received by banks from head office may be in the form of instruction circulars, information circulars and staff circulars.

WEAKNESSES OF THE PRESENT INFORAMTION SYSTEM

The present information system in commercial banks of India suffers from the following drawbacks:

1. There is a considerable duplication of effort in the collection of data from individual banks. No effort is made to use the data already available in the forms prescribed by Reserve Bank of India, although the large part of these data can be so used. Similarly the head office requisitions certain information from its branches, which can be obtained easily from the periodic statements submitted to it by the branches. This has unnecessarily increased the work load of the branches.
2. The Reserve Bank of India and the government of India often requisition certain informations from the head office of bank about which the branches do not maintain any record. The result is whatever information is supplied by branches to the head office is purely a guess estimate.

3. There is not effective system and regular compilation of information which might enable the management to evaluate the profitability of various services and the operating efficiency of the various departments.
4. A major problem of banks in India is the availability of excessive data, the relevance and quality of which are both suspected.
5. There is an absence of feedback of processed data from higher to lower levels.
6. Information relating to changes likely to take place in socio-economic, competitive and technological spheres in the country and the emergence of opportunities and threats are not complied and supplied to the top management of commercial banks as a result the private and foreign banks have a lead.
7. Due to absence of strategic perspective among the top management of the most commercial banks, no strategic planning was formulated within crucial time.

CONCLUSION AND SUGGESTIONS

In use of technology, public sector banks are behind competing multinational banks and private banks. With products and service, being more and more technology driven this will be a crippling disadvantage to public sector banks.

There are some suggestions to enable commercial banks, more effective for managing future successfully through MIS.

- Organized efforts should be made to ensure that there is a minimum duplication of efforts in collection of information.
- Each bank should have an effective statistical cell for planning and developing the statistical services. Adequate training and documentation should be provided for the operations and users of the system.
- There is an urgent need for organizing feedback with a view to involving the branch managers and others at the lower level of operation and judging their performance on the basis of facts and figures.
- A common set of forms should be evolved for each priority sector that can be easily understood and be usable without further modifications.

- There is a need for an integrated costing and financial reporting system in banks. The Management Information System should clearly bring out the inter-relationships between the volume of business, the cost and related income, so that the managerial decision-making may lead to improve profitability. It must be cost-effective.
- To achieve competitiveness both in domestic and international market, the banking sector necessarily needs to launch various efforts of innovation.

As the environment changes the commercial banks (organizations) may change their vision and objective, portfolio management, business markets and competitive strategies. Management Information System have potential to improve the performance of the organization or system by enhancing the (a) quality of decision-making process, (b) quality of services provided by the staff in satisfying the costomer needs, (c) efficiency of resource mobilization and (d) by providing a performance appraisal (accountability) of the staff involved. MIS can also be used as a training tool for improving the skills of manager and other staff. As we are living in 'Techno Era' an effective Management Information System (MIS) in organization has become panacea to exploit the opportunities and utilize its strength to combat the threats as well as its weaknesses.

REFERENCES

1. Bardalai Niranjan (2000), Planning for the New Millennium, *SBI Monthly Review*, pp. 242-256.
2. Head, V.R. (1967) Management information system . A critical appraisal, *Datamation*, Vol. 2 pp. 23-24.
3. Jayashanker, R. (1991). *Decision support systems*, Tata McGraw Hill Publishing Co. Ltd., New Delhi.
4. Jeemol and U. Rani, (2000), Globalization, Information Technology Revolution and Service Sector in India. *Indian Journal of Labour Economics*, Oct-Dec.
5. Kumar, N., Mittal, R. (2001), *Marketing Management*, Anmol Publication, Delhi.
6. Patker, V.N. (1985), Introducing MIS in an urban planning authority: Three approaches, *Nagarlok*, Vol. 17, No. 4, pp. 59-67.
7. Ragnar, G.M., Ross, J.E. (1977). Information Systems for Modern Management.

8. Subba Rao P. (1999), *Essentials of Human Resource Management and Industrial Relations*, Himalaya Publishing House, Mumbai.
9. Sharma, S.K. (2002). "Strategic Management: A necessity in India in new millennium", paper presented and published in the Souvenir of the International Conference entitled "Vedic values and corporate excellence' held at G.K. University, Haridwar (UA), pp. 27-28.
10. Singla, M.L. (1992), MIS in public sector undertakings—A perceptual study. *Indian Management*, Vol. 31, No.6., pp. 14-17.
11. Srivastava, R.M. (2000). *Management of Indian Financial Institution*, Himalaya Publishing House, pp. 409-417.

11

ASSET-LIABILITY MANAGEMENT: AN EMERGING TREND IN BANKING SECTOR

Lalita Prasad*
M.C.Pande**

Management of Risk has always been the main concern for each and every business organization. In the process of globalization banks have become exposed to greater verity of financial risk. Asset-Liability Management (ALM) provides a macro level framework and a sophisticated tool for modern risk management in banks. The study presents the role and importance of ALM in commercial banks. The Nainital Bank Ltd. has been selected as sample which is rendering its services in four states namely - Uttaranchal, Uttar Pradesh, Delhi and Harayana. Study shows that the process of globalization has arrived in India without proper advance planning. However, banks are developing their structure accordingly and doing a good job for proper management of their risks with the help of ALM.

BACKGROUND

Asset-Liability Management (ALM) is a coordination approach to a balance sheet risk management. ALM does not mean not taking risk but it means that banks should be fully aware of risk being taken, capping the risk to a pretend level and being reasonably ready with alternative plans in tune with the changing environment. ALM involves

*Research Scholar.

**Faculty of Commerce, Govt. P.G. College, Rudrapur (Uttaranchal).

planning, directing and controlling the flow, mix, cost and yield of the consolidated funds of the bank. It is also seen as strategic positioning of the asset side with the liability side and enhancing the linkage through 'off balance sheet activities'. In simple words ALM is an attempt to match the assets and liabilities in terms of their maturities and interest rates sensitivities so that the risk arising from such mismatches—mainly interest rate risk and liquidity risk—can be contained within the desire limit.

During mid-term review of the monetary and credit policy for 1998-99 the Governor of Reserve Bank of India has stated on October 30th 1998, "Banks are advised to introduce effective risk management system to cover credit risk, market risk and operational risk on a priority basis." Based on the origin and their nature, risks are classified into various categories. Risks to which banks are generally exposed to are —

1. Interest Rate Risk–
   (a) Restructuring Risk
   (b) Volatility Risk
   (c) Prepayment Risk
   (d) Call / Put Risk
   (e) Reinvestment Risk
   (f) Bases Risk
2. Liquidity Risk–
   (a) Long Term Liquidity Risk
   (b) Short Term Liquidity Risk
3. Credit Risk
4. Exchange Rate Risk
5. Operational Risk
6. Contingent Risk
7. Other Risks–
   (a) Political Risk
   (b) Human Risk
   (c) Technology Risk
   (d) Legal Risk
   (e) Systemic Risk
   (f) Price Risk

Apart from above risks many other risks may also cause harm to the health of a bank. These are Liability Risk, Compliance Risk, Tax Risk, Crime Risk, Physical Risk, Funding Risk and Market Risk, etc. Any bank may face one or more than one risk altogether.

CONCEPTUAL FRAMEWORK

The last decade has been a path-breaking era for the banking sector. The liberalization process and as a consequence, the Narsimhan Committee reforms have brought into focus the liner qualitative aspect of banking rather than the hitherto lauded quantitative parameters. The first phase of banking sector reforms which began in 1992, was focused on transparent accounting norms, cleansing of balance sheet, reducing statutory pre-emption of resources of banks and deregulation of interest. Due to the introduction of internationally accepted norms of income recognition and provisioning, the profit and loss account and balance sheet of banks have become a fair reflection of the financial health of organization.

Switching over of banks from protected sector to free market has made them risk aware. This is why the ALM has become unavoidable.

METHODOLOGY

The Nainital Bank Ltd. is an'A' class private sector scheduled commercial bank, from Uttaranchal state. Bharat Ratna Govind Ballabh Pant and others initially established it in the year 1922. In the year 1973 the management and control of this bank was taken over by Bank of Baroda, which now holds 94.59% of shares of the bank. Bank has 59 branches operating in the state of Uttaranchal, Uttar Pradesh, Delhi and Haryana. It has distinction of being the only profit making and dividend-paying bank of erstwhile state of UP since last 28 years. The areawise classification of the branches is as follows —

Metro	09
Urban	14
Semi-Urban	20
Rural	16

In the year 2002, Bank had a total deposit of Rs. 60801 lakhs and advances of Rs.13080 lakhs, which is only 21.51% of total deposits. Bank's net profit is increasing rapidly. For the year 2002, it was 572 lakhs. Bank has been successful in keeping NPA at lowest level.

The period of this study is four years. Asset-Liability Management was introduced in India when RBI notification was issued on Feb.19, 1999. The Nainital Bank Ltd. (NTB), too, initiated the process of ALM in the same year. Data up to 18 April 2003 have been taken for the purpose.

The study is basically secondary database. However, the views of officers and staff working at head office and in branches have also been included so that problems and prospects may be test checked.

OBJECTIVE

Main objective of the study is to evaluate the performance of commercial banks in the light of their objectives with a view to suggest the way and means for bringing about relatively high degree of effectiveness and efficiency in managing assets and liabilities. The model of NTB is taken, as it is comparatively a small bank having its 59 branches in metropolitan, urban, semi-urban and rural centers of four states. Following working objectives have been laid down:

1. To examine the relevance and importance of asset-liability management.
2. To examine the implementation of RBI guidelines.
3. To study the role and organization of ALCO.
4. To analyze the impact of asset-liability management.
5. To draw results in the light of RBI guidelines.

HYPOTHESIS

Following hypothesis were worked out —

1. Banks are well aware of their risks.
2. ALM has gained importance with the beginning of LPG era.
3. Indian Banks can do better with keeping pace with internationally accepted norms.
4. RBI has proper control on commercial banks.

ALM IN INDIAN BANKS

ALM has not been an issue in India till recent past because of high Statutory Liquidity Ratio (SLR) and regulated interest and exchange rates. Banks took deposits at mandated rates and lent them at higher rates fixed by the RBI. This flexibility of the commercial banking activities did not translate into interest rate risk. Similarly, the liquidity risk to a great extent was taken care by the RBI through various refinance windows like discretionary refinance, etc. However, since 1989 as part of the financial sector reforms interest rates have been withdrawn. As a result of this the risks involved in commercial banking, have become very pronounced.

In 1993-94 RBI asked public sector banks to frame the ALM policy. But, first ever comprehensive circular for establishing ALM system was issued by RBI on 19 Feb. 1999. According to this circular the process of ALM rests on three pillars –

1. ALM information system
   a) Management Information System.
   b) Information availability, accuracy, adequacy and expediency.
2. ALM Organization
   a) Structure and responsibility
   b) Level of top management involvement.
3. ALM Process
   a) Risk parameters
   b) Risk identification
   c) Risk measurement
   d) Risk management
   e) Risk policies and tolerance levels.

The central element of the entire ALM exercise is the availability of adequate and accurate information with expedience. The existing systems in many Indian banks do not generate information in the manner required for ALM. Collecting accurate data in a timely manner will be the biggest challenge before the banks, particularly those having wide network of branches but lacking full-scale computerization. In these banks ALM needs to be addressed by following an ABC approach, i.e. analyzing of asset and liability products in the sample branches accounting for significant business and then making rational assumptions about the way in which assets and liabilities would behave in other branches.

For successful implementation of ALM, banks require strong commitment on the part of the senior management in the bank. Two committees work for this purpose —

i. Management Committee of Board (MCB) on ALM and risk management.
ii. Asset-Liability Committee (ALCO)

ALM process includes Measuring, Monitoring and Managing the Market Risk, Liquidity Risk, Interest Rate Risk, Currency Risk and other risks. They follow a system as per the size and business of their organization. Collection, communication, coordination and control are keys of good ALM process.

CASE STUDY

The Nainital Bank Ltd. (NTB) is a fast growing bank. During last decade it has shown a sharp increase in branch expansion, business growth and management of NPAs. This bank has been taken as model for study.

In Nainital Bank, there is a Management Committee of Board on ALM and Risk Management (MCB). It includes six directors (including the chairman). MCB clearly communicates to the management the acceptable level of risk in terms of the parameters chosen. It is also board's responsibility to ensure that the bank puts in place software, management system and expertise to regularly monitor report of these risks. The committee usually meets on quarterly intervals.

Asset-Liability Committee (ALCO) was constituted in 1999 comprising Chairman, GM, DGMs and heads of accounts, credit and planning and investment depts. This committee is responsible for ensuring adherence to the board limits as well as deciding the business strategy of the bank. The ALM desk consisting of operating level staff assists ALCO. This desk is responsible for analyzing, monitoring and reporting the risk levels to the ALCO.

In the bank, market risk policy has been put in place, prudential limits are fixed and reporting system works on fortnightly basis. The Bank does not deals in trading so far, independent middle office other than treasury department to track the magnitude of market risk on a real time basis has not been set up.

Reserve Bank of India, in its inspection in 1999-2000, has appreciated the performance of the bank. On comparison with RBI stipulation following scene appears—

Parameters	*RBI (%)*	*Nainital Bank (%) (as on 30-09-99)*
CAR	09	15.11
SLR Security	25	31.13
CRR	08	09.17
Priority Sector Advances	40	54.48
Provisions for NPA	As per RBI guidelines	Full provided
Provision for Standard	0.25	0.30

The Bank also fulfils the expectations of Varma Committee parameters. This Bank has fairly proved its worth in various fields. Tables 1 and 2 shows bank's growth and profit earned during last decades. The bank is not only fulfilling the expectations of RBI and other controlling authorities but also improving its position day by day. Bank's Capital Adequacy Ratio is 20.93% in 2002-03. Return on equity is also appreciable.

Table 1: NTB's Growth of Business

Year	*Total Business (Dep. + Adv.) (Rs. in lakhs)*	*No. of Branches*	*Business Per Branch (Rs. in lakhs)*	*Growth Indices*
1971	234	9	26	100.00
1976	648	12	54	207.69
1981	2580	30	86	330.77
1986	10619	41	259	999.15
1992	17429	48	363	1396.15
1997	35343	51	693	2665.38
2002	75922	58	1309	5034.62

Table 2: NTB's Statement of Profitability

Year	*Profit Rs. in lacs*	*No. of Employees*	*Profit per Employee*	*Growth Indices*
1971	-1	89	–	–
1976	2	115	0.02	100.00
1981	4	269	0.01	50.00
1986	15	554	0.03	150.00
1992	80	579	0.14	700.00
1997	74	585	0.12	600.00
2002	572	644	0.88	4400.00

Statement of *structural liquidity* is given in Table 3. As on 18 April 2003 bank's total flow was Rs. 77,175, which was spread in 8 buckets as under—

1. 1-14 days
2. 15-28 days
3. 29 days-upto 3 months
4. Over 3 months—up to 6 months
5. Over 6 months—up to 1 year
6. Over 1 year—up to 3 years
7. Over 3 year—up to 5 years
8. Over 5 years

Analysis clearly states that bank achieved positive gap in bucket 1, 2, 3, 5, 7 and 8. Two buckets with negative gap are 4 (over 3 months—up to 6 months) and 6 (over 1 year— up to 3 years). In time bucket 4, negative gap is only 21.49% but in time bucket 6, the negative gap is 60.38% as against the tolerance limit of 55%. The bank needs to look into the matter. However, it is not so serious matter as cumulative mismatch up to three years is 46.42% (negative), which is within the tolerance limit.

Table 4 shows the statement of *interest rate sensitivity* as on 18th April 2003. There are positive gaps in 1st, 2nd, 3rd, 5th, 7th and 8th time buckets. Gaps in 4th and 6th time bucket are found negative on this date. The cumulative gap up to one year is also negative. The bank needs to restructure its lending rates in such a manner that negative gaps may be made positive. Short-term loans should be encouraged recovering the negative gap. Surplus of this bucket may help the bank in eliminating the cumulative negative gap. RBI has given the freedom for adjusting the rate of interest under prescribed limits.

PROBLEMS AND PROSPECTS

Success of ALM is the end product of joint efforts of branches and their corporate office. Consolidation, compilation and analysis of data (supplied by branches) are done at head office. During the course of study it was found that the slow pace of computerization is barring the progress of ALM in bank. NTB was having its only 19 branches fully computerized. This number does not cover even metro and urban

Table 3: Statement of Structral Liquidity as on 18.04.2003
(Bank Code: 826)

OUTFLOWS

(Amount in lacs)

	1-14 days	*15-28 days*	*29 days upto 3 months*	*Over 3 months upto 6 months*	*Over 6 month upto 1 year*	*Over 1 year upto 3 year*	*Over 3 upto 5 year*	*Over 5 year*	*Total*
1. Capital	0	0	0	0	0	0	0	1,500	1,500
2. Reserve and Surplus	0	0	0	0	0	0	0	4,255	4,255
3. Deposit	4,800	1,074	3,260	4,814	7,820	41,339	3,172	1,045	67,324
3.1 Current Deposits	949	0	0	0	0	5,377	0	0	6,326
3.2 Saving Bank Deposits	2,619	0	0	0	0	23,572	0	0	26,191
3.3 Term Deposits	1,232	1,074	3,260	4,814	7,820	12,390	3,172	1,045	34,807
3.4 Certificates of Deposits	0	0	0	0	0	0	0	0	0
4. Borrowings	0	0	0	1	2	6	5	0	14
4.1 Call and Short Notice	0	0	0	0	0	0	0	0	0
4.2 Inter Bank (Term)	0	0	0	0	0	0	0	0	0
4.3 Refinances	0	0	0	1	2	6	5	0	14
4.4 Other (Specify)	0	0	0	0	0	0	0	0	0

5. Other Liabilities and Provision	93	323	437	91	32	105	186	859	2,126
5.1 Bills Payable	41	260	310	80	0	0	0	0	691
5.2 Inter-Office Adjustment	0	0	0	0	0	0	0	0	0
5.3 Provision	0	0	0	0	20	60	120	709	909
5.4 Others	52	63	127	11	12	45	66	150	526
6. Lines of credit committed to	0	0	0	0	0	0	0	0	0
6.1 Institutions	0	0	0	0	0	0	0	0	0
6.2 Customers	0	0	0	0	0	0	0	0	0
7. Unavailed portion cash credit	500	450	358	0	0	0	0	0	1,308
8. Letters of Credit/Guarantees	81	0	0	0	0	0	0	0	81
9. Repos	0	0	0	0	0	0	0	0	0
10. Bills Rediscounted (DUPN)	0	0	0	0	0	0	0	0	0
11. SWAPS (Buy/Sell)	0	0	0	0	0	0	0	0	0
12. Interest Payable	11	3	30	50	70	60	0	0	224
13. Other (specify) profit	0	0	0	0	0	0	0	343	343
A. Total Outflows	**5,485**	**1,850**	**4,085**	**4,956**	**7,924**	**41,510**	**3,336**	**8,002**	**77,175**

INFLOWS

(Amount in lacs)

	1-14 days	*15-28 days*	*29 days upto 3 months*	*Over 3 months upto 6 months*	*Over 6 month upto 1 year*	*Over 1 year upto 3 year*	*Over 3 upto 5 year*	*Over 5 year*	*Total*
1. Cash	630	0	0	0	0	0	0	0	630
2. Balance with RBI	1,081	261	83	184	223	357	1,868	151	4,208
3. Balance with other Banks	3,193	1,600	2,035	2,630	6,490	715	43	0	16,706
3.1 Current Account	1,336	0	0	0	0	250	0	0	1,586
3.2 Money at Call, Short Notice, Term Deposit and Other Placements	1,857	1,600	2,035	2,630	6,490	465	43	0	15,120
4. Investments	0	2454	713	329	610	5792	4698	19661	34,257
5. Advances (performing)	1,413	1,241	1,410	443	607	9,366	1,379	1,356	17,215
5.1 Bills Purchased and Discounted Bill under (DUPN)									
5.2 Cash Credit, Overdrafts and Loan Repayable on Demand	1,147	1,111	1,147	81	36	8,028	0	0	11,550
5.3 Term Loans	95	130	263	362	571	1338	1379	1356	5,494

6. NPAs (Advances and Investments)	0	0	0	0	0	0	268	162	430
7. Fixed Assets	0	0	0	0	0	0	0	507	507
8. Other Assets	1,052	289	128	55	1	15	20	69	1,629
8.1 Inter-office Adjustement	739	0	0	0	0	0	0	0	739
8.2 Leased Assets	0	0	0	0	0	0	0	0	0
8.3 Others	313	289	128	55	1	15	20	69	890
9. Reverse Repos	0	0	0	0	0	0	0	0	0
10. SWAPS (Seel/Buy)/ maturing forward	0	0	0	0	0	0	0	0	0
11. Bills Rediscounted (DUPN)	0	0	0	0	0	0	0	0	0
12. Interest Receivable	68	25	175	250	425	200	250	200	1,593
13. Committed Lines of Credit	0	0	0	0	0	0	0	0	0
14. Other (Specify) Loss	0	0	0	0	0	0	0	0	0
B. Total Inflows	**7,437**	**5,870**	**4,544**	**3,891**	**8,356**	**16,445**	**8,526**	**22,106**	**77,175**
C. Mismatch (B-A)	**1,952**	**4,020**	**459**	**– 1,065**	**432**	**– 25,065**	**5,163**	**14,104**	**0**
D. Cumulative Mismatch	**1,952**	**5,972**	**6,431**	**5,366**	**5,798**	**– 19,267**	**– 14,104**	**0**	**0**
E. C as % to A	**35.59%**	**217.30%**	**11.24%**	**–21.49%**	**5.45%**	**–60.38%**	**153.52%**	**176.26%**	**0**

Table 4: Statement of Interest Rate sensitivity as on 18-04-03

LIABILITIES

	1-14 days	*15-28 days*	*29 days to 3 month*	*Over 3 month upto 6 months*	*Over 6 months upto 1 year*	*Over 1 year upto 3 year*	*Over 3 year upto 5 year*	*Over 5 year*	*Non-sensitive*	*Total*
1. Capital	0	0	0	0	0	0	0	0	1,500	1,500
2. Reserve and surplus	0	0	0	0	0	0	0	0	4,255	4,255
3. Deposits	1,232	1,074	3,260	28,386	7,820	12,390	3,172	1,045	8,945	67,324
3.1 Current Deposits	0	0	0	0	0	0	0	0	6,326	6,326
3.2 Saving Bank Deposits	0	0	23,572	0	0	0	2,619	26,191		
3.3 Term Deposits	1232	1074	3260	4814	7820	12390	3172	1045	34,807	
3.4 Certificates of Deposits	0	0	0	0	0	0	0	0	0	0
4. Borrowings	0	0	0	0	0	0	0	0	14	14
4.1 Call and Short Notice	0	0	0	0	0	0	0	0	0	0
4.2 Inter Bank (Term)	0	0	0	0	0	0	0	0	0	0
4.3 Refinances	0	0	0	0	0	0	0	0	14	14
4.4 Other (Specify)	0	0	0	0	0	0	0	0	0	0

5. Other Liabilities and Provision	0	0	0	0	0	0	0	0	2,126	2,126
5.1 Bills Payable	0	0	0	0	0	0	0	0	691	691
5.2 Inter-Office Adjustement	0	0	0	0	0	0	0	0	0	0
5.3 Provisions	0	0	0	0	0	0	0	0	909	909
5.4 Others (Specify)	0	0	0	0	0	0	0	0	526	526
6. Repos	0	0	0	0	0	0	0	0	0	0
7. Bills Rediscounted (DUPN)	0	0	0	0	0	0	0	0	0	0
8. Swaps (Buy/Sell)	0	0	0	0	0	0	0	0	0	0
9. Other intt. payable & profit	0	0	0	0	0	0	0	0	0	0
A. Total Liabilities	1,232	1,074	3,260	28,386	7,820	12,290	3,172	1,045	17,407	75,786

Excluding provision for NPAs and Investment

ASSETS

	1-14 days	15-28 days	29 days up to 3 months	Over 3 months upto 6 months	Over 6 months upto 1 year	Over 1 year upto 3 year	Over 3 year upto 5 year	Over 5 year	Non-sensitive	Total
1. Cash	0	0	0	0	0	0	0	0	630	630
2. Balance with RBI	0	0	0	2,135	0	0	0	0	2,073	4,208
3. Balance with other Banks	1,857	1,600	2,035	2,630	6,490	465	43	0	1,586	16,706
3.1 Current Accounts	0	0	0	0	0	0	0	0	1,586	1,586
3.2 Money at call, Short Notice & Term Deposite	1,875	1,600	2,035	2,630	6,490	465	43	0	0	15,120
4. Investments	0	2454	713	329	610	5792	4698	19658	3	34,257
5. Advances (performing)	95	130	10,424	362	571	1,338	1,379	1,356	171	15,826
5.1 B.P. and Discounted (incld. Bill under DUPN)	0	0	0	0	0	0	0	0	171	171
5.2 Cash Credits, Overdraft and Demand Loan	0	0	10,161	0	0	0	0	0	0	10,161
5.3 Term Loans	95	130	263	362	571	1338	1379	1356	0	5,494
6. NPAs (Advances & invest)	0	0	0	0	0	0	0	0	430	430

7. Fixed Assets	0	0	0	0	0	0	0	0	507	507
8. Other Assets	0	0	0	0	0	0	0	0	3,222	3,222
8.1 Inter-office Adjustement	0	0	0	0	0	0	0	0	739	739
8.2 Others	0	0	0	0	0	0	0	0	2,483	2,483
9. Reverse Repos	0	0	0	0	0	0	0	0	0	0
10. SWPS (Sell/Buy)	0	0	0	0	0	0	0	0	0	0
11. Bills Rediscounted (DUPN)	0	0	0	0	0	0	0	0	0	0
12. Other (Specify) Loss	0	0	0	0	0	0	0	0	0	0
B. Total Assets	**1,952**	**4,184**	**13,172**	**3,321**	**9,806**	**7,595**	**6,120**	**21,014**	**8,622**	**75,786**
C. Gap (B-A)	**720**	**3,110**	**9,912**	**-25,065**	**1,986**	**-4,795**	**2,948**	**19,969**	**-8,785**	**0**
Other Products	0	0	0	0	0	0	0	0	0	0
1. FRAs	0	0	0	0	0	0	0	0	0	0
2. Waps	0	0	0	0	0	0	0	0	0	0
3. Futures	0	0	0	0	0	0	0	0	0	0
4. Options	0	0	0	0	0	0	0	0	0	0
5. Other (Specify)	0	0	0	0	0	0	0	0	0	0
D. Other Products Total	0	0	0	0	0	0	0	0	0	0
E. Net Gap (C-D)	**720**	**3,110**	**9,912**	**-25,065**	**1,986**	**-4,795**	**2,948**	**19,969**	**-8,785**	**0**
F. Cumulative Gap	**720**	**3,830**	**13,742**	**-11,323**	**-9,337**	**-14,132**	**-11,184**	**8,785**	**13,601**	
G. E as % To B	**36.89**	**74.33**	**75.25**	**-754.74**	**20.25**	**-63.13**	**48.17**	**95.03**	**-101.89**	
	%	**%**	**%**	**%**	**%**	**%**	**%**	**%**	**%**	

centers. Bank's 18 branches were running on ALPMs. This system does not cover credit business. Computerization in 16 rural branches is a big challenge, because on those centers computerization is neither economically viable nor technically possible.

Several branches of NTB are facing the shortage of staff. Change in banking environment has increased their accountability. Customer satisfaction is a must for the existence in market. ALM is a back office work and sometimes, despite all strategies of RBI and Head Office, it becomes secondary in comparison to front office work. Manipulation of data is possible in such condition.

Treatment of mismatch is based on flexible grounds, so there is ample chance of manipulation and window-dressing. For example, in a bank there are liabilities of Rs. 500 crore and in assets side investment + loans are of Rs. 400 crores in 1-14 days bucket. This shows a negative mismatch of assets and liabilities. Bank keeps investment in three categories, i.e. held for trading, available for sale and held to maturity. In this case, bank will show held for trading investment because they are to be traded within a period of 90 days from the date of its classification. For remaining gap bank may show its investment in available for sale categories in first bucket to fulfill the gap as they were kept for this purpose. This flexibility will make the bank safe and bank will show rosy picture of its affairs.

Reserve Bank of India has suggested the classification of saving bank and current deposit into volatile and core portions. It is suggested that 10% saving bank and 15% of current deposit may be treated as volatile and can be placed in first time bucket that is 1-14 days. The core portion may be placed in over 1 to 3 years bucket. RBI has given a freedom for better-equipped banks to estimate the behavior pattern, roll in roll out, imbedded options etc. on the basis of past data. In Nainital Bank Ltd. 10% of savings and 15% of current account is treated as volatile portion. Remaining 85% current and 90% of saving bank account is treated as core portion. This bank keeps the core portion of saving bank account divided into two buckets of 45% each, i.e. 1-3 years and 3-5 years. This ratio is fixed on the basis of bank's previous experience.

RESUME OF CONCLUSION

ALM is mandatory for all banks. Reserve Bank of India regulates them. Detailed guidelines for establishing Asset and Liability Management System in banks were issued on 19-02-1999. Gradually all banks adopted the system to manage their assets and liability. The Nainital Bank Ltd., like other banks, has formed an ALCO and a committee at directors' level. Monthly monitoring system is implemented in this bank. A separate cell at head office level is formed for this purpose, which collects, compiles and compares the data. Implementation of policy decisions is the prime duty of this cell. Bank presents report on interest rate sensitivity and short-term liquidity before its board of directors. The bank looks to be in comfortable position. It is progressing day by day. Its NPA is at negligible stage and profits are rising high. ALM system, though not very old, is working properly. ALM has been proved of great use in curtailing NPAs, increasing profitability and facing competition with other banks (specially foreign banks). Commercial banks should improve their Management Information System as per the needs of ALM. This will help banks in improving their strength.

REFERENCES

1. Annual Report (2002-03), The Nainital Bank Ltd.
2. Deep Chandra (2000), Asset Liability Management in Commercial Banks (Project Report – IGNOU).
3. Khurana, S.K. (1999), *Security Analysis & Investment Management, Skylark Publication*, New Delhi.
4. Payant W. Randall (Aug. 11, 1995), *Credit Union News*.
5. Ravi Kumar, T. (2000) *Asset Liability Management*, Vision Books, New Delhi.
6. RBI (1999), Circular BP. BC 8/21.040098/99 dt.10-02-1999.
7. Sabnani Prahlad (July 2002), *IBA Bulletin* (Mumbai).

12

STRATEGIC HUMAN RESOURCE MANAGEMENT – A PANACEA FOR COMMERCIAL BANKS

S. Hussain Ashraf*

The most striking change that the HR function has undergone in recent time is its increasing involvement in developing and implementing business strategy. There is clear shift from the role of protector to planner and change agent. The HRM works at three different levels—strategic level, operational level and corporate level where it influences the whole organization. The strategic HRM aims at developing a well-trained workforce which is responsive to customer demands. The enhanced role of technology in banks requires high skill level from the staff. The author advises that the banks will have to focus on aligning their HRM practices to corporate strategy.

In the emerging competitive environment the banking industry is witnessing several changes in the ways of doing business. In a free market environment, the survival of a bank depends on its ability to enjoy a competitive edge in the market. With the process of financial reforms which began in 1992 banking have undergone a complete transformation. The twin forces of deregulation and liberalization have brought about a paradigm, shift in the industry. With the removal of protective cover they were enjoying, banks today have more freedom to decide upon their strategies. At the same time, the changes in the

*Reader, Department of Commerce, Aligarh Muslim University, Aligarh, U.P., India.

operating environment in the form of enhanced competition and the revolution in technology of computing and communication have compelled banks to redraw their strategies to protect their market share and sustain their profitability. While liberalization has opened new business opportunities, technology has widened the markets.

Technology has emerged as one of the key drivers of our business, we had to factor its impact on our strategy and human resource policy. While banks have invested substantially in technology there is a strong need for suitable changes in human resource policies as HRM is the weakest area in the Indian banking system. Human resource, the invisible intangible asset, are the most valuable asset in any industry more so in case of a service industry like banking, where interaction with people is among the highest. In banking the first customer is the employee and every effort needs to be made to take care of this assets. Human resources are amongst the most critical elements of competitive strategy in the modern era.

Human resource management refers to a strategic and coherent approach to the management of an organization's people who individually and collectively contribute to the achievement of sustainable competitive advantage. Competitive advantage of the organisation is to be achieved through harnessing the potential available in the employees by creating a positive culture and enlisting the support of all the employees to the organisational goals. The HRM philosophy believes that people are social capital which is capable of development through appropriate interventions and by opening channels of communications to build trust and to enlist their commitment. The emphasis is on 'commitment' and not 'compliance'. Therefore HRM strategy will have to foster the commitment of employees to the organization, unleash the latent creativity and energise the workforce. But commitment comes when there is mutuality. According to R.E. Walton of Harvard Business School: The HRM model is composed of policies that promote mutuality–mutual goals, mutual influence, mutual respect, mutual rewards, mutual responsibility... mutuality will elicit commitment which in turn will yield both better economic performance and greater human development". Thus the thrust of HRM is to foster commitment in employees, which in turn will be directed towards gaining competitive advantage and to establish an environment in which the latent creativity of the workforce will be unleashed.

The most striking change that the HR function has undergone in recent times is its increasing involvement in developing and implementing business strategy. There is clear shift from the role of protector to planner and change agent. The primary emphasis needs to be an integrating human resource management strategies with business strategy. HRM has become an integral part of business strategy and is a source of competitive advantage. Every strategy that the organization formulated will demand matching response from its employees who in turn should be supported by consistent human resource policies.

STRATEGIC HUMAN RESOURCE MANAGEMENT

The field of strategic human resource management seeks to examine the role that human resources play in firm performance, particularly focusing on the alignment of human resources with firm strategy as a means of gaining competitive advantage. The basic theory behind 'Fit' is that the effectiveness of any human resource practice or set of practices for imparting organization performance depends upon the organizations strategy (or conversely, the effectiveness of any strategy depends upon having the right human resource practices).

Wright and McMahan defined SHRM as "the pattern of planned human resource deployments and activities intended to enable the firm to achieve its goals". This definition implied at least four components to strategic HRM. First, it focuses on the firm's 'human resources' (i.e. people) as the primary resource to be strategically leveraged as a source of competitive advantage. Second, the concept of 'activities' highlights HR programs, policies and practices as the mean through which the people of a firm can be deployed to gain competitive advantage. Third, both 'pattern' and 'plan' describe the goal and process of strategy; a consistent alignment or design which could also be described as 'fit'. This fit could consist of both vertical (with the firm's strategy) and horizontal (all the HR activities aligned with one another) aspects. Finally, within this definition, the people, practices and planned pattern are all purposeful, that being "goal achievement".

SIGNIFICANCE OF STRATEGIC HRM

The way in which HRM seeks to contribute to organizational performance are through organizational design, through HR system, programmes and policies and through cost control. The extent to which HRM achieves these contributions is the extent to which the function can be effective.

In fact HRM has to work at three different levels—the strategic level, the operational level and at a broad corporate level—if it is to influence the whole organization. Their ultimate aim should be to develop a well-trained workforce, flexible and responsive to customer demands.

HRM should focus on developing skills, values and behaviours consistent with a high level of personal effectiveness in the following five broad areas:

- Technical skills which are specific to a job (e.g., marketing, book-keeping).
- Behavioural skills which cover traits like motivation, judgement, resilience and initiative as well as generic skills like communication, team working and self management.
- Business awareness which would include wider knowledge relating to the organization, its key products, competitors, etc.
- IT skills which includes understanding and exploitation of IT systems to enhance business performance.
- Risk management skills which relate to the identification of risk and mitigation thereof.

The main objective is to create a cooperative team with positive attitude towards work, towards the organization and above all towards the customers. This can lead to creation of right attitudes which calls for clear direction, belongingness and identity. While direction would come from the organization's vision, belongingness can be brought by appropriate HR policies that create confidence in the employees. A sense of identity can come once the performance levels improve and the good work done is recognized by the organization. Thus, HR has a crucial role to play in improving the work culture, the performance levels and ultimately in achieving the business goals of the organization.

In the changing environment that the banks are facing today where they have to outperform their competitors in an attempt to survive, there is constant pressure in the banks to adopt SHRM (Strategic Human Resource Management) so that the business goals could be achieved successfully by aligning HRM strategies with business strategies. The factors that are forcing banks to think in terms of aligning their HR strategies with business strategies include:

Changing business environment: Banks are getting affected by the changing tides on economic, social, political and technological fronts. HR personnel have to keep themselves updated about the global events and chalk out strategies to improve the skill level of the staff and formulate policies which would help them in retaining their trained staff.

Consumer demands and the need for flexibility: There have been many changes in the recent times in the way the banking business is being conducted. The technological revolution has forced banks to introduce 24-hour banking and accompanying service culture. Although banks are relying on technology to provide such services, they also need flexibility in staffing.

Impact of technology: Dramatic improvements in computing and communications technology have brought down the costs of information and transaction. These changes have also affected the competitive functioning of the financial sector at both the production as well as distribution levels and have led to output efficiencies. Technology has been a major driver of change in the financial sector. However, we can also view technology as a response to change in customer demand. Technology, on the other hand, demands higher skill levels from the staff.

Changing organisational structures: Many banks are reducing the layers in the hierarchical set-up and becoming flatter in an attempt to reduce costs. However, such structures do not easily lend themselves to conventional promotion opportunities for employees. This may lead to a loss of commitment at the individual organization level.

ROLE OF SHRM IN BANKS

It is clear from the above discussion that what is critical is achievement of the "strategic fit" between business strategy and HRM so that there is consistency between policy goals of HRM and that of the business. No doubt, such "alignment" of strategy is required with other parameters like structure and form, culture and leadership. But all these are mutually exclusive and reinforce one another. Aligning HRM and business goals would naturally involve some amount of strategic planning on the part of an organization which would require integration of both business plan and human resource plan that would enable the organization to plan for growth and draw plan to achieve the vision. A strategic plan would involve planning different options regarding what other products and services can be offered in the future and the ways in which banks can provide them and even to the extent of identifying takeover options. A strategic plan reflects the path which will enable an organization to reposition itself as a competitive and progressive organization in future. While making a strategic plan, one would have to assess the organization's current position and strengths and weaknesses, determine the organization's future desired position and evaluate the market opportunities. Thus strategic planning can position an organization to see beyond the present by focusing on what clients will want in the years ahead, what training staff will need to meet strategic objectives and what the financial conditions will demand of the organization.

While it is desirable that HRM strategies are as closely aligned as possible with business strategy, yet the former should not over–influence the latter. After all, the HRM strategy is aimed at making business strategy work and therefore, should subserve the overall business strategy. Specifically, the alignment process will span areas like resourcing, skill acquisition and development, culture, values, commitment, performance management, rewards and employee relations. In the ultimate analysis, HRM strategies should be imaginative, innovative while at the same time, flexible to adjust rapidly to change. It should be constantly reviewed keeping in view what is happening in the business and where the business is heading towards.

In fact under the present circumstances, a strategic plan would also have to provide for another separation scheme in case the bank still has excess staff or may be plan for a separation scheme which is cadre specific as some of the banks are feeling that they have more of clerical and subordinate staff in proportion to officers. Further, the bank also has to plan for aging of its employees and reducing the average age of its employees. The fresh recruitment drive has to take care of the likely vacuum that would be created when the existing staff starts reaching superannuation age. The HR has to take stock of extent of future computerization, the likely business forecasts and the expected environmental changes at global level for drafting a suitable HR policy that would be able to achieve the business goal of the organization.

An effective strategic plan is that which can turn the vision into reality. HR planning is a critical and integral part of such a planning exercise as it helps in identification of gaps in terms of capabilities as well as issues of utilization of talent. It is a challenge for HR personnel to "develop teams consisting of knowledge workers, who have a focused vision, believe in their mission, and empower each other with their initiative and skill development".

In the post-VRS scenario, banks had to adopt a host of HR strategies. The employees had to be relocated to fill the gaps arising out of voluntary separation of employees. The training systems had to provide greater focus on the emerging business environment including risk management. In addition, it was crucial to retain the trained staff and faster career options had to be made available to them. The banks which took care of these changes by suitably amending their policies and integrating their HRM practices with business goals have gained in the process.

Banks may seek strategic advantage through cost leadership, product or service differentiation, market segment focus or they may even follow a mix of these strategies. In fact many banks have been taking specific "focus" and "niche" strategies like being a one-stop financial service provider, acquiring new customers, cross-selling of new products, establishment of alternate delivery channels etc. It is important to note that each strategy may imply its own imperative for human resources. Thus, adoption of the most suitable HR strategy is crucial to the process of alignment of the same to business strategy.

CONCLUSION

Bank managements have, no doubt, become more sensitive to business performance and business strategy. However, to align the performance of staff with business strategy, they would need to give attention to quality of recruitment. Besides, rewards system based on performance would have to be introduced. The rewards system today is viewed as "the complete suite of monetary and non-monetary rewards and work environment offered to employees". This includes extrinsic rewards like pay, benefits, recognition awards and incentives and intrinsic rewards like training, skills, communication skills etc.

In the emerging financial landscape, quality of service will command a premium. Building competitiveness would be the only route to survival and growth and towards this end, the banks have to sooner or later adopt initiatives like SHRM. The speed with which such initiatives are implemented will be critical in deciding the competitive position of banks. Thus, banks will have to focus on increasingly aligning their HRM practices to corporate strategy. All the bank branches must be aware of the bank's vision. The bank's values regarding customer satisfaction and its goals regarding business development need to be shared with all the employees through communications from top management or through participative programmes. It is crucial to discuss the bank's policies with the staff as that enforces a sense of belonging in the organization, which results in improved productivity. Further, stress also needs to be given on improving the productivity and skills of the employees and sending them on trainings related to their job profile. All these initiatives will go a long way in achieving the business goals and are steps in aligning the HR practices to corporate strategy.

REFERENCES

1. Dr. Jacob Mankidy, 1988. Human Resource Management in Banks—Contemporary Issues, *NIBM*, Pune.
2. NR Sheth, 1992. "*Some thoughts in HRM*", *Emerging Issues in HRM*, Oxford & IBM Publishing Co.
3. Reeta Kaul, 2003. Beyond VRS: Towards Strategic Human Resource Management, *PNB Monthly Review*, Vol. 25, No. 6, New Delhi.
4. SS Kohli, 2002. Aligning Human Resources with Corporate Goals, *PNB Monthly Review*, Vol. 24, No. 3, New Delhi.
5. Stephen P. Robbins and Mary Coulter, 2000. "*Human Resource Management*" – Management, Prentice-Hall of India Pvt. Ltd., New Delhi.

13

HRD IN BANKING: FEW PSYCHOLOGICAL INPUTS

R.K. Srivastava*

It is emotional association, which binds up with the organization. The degree of emotional association can be improved by raising the emotional quotient level. Emotional fitness and emotional depth affect one's performance at the work place.

The concept of emotional intelligence is equally relevant in the area of customer relations. The emotional association with the customers can fetch a lot in banking business. The customer relations need to be tested on emotions yardstick.

The emotional intelligence mitigates the stress level at work. It helps making the work environment conducive in the bank. It provides better handling of grievances. It alleviates the complaints.

Our decisions are not only logic based but they are largely emotion based. We are mainly directed by our emotions. The emotional intelligence includes—self-awareness, managing emotions, motivating oneself, recognizing emotions in others, and handling relationship.

We are in the era of turbulent competition. Now, the total quality management is the norm rather than the exception. So, every organisation, including the Banks, strives for its total quality management. The total quality management encourages the management to create an environment in which the desired corporate culture evolves. It emphasises a continuous improvement. Ultimately,

---

*Faculty of Education, HNB Garhwal University Campus, Badshahi Thaul, Distt. Tehri Garhwal, Uttranchal.

it leads the organisation on the path of Corporate-Excellence. The word "Corporate" in general means "a united body" and the "Excellence" refers to surpassing quality or merit and an outsourcing performance in one's field of work. It includes vital force for growth, it sets standard of behaviour and galvanizes people in doing something remarkable. Generally, the corporate-excellence depends upon the work-culture of any organization, even of the Banks too. The continum of work-culture, normally constitutes of employees' job satisfaction, job-involvement, work-commitment, value-expectancies, value-striving, work-motivation, social-personal obligations and the work-values.

Every human being is assigned some type of work in every organisation. He is expected to involve with it deeply for its great success. His work may be a task, a duty, or an accomplishment. It may be mental, physical or both. Work has not only an economic and mechanical aspect but it also has a psychological aspect. Regardless of its meaning or nature "work" can not be considered separate from the individual who performs it. Besides, the physical input, the psychological inputs influence one's performance to a task. Like other organisation, the bank-management has to prepare its personnel to pay their attention on the following points covering in their psychological domain:

(a) **Work-Motivation:** Motivation to work is a human state where competence to work and will to work fuse together. In the absence of one, the other does not produce results. Work-motivation has been defined as an environment which affects the arousal, direction and maintenance of behaviour in pertinent work-settings. It is like other types of motivation (Vroom, 1964; Landy and Trumbo, 1976) giving special attention to behaviour (relevant to the work-environment). The continum of work-motivation consists of at least the seven areas of work, viz. personal growth, self-control, achievement, momentary gain, non-financial gain, social affiliation, and self actualization.

(b) **Work-Values:** The values pertaining to work are termed as one's work-values. They constitute various aspects of work, which guide and influence one's behaviour (Dhar, 1967). As such, one's work-values shape and direct one's behavioural activity in that organisation. One's work-values, may guide him to adopt a particular behaviour at a particular time while he is on a particular work. D.E. Super (1968) has identified the fifteen work-values: variety, creativity, management, achievement, surroundings, relation with superior, relation with colleagues, security, life-style, aesthetic, prestige, independence, intellectual stimulations, adventure and economic-returns.

(c) **Job-Involvement:** The notion of job-involvement is closely related to motivation. The psychological variable of job-involvement influences the employee's job-performance. It provides a link between productivity or role performance on one hand and the employees' needs and the quality of working life on the other. Bass (1965) mentioned different conditions that strengthen job-involvement of employees such as opportunity to make decisions, self-determination, recognition and freedom to set one's own work pace. Reddy and Rajasekhar (1991) defined the Job-involvment, "It refers to the degree to which a person is identified psychologically with his/her work and the importance of work in the total self-image."

(d) **Decision-making:** The process of decision-making is vitally important. Yet some form of decision-making is practised by everyone each day of life. Like breathing, it can be a routine act. Decision-making mainly involves problem-solving. It can be stated that in making decisions there involve two most important tasks, "Finding the right questions, and making the solutions effective.". There are seven functional stages through which all decisions are processed. These stages are:

(i) information (Problem identification and detailed information about the problem)

(ii) Recommendation (Formulation of alternatives)

(iii) Prescription (Sanctioned selection of alternatives)

(iv) Invocation (Provisional enforcement)

(v) Application (Specific Implementation)

(vi) Appraisal (Monitoring and review of decision process and its effects)

(vii) Termination (Renewal, revision or repeat)

In critical situations, the shared decision-making process is adopted. So that decision may become more rational and useful and be better tuned to the need of the people or/and the organisation. The effective decision-making depends on one's understanding of the decision-making process and the setting in which decision-making takes place.

(e) **Emotional-Intelligence:** Emotions are our axis on which we rotate throughout our life. If we have close analysis of our own self, we shall find that reason and logic play the least role in our life. We are dictated by our motions. According to Goleman (1995), E.Q. (emotional quotient) is a necessity for an effective use of IQ (Intelligence-Quotient). He writes: "In a sense we have two brains, two minds and two different kinds of intelligence, "rational" and "emotional", How we do in life is determined by both — it is not just IQ but emotional intelligence that matters." Solvey (1990) defines emotional intelligence as a type of social intelligence that involves the ability to monitor one's own and other's emotions, to discriminate among them, and to use the information to guide one's thinking and actions. The scope of emotional intelligence includes abilities in five main areas:

(i) **Self awareness:** Being "aware of both our mood and our thoughts about that mood."

(ii) **Managing Emotions:** Handling feelings so that they are appropriate, and keeping the distressing emotions in check.

(iii) **Motivating oneself:** Being able to focus on a goal

(iv) **Recognising emotions in others:** Empathising with others and building up people skill.

(v) **Handling relationships:** Being socially competent to be effective in interpersonal relationship.

Emotional-intelligence helps to avoid stress at work place also. Application of emotional-intelligence at the work-place enables to form a conducive work environment in three important ways. Firstly, it helps to see grievances a helpful critiques. Secondly, it helps in creating an atmosphere in which diversity is valued. Thirdly, it enables to create effective networks where differences are respected and people are motivated to work towards a common goal. It adds to group IQ, i.e. the ability of group members to harmonize and work together effectively. There are four corner stones of Emotional-Intelligence:

(i) **Emotional literacy:** Involves developing a clear and useful vocabulary for emotional-literacy and recognising, respecting and valuing the inherent wisdom of feelings.

(ii) **Emotional fitness:** Means authenticity, resilience, renewal and constructive discontent. It refers to those qualities that illuminate our personal values and character and feeling that enliven and drive them.

(iii) **Emotional depth:** Calls forth one's core character, unique potential and purpose of destiny. It is the manifestation of person's commitment, drive, initiatives, conscience and accountability.

(iv) **Emotional Alchemy:** It is a blending of forces that enable us to discover creative opportunities and transform lesser ideas into greater ones, it shows light to the range of hidden solutions and untapped opportunities.

It is the emotional association which binds us with our family, friends, relatives and our organisation wherein we work. The degree of the emotional association can be increased remarkably by applying our emotional intelligence which gives the more opportunities for our success in the work and in the job.

It is expected that by imparting the knowledge and understanding on the above mentioned points into the bank employees on their psychological continuum aspects, it will certainly empower them for seriousness to self and to work but it will also strive them to sharpen their abilities and capacities at work. They will feel refresh on their improving degree of performance beside increasing their loyalty and obedience in the framework of these job. As such, by paying attention on above mentioned issues, the banking endeavour can be accelerated remarkably.

REFERENCES

1. Bass, B.M. (1965): *Organizational Psychology*, Boston: Allyn and Bacon.
2. Dhar, C.K. (1967): A study of work-values of adolescent boys. *Guidance Review*, 3 (1).
3. Goleman, D. (1995): *Emotional Intelligence*, New York: Bantom Books.
4. Landy, F.J. and Trumbo, D.A. (1976): Psychology of Work Behaviour. *Homewood*, 1, 11 : Dorsey Press.

5. Reddy, K.S. and Rajasekhar, T. (1991): Job-satisfaction, Job-Involvement and Work-Involvement of Permanent and Temporary Employees. Madras: *Indian Journal of Applied Psychology*, 1991, Vol. 28 (1), pp. 5-10.
6. Salovery, P. and Mayer, J.D. (1990): Emotional-Intelligence. Imagination, Cognition and Personality, 9, 185-211.
7. Super, D.E. (1968): *Work-Value Inventory (Manual).* Houghton: Miffin Company, New York.
8. Vroom, H.V. (1964): *Work and Motivation*. New York: Wiley Eastern Ltd.

14

PLANNING FOR HUMAN RESOURCE DEVELOPMENT IN THE BANKING INDUSTRY

Mohd.Younus Ali Khan

HRD is a supportive system, which helps the line manager and personnel people becoming more effective. Before implementing the formal HR policies there is always a need of an informal policy on HRM. Before introducing the HRD as a system it is essential to create a conducive HRD climate in the bank. For an approach paper on HRD strategies, the services of external consultants are taken in many of the organizations. Thereafter, seminars are arranged at all the management levels–apex management, senior managers, line managers. The union and associations participation is also advisable in the seminars for HRD planning. Individuals from other banks can also be invited for sharing their experiences pertaining to the HR practices in the appropriate forums.

"Banking is an activity which thrives on the strength of people power". People are the direct factors of productivity of its services and people are its sole consumers.

The HRD is an emerging concept today, which no organisation with long-term objectives can afford to ignore or take lightly in case it wants to achieve the standards of excellence. The significance of HRD is felt in all types of organisations like manufacturing, trading, services etc. Proper development of human resources is all the more

*Postgraduate Teacher, Commerce Section, Aligarh Muslim University, Aligarh.

relevant in result-oriented organisations like banks which are not only service organisations but are also considered as wheels of social change for improvement of general standards of prosperity of the society along with public accountability.

Banking was a thriving industry in ancient India. Initially, the industrial houses pioneered banks with a view to generating funds for productive activities and at the same time offered considerable security, liquidity and fair returns to the depositors. In a way, banking continued to be a traditional industry till 1969 when major banks were taken over by the Government of India. With nationalisation, banks ceased to be funding agencies only for industrial sector and became a vivacious instrument of social change. More statistical data are available in support of the proposition that there is a phenomenal growth of banking industry since 1969 in terms of number of branches, advances, deposits and manpower.

The prime mover of the turbulence one is witnessing all around in Indian economic and social life, has been the Government of India's (GOI's) initiative in launching the structural changes in the economy. These, along with and incorporating the financial sector reforms have brought about a revolutionary change in the environment in which the Indian banker has been operating. The key changes so far as the banker is concerned are liberalisation of the economy, globalisation, technology explosion, consumer supremacy, profitability crunch and competitive pressures. These factors are interrelated – they influence and are influenced by one another. The Indian banker suddenly finds his semi-protected, monopolistic, rule bound, consumer-insular world integrating into a fiercely competitive, profit driven world, for facing which he is unprepared.

The Indian banker's strategic response to the challenge has to be wide ranging. He has to look at his organisation structure, the systems, and the processes and to bring about the much needed changes. But most of all, he has to equip and rally round his men to meet the challenges. A challenge is also an opportunity. The Indian banker has to snatch this opportunity and snatch it fast before the competition overtakes him. Since in a service industry like banking the raw material is men, HRD emerges as the single most potent element of the banker's strategic response to the challenge of change.

HUMAN RESOURCE DEVELOPMENT

A look at the banking industry revealed that there is ample scope for further improvements is each of the three aspects of HRM, viz., managerial beliefs, work technology and organisational climate. In the sphere of managerial beliefs a more 'positive' attitude towards the employees is called for. To the extent that employee behaviour is a response to the organisational systems and procedures, there is a need to examine the factors within the management system which contribute toward strained employer-employee relations. The management must examine, in addition, its own beliefs about the employees and how these beliefs influence the policies and procedures in the banks.

In the sphere of work technology, there is again greater scope for innovation to reduce boredom and alienation. Research findings made it abundantly clear that 'work technology' has a direct influence on employee attitudes and feelings. While, on the one hand, the design of bank jobs remains as old as the industry itself, on the other hand, the profile of new entrants to the banking industry has undergone a radical change. The repetitive and routine nature of the bank jobs easily bores today's employees being highly educated and ambitious.

Lastly, there is a plenty of room for a critical examination of the personnel policies and procedures, which is one of the dimensions of organisational climate. It seems that for a long time indeed the banking industry has been concentrating on providing 'monetary benefits' and various facilities and amenities to the employees. These aspects of climate have almost reached saturation point. If the industry has not been able to reap the fruits of these investments in the form of employee behaviour, it is because several other aspects of climate have remained neglected. Hence, the following dimensions of climate such as discipline and control, leadership style, delegation of authority, recognition and appreciation, grievance handling and participation in management require attention of the management as these are either neglected or only moderately well looked after.

ISSUES AND PLANNING FOR HRD IN BANKS

HRD must be relevant to an organisation and must be so designed as to introduce in a manner suitable for that organisation. Obviously HRD cannot be introduced uniformly in all the banks. However, there are some issues which are based on the experience can be raised in relation to introduction of HRD in banks and they are as follows:

ASSESSING THE CULTURE AND TRADITIONS OF THE BANK

Before introducing HRD in banks it is necessary to assess the culture and tradition of the bank. Each bank has its own history with the relative culture and tradition. Some banks emerged from family ownership, while the government set some others up right from the beginning. The banks developed their own identities and even after nationalisation these identities and uniqueness were continued which differentiate one from the other.

Some banks were concentrated in specific areas and sectors and developed strength and identities related to them. In some banks there was much more informal culture, much more openness to each other, traditions of sitting together to look at certain problems they faced. In other banks the culture was more bureaucratic coupled with the system of confidential assessment reports, etc. Obviously, one cannot introduce HRD uniformly in the bank with such diverse tradition and cultures. Being sensitive to the culture, one may give ideas about different methods of introducing HRD.

CREATION OF HRD CLIMATE

In the early stages before the introduction of HRD as a system, it becomes essential to create a conducive HRD climate. This instrument developed by social scientist can be used to ascertain how much of a favourable climate exists in a particular bank for implementing HRD. If the climate for introduction of HRD is low, methods can be adopted to create a suitable climate. An appropriate climate can be created by stressing the importance of development of people, creating effective teams, solving problems by bringing them out and working together to find solutions to problems. HRD climate can also be created by exposing most employees in the bank to the general approach of HRD and helping them to understand what is involved in HRD. Individuals from other banks can be invited to share their experiences in the appropriate forums.

It is more important to note that the development of human resource requires 'development climate' – an HRD climate in the bank which is characterised by the presence of values of 'openness', 'confrontation', 'trust', 'authenticity', 'proactivity', 'autonomy' and 'collaboration' (OCTAPAC). Apart from the OCTAPAC culture, a general supportive atmosphere is also needed. This includes commitment of top management and line management, an effective and fair personnel policy and positive attitude towards development.

DEVELOPMENT OF HRD STRATEGY

The first step in the introduction of HRD may be taken by inviting an external consultant to study the bank and prepare a strategy of introducing HRD functions therein. Once the external consultant has prepared an approach paper and strategy of introducing the HRD function, it will be useful to have a discussion on the implications at various levels in the bank. The first seminar should be conducted at the top level. In the light of the discussions, the approach paper on the HRD strategy may be revised for discussion at the level of senior managers. Again, using the feedback from that level, seminars may be conducted simultaneously at two or three levels in the bank, in which representatives of the unions and staff associations can also be invited. If necessary, separate seminars may be held for union or associations. Sometimes, there is a fear that unions and staff associations may put obstacles in the introduction of HRD in a bank. Experience has shown that not only is this fear unfounded but that the unions may make a significant contribution to some ideas of HRD, relevant for that bank and may become partners in the process of implementation of HRD. In fact, unions have a right to have their say in any area which affects human beings in the bank. Their suggestions and contributions in the discussions are valuable for HRD and would certainly facilitate its implementation.

INDUCTING HRD SPIRIT

In the earlier stages of HRD, much more emphasis needs to be given on the spirit rather than the ritualistic part of it. There are two specific methods in which the spirit of HRD can be inducted before HRD systems are implemented in a bank. Firstly, emphasis can be given to the development of individuals through the help of their supervisors. Secondly, solving problems by working together can be emphasised. The first can be accomplished by introducing performance counselling before the introduction of formal Performance Appraisal System. If a new PAS, however scientific and well planned it may be, is introduced before the managers could know how to conduct performance counselling. The system might degenerate into a ritual and may generate more resistance on behalf of the employees. Introduction of performance counselling as an informal way of helping employees by their supervisors is very useful to create a healthy HRD in a bank.

While performance counselling is introduced as legitimate responsibility and activity of the supervisors to work with their employees, OD activities may also be introduced as a way of solving problems. If OD spirit is to be inculcated at the beginning it may be useful to select branches or other parts of the bank which have positive attitudes and whose managers are enthusiastic in experimenting innovative ways of solving problems. Another message, which may be clear from such a step, is that standardised solutions of problems are not possible and problems can be diagnosed and solved only by persons who are facing the problems although they can learn from the experience of others.

REVAMPING THE TRAINING FUNCTION

Introduction of simple OD in the beginning may also require change in the conduct of training in the bank. Training is needed to move more towards OD and problem solving. This would mean that instead of standardised training system, more and more training should be focused on action to be taken for improving some parts of the functioning of a bank.

PHASED INTRODUCTION OF APPRAISAL SYSTEMS

After the spirit of HRD is internalised in the bank for performance counselling and OD, formal systems of HRD may be introduced. For example, performance and potential appraisal may be introduced at this stage. It may be useful to prepare a phased plan of introduction of such HRD systems. This phasing may be done in two ways. One way of phasing is to introduce the system in one part of the bank (geographical phasing) and to spread the system to other parts of the bank after it has been seen as useful by the part in which it was introduced first. The second way of phasing is in the sophistication and depth of the HRD system.

PREPARATION OF A DETAILED PLAN

It may be useful to prepare a clear phasing of HRD along with the dates and parts of which it would be introduced. Some systematic plan like PERT chart for introduction of HRD may be useful. The sequence of HRD implementation may be shown in the chart, with dates and alternative actions if certain parts of the sequences do not work out successfully.

STRENGTHENING LINE MANAGEMENT AND PERSONNEL FUNCTION

When HRD is introduced in a bank, emphasis may be given on strengthening the roles of the line managers and the functioning of the personnel and industrial relations function in the bank. HRD is supportive system, which helps the line manager and personnel people to become more effective. It may be necessary for HRD people to work in close collaboration with personnel and IR people. In fact, both personnel and IR functions need to have the spirit of HRD of involving employees in personnel and IR problems to jointly find solutions for them.

CREATION OF FORMAL HRD FUNCTIONS

At this stage, the bank will be ready to have distinct HRD function, which may be placed independently or in some other group like personnel, depending on the performance of a bank. In the long-term, HRD must be a distinct function. But the way it is introduced in a bank can differ. However, it is necessary that HRD responsibility is assigned at a very high level, like a deputy general manager being in charge of such functions. One cannot prescribe any standard structure for HRD. It will differ from bank to bank. There is enough experience available as to how HRD function can be structured and designed. However, after the function has been formally introduced and structured, the HRD people along with junior line managers need to prepare long-term and short-term steps for strengthening the HRD activities in the bank. Line people should review such plans and a plan for the entire bank may be prepared for discussion at the highest level for its implementation.

In the end, there is no single way of introducing the HRD function in the banks. While each bank has to find its own steps to introduce the HRD, some general directions may be observed. It is necessary to introduce and inculcate the spirit of HRD (developing people and solving problems by joint efforts of those who face such problems). Training function should be reoriented towards designing training for improving action of a specific group. Performance counselling skills may be given to the line managers so that they can help their employees to take steps to improve their performance and working. Simple OD work to deal with the problems identified by people themselves may be introduced in the initial period. After such practices are accepted and used, formal HRD systems may be introduced in one part of the bank and later, after its success, to other parts of the bank. Sophistication in the HRD systems may be introduced in phases. Finally, the HRD formal function may be introduced and detailed short-term and long-term plans may be implemented.

REFERENCES

1. Government of India, 1977, Report of Working Group on Customer Service in Banks.
2. Joshi, K.R., September 1996, Personnel Administration, *IBA Bulletin*, HRD – An Emerging Approach to Banking.
3. Khan, F.H., December 1993, Human Resource Development in Bank. *State Bank of India Monthly Review,*
4. Kulkarni, L.G., January 1994, Human Resources Development, *IBA Bulletin.*
5. Madhu Neglur, December 1994, HRD – A Journey, Not a Destination, *Canara Bank Monthly Review.*
6. Prasanna Bhat, V., December 1990 – Changing Organisation Needs – *The Journal of the Indian Institue of Bankers.*
7. Shanker, K., The Banker July 1992, Training in Banks: Need for Innovation.

15

PANORAMA OF CRM IN COMMERCIAL BANKS

Subodh Kumar*

Nurturing the customer relations is the future of any business, particularly in service industry. The private and foreign banks have created a lot of competition pressure in the market. A single imperative answer to the rising competition is attracting new customers and retaining the customer base in the business. In banking the customer relationship is life long and it goes on generation by generation. Bank started saying clients instead of customers as 'customer' refers to short-term dealing and 'client' to long-term relations.

Now, the market is buyer's market. The buyer has many options to switch over his loyalty. Today's customer is demanding one. The bank customer is in search of solutions to his life events. The customer care is essence of whole marketing process. The present time is of relationship banking instead of mass banking. The whole workforce in the bank needs to be customer friendly. The CRM training is required to all the levels in the bank staff.

The concept of Customer Relationship Management is getting utmost attention in the banking industry. The main reason behind its growing concern is competition pressure in the business. The liberalization has brought greater competition among banks, both domestic and foreign, as well as from mutual funds, NBFCs, post offices. There is multi-facets competition in the banking, like price competition, product

*Senior Lecturer, Dept. of Commerce, HNB Garhwal University SRT Campus Badshahi Thaul, Distt. Tehri Garhwal, Uttaranchal .

range competition, segment competition, technology competition, cost competition, place competition, first entry competition, profit based competition and competition in marketing. In the light of negotiations under WTO the further liberalization of service sector is anticipated and likewise the banking sector will be affected. It will advance the competition in the market. One imperative answer to the rising competition is attracting and retaining the customer base in the industry. The solution lies in maintaining good customer relations. One way to prepare for globalisation is better understanding and practicing the CRM by the banks.

The CRM is a process where three components are involved— customer, service provider, products range. The concept has always been in the existence in business but it keeps revising as per moderations in the marketing practices. It is an integrated business strategy that keeps the customer in the center of whole business activity. There is a big shift from product centric to customer centric in all over organisation planning. The CRM is establishing good relationship with the customers and maintaining it in order to acquire customer loyalty.

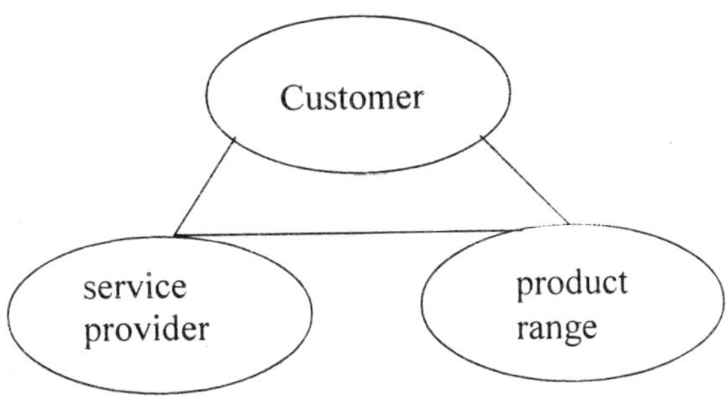

The financial sector reforms resulted restructuring of banking industry. The new private banks and foreign banks started working in our market. The entry of new private banks and foreign banks caused many big changes in the environment of banking business. Before the reforms era, it was the social banking period. The technology revolution transformed the whole banking in a very short period. The technology affected the banks in many ways. The computerization resulted in surplus manpower in banks. The major shifts in banking in post-reforms period are listed hereunder.

Table 1: Major shifts in Banking during Post-Reforms Era

From	*To*
Dominance of public sector banks	Entry of new private and Foreign banks
Absence of competition	Multiple competition-price, product, cost, quality, marketing competition
Few products	New product range–credit card, debit card, insurance, ATM card, bills payment
Mass banking	Relationship banking
Product centric approach	Customer centric approach
Corporate banking	Retail banking
Absence of International standards	Occurrence of ISO certificate, service efficiency rating
Regulated interest rate	Deregulated interest rate

AMENDING CUSTOMER PERCEPTION

The customer perception is a dynamic phenomenon. In the fifties the customer perception was 'serving the customer'. In the next decade, it was 'satisfying the customer'. Further, it became 'pleasing the customer' during eighties. It shifted to 'delighting the customer' in nineties. In the new millennium, it is set to 'retaining the customer'. Now, the word 'customer' is replaced by the word 'client'. Bankers started saying client in lieu of customers. It gives an impression of long term relationship while the customer refers to short-term connection or one time transaction. In banking the customer association is life-long but it can go on generation by generation.

The studies on CRM indicate that new private banks are successful in having better knowledge of the customers need. They conduct regular customer surveys. Our Public sector banks leg behind in this regard. There is always a poor attendance in their customers meet. The banker has to know the customer well. He has to know the customer's fore coming life events. Then he can offer relevant solutions to them.

Table 2: Emerged Marketing Patterns in Banking

From	*To*
Sellers Market	Buyers Market
Customer	Client
Transaction	Relationship building
Monologue	Dialogue
Short term dealing	Life time interaction
Easy customer	Demanding customer
Focus on gaining new customers	Retaining the existing customer

TRACKING CUSTOMER SATISFACTION

The present market is buyers' market. The buyer has many options to switch over his loyalty. Further, today's customer is demanding one. He is time conscious. He no longer can wait standing in long queues. He is not going to accept indifferent behaviour. In addition to all service he aspire for humanly respectful treatment from his banker. The customer is not only to seek financial services rather he is in search of solution to the events happened in his life time to time. Thus, there is a need of relationship between banker and the customer so that the customer can be served better and could be retained for a longer span of time. The banks are also going to be developed as financial service provider wherefrom his all financial needs are fulfilled.

There is a shift in marketing that the focus is on retaining the customer than gaining new ones. In many ways the retention of customer fetch more than that from new customers. It costs less than attracting new people. It is reported that the nationalized banks along with old private banks take better care of their old customers than other bankers. The retained customers bring in many other new customers. The studies report that the satisfied customer stays longer and he purchases more. The satisfied customers talks and remarks in favour of the products purchased. Thus he is a good advertisement for the seller.

It is said that the PSBs did not succeed in maintaining good customer relations. New private banks and foreign banks stand better in this regard. There are certain hindrances in the way. Firstly some negative attitude of the higher authority is the problem. Secondly, the non-cooperative junior staff is the obstacle in the other case. Thirdly, lack of promotion chances for the staff works as negative charge in the way. Fourthly, there is a communication crisis between manager and staff. Fifthly is the gap between customer expectation and banker perception. Further, the bank employee is a human and customer is also a human so many psychological traits come in the way. However, few measures are suggested for tracking the customer satisfaction better.

Tracking Customer Satisfaction

- Customer data base
- CRM software
- Customer friendly premises
- Training in CRM
- Relationship managers
- Incentives to staff

- To know the customer well, it is imperative that the customer profile is prepared. The new private banks and the foreign banks invariably maintain customer profile. For product development, surveys are conducted at macro level but for CRM purposes the surveys are needed at micro level. The occupational structure of the target customers is to be analysed. Banks have started schemes for pensioners. In addition to professional details like family information, history, purchase and payment pattern and account with other banks are the details which should be in our customer profile.
- The IT companies prepare CRM software programme for their clients. The programme covers all the possible situations related to the particular product. The software makes the CRM function very easy and effective. It is worth mention that the software costs a lot. A software of one product can be integrated with the other product software.
- The bank premises are required to be maintained in a manner that they are customer friendly. New private banks are much conscious in this regard. It is observed that our nationalised banks do not have the customer friendly environment in their branches. Some foreign banks put works of famous artists in their branches. Some banks provide a cup of coffee to their customers. In a big branch a coffee shop can be started within the bank premises. In some branches light music is available in banking hours. Few green plants can make a difference in a bank branch.

- The training is a major tool for human resource development.All the banks have some training arrangements for their employees but they are quite inadequate. It is important that for CRM the training should be given to the staff at all the levels. The CRM techniques are required to be impressed upon every one working in the bank. The complete bank work force need to be customer friendly.
- The present time is of relationship banking instead of mass banking. Unless the banker is rightly concerned with the customer, he cannot know the customer demands and expectations. The main problem in good relations is gap between customer expectation and banker perception. The gap needs to be reconciled.
- One of the important problems in our banks is that promotion chances for bank staff are remained very few. In absence of promotion opportunities, the employees get frustrated. It becomes rather difficult to seek their full cooperation. Since the banks have entered in insurance business, promotion venues should be developed for the work force in banks. Some consideration in the form of marks for promotion can be kept for maintaining better customer relations.

CUSTOMER RELATIONS ASSESSMENT

The customer relations in a service industry become more important as compared to the commodity market. The relationship is very long term in banks and regularity and continuity is seen there. A chain of transactions is there. The relations are based on trust and faith. Further, the customer aspires for security. The banks have started insurance business. In insurance dealings the relations are for much more longer span of time. The utmost faith is not an obligation in insurance but observance of utmost faith is a pre-requisite for a valid insurance contract. A check list is given hereunder for supervising the customer relations in banks.

Customer Relations Check List

- know the customer expectation
- Fulfill the promise
- Co-operative and courteous behaviour
- 'Win Win' approach

- Apology for errors
- Feed back exchange
- Care of cutomer

- The customer profile is found very useful in knowing the customers expectation. The customer satisfaction survey is the other tool that is helpful in good relations. In bank like business it is imperative to keep a watch over satisfaction level of customer.
- A caution should be taken in giving an assurance. Once promised, it should be fulfilled. Even in small things, a word given should be kept. This is considered good for human relations. Whenever complying the word is not possible, reason thereof needs to be explained before the affected man. The party is to be convinced the genuine circumstances that led not to fulfill the word.
- A cooperative and helping attitude is expected from the banker. Not merely helping attitude but the customer comes to seek solution to his puzzles. The human side of the relations can never be ignored as he aspires for respectful appropriate treatment all the time.
- In human relations, the psychologists suggest to take recourse at 'Win Win' approach. Satisfy the consumer and be satisfied. Both the parties should be happy in the dealings. One's happiness is incomplete without other's happiness. Make the customer happy and be happy. Ideal situation is that both are happy.
- To err is human. Bankers are also human. There is no way which can claim that the errors can be checked at cent per cent level. In case of a mistake on the bank's part, apology is must to be expressed. The admission of guilt itself gives enough mental satisfaction to the customer. It mitigates the complaints in good number.
- It is necessary that feedback is obtained and given periodically. The feedback is an evaluation way for the between relations. It suggests curative measures for the improvement in the track. The feedback helps in understanding each other.
- The customer care is the essence of the whole marketing

process. The emerging marketing pattern is to put the customer at ease. The individual customer care helps the bank in diagnosing the customer needs. If a customer feels that he is looked after, it is enough to say that there is a good relation.

REFERENCES

1. Chairman speech Jul. 24, 2003, *SBI Monthly Review.* Sept. 2003. 434-447.
2. Dhillon, J S. *et al.* Paradigm Change: Relationship Marketing and Service Quality of Banking Services. *IBA Bull.* Jun 2003. 26-32.
3. Ramchandra, S.T. Customer Relationship Management: Emerging Strategies. *IBA Bull.* Sept. 2002. 46-51.
4. Shaw, Sujay Kumar. Grahak Sambandh Prabandahn. *IBA Bull.* Sept. 2003. 54-56.

16

CUSTOMER—AN UNPAID SALES PERSON (A Study of Public Sector Banks)

P.K. Garg*

Customer Satisfaction is the base for business expansion because of the stiff competition prevalent in the banking industry. With the advent of new private banks in 1995 "the concept of customer service" has become an important and pivotal issue in banks. Either it is in the public sector, private sector, cooperative sector and NBFC. The survival of banking business is dependent on customer services.

"By entering into your premises, customer is giving an opportunity to serve him. You are not doing favour by serving him."

Mahatma Gandhi

Liberalisation and globalisation of Indian economy has taken place almost a decade ago. The focus point in any service organisation is customer service more so in the banking industry. The phrases such as "Customer is the king in our business". "Service to customer is service to God" are no more a myth but turned out to be a reality.

CHANGING PERCEPTION OF CUSTOMER

The customer perception is changing day by day. Peter Drucker said twenty-five years ago. "The purpose of a business is to attract and retain a customer." It sounds simple but too many businesses have forgotten it to their cost. There is a phenomenal change and paradigm shift towards customer focus for the past five decades.

---

*Reader in Commerce, Govt. Raza P.G. College, Rampur (U.P.), India.

Serving the customer	1950 to 1960
↓	
Satisfying the cutomer	1960 to 1980
↓	
Pleasing the customer	1980 to 1990
↓	
Delighting the customer	1990 to 2000
↓	
Retaining the customer	2000 and beyond

NEED FOR CUSTOMER FOCUS

The customer choice and awareness have been increasing tremendously during this decade due to more open economy, the advent of information technology and Media revolution, besides hectic competition for resources by banks and non-banks. Banks are attempting by creating exclusive delivery channels for specific customer segments. As markets become increasingly competitive, customers can now immediately go elsewhere if they don't get what they want. Continuous improvement, gaining the competitive edge, increased market share, higher profits—none of these things is possible unless businesses can find new ways of maintaining the loyalty of existing customers. Customer focus is the ability to provide predictable positive experiences that consistently meet or exceed to customer's expectations. Customer focus should be managed by moments of truth.

A 'moment of truth' refers to 'any incident when a customer comes into contact with any aspect of the service offered and on the basis of the contact, forms an opinion about the quality of the service and the quality of product offered.'

CUSTOMER GRIEVANCES

Receiving customer complaints, listening to the grievances patiently and solving the problems is one of the important areas of customer service. For this a separate mechanism is provided by banks, such as "customer grievance cells" in individual banks and ombudsman at each state. Customers are free to contact the grievance cells in banks to make complaints, about the service problems etc. Banks will immediately attend such grievances and settle the issues. The ombudsman at state level is appointed by the Government and this official will receive the grievances from the customers of all banks and provide solutions to the issues. It is the duty of ombudsman to solve the issues within a time frame. If required, an enquiry is made by the ombudsman into each case and advise the banks for further proceedings. This is one of the important aspects of customer service. Today customers are more discerning and have very low tolerance regarding poor service. Customers have a greater propensity to switch over to another service provider. That's why, they should be satisfied to the maximum possible extent, to retain by the bankers.

Solving customer problems therefore is an important aspect in retaining customer loyalty. Once good service is extended a loyal customer will work as an Ambassador to the bank and facilitate growth of business.

CUSTOMER COMPLAINTS

Like in any other business organisation, in banks too there are machineries for dealing customer complaints effectively. Successful organisations are those that have realised that prompt attention to customer complaints is an essential ingredient of a profitable customer relationship. A Cliche often used in describing this is–"A Satisfied Customer is the Best Ambassador". What is equally worthnoting, however, is that just as a satisfied customer tells others about it, an unhappy customer too tells others about his experience and indeed more so.

In Service organizations like banks, handling of complaints should be a high priority item. Following are some of the strategies for effective redressal of customer complaints:

- Complainants to be received and attended to by the senior level.

- Sincere efforts to be made to understand the nature of the complaint; the person handing the complaint should always be attentive.
- Any irritated customer, in particular, to be tactfully handled.
- The complainant should not be given the impression that the bank officer is too anxious to get rid of him.
- Complainant should not be made to run from pillar to post; he should be guided to the right person/department. No customer likes to repeat his grievances to several persons in the organization.
- Adequate information should be made available to the customers apart from factual details.
- The customers should not be driven to approach the authority outside the bank, customer organisation etc. Such instances will surely cause considerable damage to the bank's image.
- Phony or biased calls also to be handled with tact, sincerity and patience.

A customer will feel special if the banker will actually reward, recognise and encourage his loyalty and in the long run either personal or business, given the right elements and environment he would prefer to be consistent.

When put together each one of the above elements will accelerate customer satisfaction beyond even their wildest dreams. The customers will become increasingly more loyal and profitable if the banker begins to implement ideas based around the above elements and make them a constant focus of attention.

BUSINESS PROCESS RE-ENGINEERING (BPR)

Public sector banks are still operating in the old fashion and therefore, unable to spare time for customer service, which is badly affecting the image and also the business.

There is an imperative need for adopting a change in public sector banks and restructure the working of branches by implementing the re-engineering process. Otherwise, the competition of private sector banks cannot be faced by public sector banks. Besides this, mind set of the personnel working in the banks, needs drastic change. Continuous training of the staff and counselling through programs will help to change the attitudes of the people, and make them more customer oriented. In this context, bank managements should have an immediate thought to provide prompt and better customer service to reach their maximum level of business.

BPR concept is unique, since it bifurcates the front office operations and back office operations. This is more or less like a manufacturing centre, i.e. Factory and showroom, i.e. front office. BPR implementation will help and branch office personnel to pay more attention to the customer needs. ATM cards/debit cards and issuance of statement of accounts, opening of accounts, issuance of cheque books and related correspondence are looked after by the back office at processing centres. This processs will help the front office staff to spare more valuable time to serve the customers and fulfil their needs. BPR implementation will enable banks in improving relationships and ultimately for business expansion.

IMPORTANCE OF CUSTOMER SATISFACTION

The importance of customer service for capturing business in banks has become as focus point in all stages of marketing of banking services, since almost all banks offering more of less the same products with little changes in nomenclature. In the present day situations, customers becoming more and more demanding, bankers have had to evolve new approaches, new and innovative products to keep pace with growing expectations. With the opening up of the economy customer satisfaction has acquired new meaning and different dimensions" as banks are discovering more and more innovative products to meet increasing competition among themselves.

Truly the customer is the king in the present day banking, since the banks are providing tailor made service to the changing needs of customer to face the competition from the rival banks. Customers are not ready to accept any delay in service today and are in need of information for instant decisions. Therefore, customer satisfaction is more important in servicing.

It has become a challenging and tough job for bankers to retain the existing customer and winning the new customers. Otherwise sustaining in the banking business is a tough phenomena. Bankers are in the peoples business and it is the goal of the bankers to make the customers happy to achieve their targets. To achieve this challenging task of customer satisfaction bankers are turning towards technology for help.

TECHNOLOGY

Though technology is helpful in upgrading the services to meet the competition, it will become fallout if not operated effectively and efficiently.

Technology-driven products such as, debit cards, credit cards, telebanking, mobile phone banking, internet banking, fax, e-mail, help desk services etc. have given more access to customers to communicate their needs instantly and transact their business promptly. For technological upgradations banks have to recruit specialists in each field, efficient people at all levels to provide these services. Bankers have to gear up to keep up the customers expectations. Bankers have to learn the use of technological advancement to gain the maximum advantage in the business.

Customer Service Model

Customers who contact any bank, want two things:

1. They need a solution to a problem relating to investment/credit.
2. They want to feel in some way "special".

   Looking at number one, when the bank is providing appropriate solution for the problem, say–

   (a) Keeping the amount in savings/term deposits suiting to the needs of the customer.

   (b) Offering a loan for purchase a house, car or motorcycle.

   (c) Issuing a demand draft.

The following can be considered as some important elements in making a customer feel "special"—

Speed and time measures are very important factors to many customers. The speed with which the banks offer their services will actually gain a competitive advantage and allow them to offer higher satisfaction. On account of technological revolution at present products are offered to take care of the element of "speed and time" like.

1. Anywhere banking
2. Debit cards
3. ATM
4. Internet and mobile banking etc.

Very often the only time that customers contact the bank is when they have a problem with some services that they have availed/they want to avail—say,

1. Delay in getting a term deposit receipt
2. Delay in getting a loan
3. Delay in getting a demand draft.

RELATIONSHIP BANKING MANAGEMENT

A new approach to the marketing of bank services that is receiving growing attention in banks is "relationship banking". The emphasis here is on viewing the customer as a long-term business relationship rather than confining attention to the particular transaction. Banks made strategic plans to meet the total banking requirements of the customers and expect respective business from them. Banks take on the role of all weather friends and establish a firm relationship wherein the customers confine all their banking transactions to them. For building up profitable customer relationships, it is inevitable on the part of the bankers, first of all to know more about the customer and his banking needs and to this end, banks need to prepare customer profiles. Building a long-term profitable relationships with customers calls for systematic efforts. In order to ensure customer satisfaction bank staff should guide the customers in making the right choice from among the available range of services and facilities.

Relationship Manager's role in providing a better service to the customers is pivotal for the expansion of banking business. These RM's maintain rapport, particularly with high new worth (H.N.W.) customers and provide them with all the services they need. This will help in not only retaining the existing customer base but also to capture the new clientele. Relationships are more important to provide good customer services. Alternatively good service will help the bankers to build up relationships. Unless the service is provided to the fullest satisfaction of the customers, taking further references from the existing customers to establish new relationships is difficult. Again this requires the service to the existing customers and their patronage to bank.

In order to provide the best service to the existing HNW customers through the relationship managers, properly trained, qualified persons, with good communication skills need to be appointed by the banks. This is a Herculean task of HRD in banks. Relationship building particularly in the new private sector banks, is a tough task where there is a stiff business competition prevailing.

Public sector banks are also becoming stiff competitors to the private sector banks, since they are also upgrading technology and providing modern bated services. The misnomer among the public about the safety and security of their money with private sector banks is standing as a competition to private banks. In this context, relationship banking will not only help to build confidence in the people but, also to maintain relationship with customers. The ultimate objective is to provide best service to the customers by banks.

CUSTOMER CARE AND NEW TECHNOLOGIES

The banking sector occupies a pivotal position in the global economy. The sector has been subject to many external and internal forces in many countries, particularly in developed and developing countries, since the 1980s. Of the external forces, technological change is likely to have the most far-reaching impact on the sector. Information and Communication Technology (ICT), in particular the Internet, is a key drive of internal changes. Within the sector external forces have attracted new entrants and increased customer influence. Internal change has been greatly amplified by the internet. The Internet is causing major delivery change. The synergies of these forces will bring about a major transformation of the banking sector.

In respect of customer relations, technology can be divided into a number of types:

- Technology that makes the operation safer for both the banks and for the customer.
- Technology that provides the customer with something completely new.
- Technology that provides the customer with a comfortable and convenient service.
- Technology that provides the customer the service in a minimum possible time.
- Technology that provides the supplier with more information about the customer.

The system is a little slower than having cash readily available but the trade-off is in the safety provided for the customers and the staff. The use of Credit and ATM-cum Debit Cards etc., can have a safety aspect.

The synergy between the computer and ICT (information and communication technology) has led to the increased use of the Internet and promises for the customer convenience. It also offers a massive challenge to maintain and strengthen the relationship with the customer.

ON-LINE BANKING (INTERNET): A NEW PHASE IN BANKING SERVICES

To exploit the full convenience of Internet banking, customers must be able to make applications for core banking services and open new accounts (savings accounts, loans, etc). Relatively few banks offer the facility of making application and enabling new services. It is important that both existing and potential customers be encouraged to make applications and acquire new services. If the entire process cannot be completed over the Internet due to regulatory barriers (e.g., money laundering regulations) at least the customer should be allowed to feed in personal details so that the process is expedited. The absence of these features is a lost opportunity to recur new customers and increases the danger of loosing existing ones, since a customer is only a few key strokes away from mòving to a competitor with more on-line functions.

Increasingly customers are looking for opportunities for transacting a number of diverse products and services under one roof. Banks are increasingly offering non-core banking products and services. Therefore it is logical that these products and services are made available through the Internet. Such facilities include insurance, credit cards, mortgages, etc.

A delighted customer will come back to the bank and will convey his friends about his experience and will become an ambassador for the bank's business—an unpaid sales person.

A satisfied customer is one whose expectations are equal to the experiences.

PROMOTION/COMMUNICATION STRATEGY

Some of the banks spend larger sums on advertising. If they have the right products at the right customer, it is pointless if anybody knows about it. Promotion, including advertising, lets customers not only to know products and services but also helps them to retain in the memory. Individual working for banks has two roles to play:

(a) They need to know the promotions that their banks has underway so that they anticipate customers request and queries.

(b) The way they deal with customers can be an advertisement itself.

Most of the customers share their experience and feelings with friends and colleagues and focus on the good and bad of the products and services. These personalised sharing and recommending are very important in decision-making.

SUGGESTION FOR IMPROVEMENT AND CONCLUSION

Banks should realise that the customer is the "focus point" to improve the business. Banks have to evolve plans and strategies to cater better service and enhance satisfaction levels and try to create a brand image.

Excelling and managing customer relationships is the future of any business, or everybody's business. Customer focusing is not to be viewed as just a business strategy but should become a corporate mission. Unless this mission percolates throughout the organisation at all levels, the chances are that the attempts to address customer issues will receive only lip sympathy. Building value for customers should be seen as equal to building shareholder value. The challenge for banks will be in the area of people (changing their beliefs and attitudes), technology and competition.

Customer satisfaction through service should be the main motto for improvement of business.

Technology implementation should be speeded up, such as computerisation, electronic banking through e-mail, tele-banking, mobile phone banking and wide net of ATMs through channel migration process.

All these factors will help to increase customer service. Ultimately banks should prove that they are providing essential services as already branded for development of the economy.

The challenge that lies ahead for banks is fourfold. First, they need to satisfy customer needs that are complex and difficult to manage. Second, they need to face up to increased competition from within the sector and from new entrants coming into the financial services market. Third, they need to address the demands based on the supply chain. Finally, they must continually invent new products and services in the light of envisaged changes discussed in this paper.

REFERENCES

1. Anthony Ovenden, Keep Your Customers Happy and Your Competition will Slowly Fade Away, *AQM Magazine*, Vol. 13, No. 5, 2001.
2. Bhaskar, P.V. Anantha, *Customer Service in Banks Cell.*
3. Dhar, S.K., Marketing of Services, *Yogakshema*, Vol. 40, No. 7, 1996.
4. James Barncs. "Establishing Meaningful Customer Relationship;" Why Some Companies and Brands Mean.
5. Kotler, Philip, *Marketing Management*, PHI, New Delhi, 2002.
6. Richard, M.S.W. and Elin Gilligan. *Strategic Marketing Management*, Viva Books, New Delhi, 1999.
7. Shankar, A. Gauri, "*Customer Service in Banks*", monthly Journal by *I.B.A.* Vol. 26, 2004.
8. Steve Farner, Fred Luthans and Steven M. Sommer. An Empirical Assessment of Internal Customer Service, Managing Service Quality, Vol. 11(5) 2001.

17

MARKET ORIENTED STRATEGIES AT BANK BRANCHES

Rajendra P. Bharti*

Bank marketing deals with providing services to satisfy customers' financial needs and wants. Banks have to discover/ ascertain/ anticipate the financial needs of the customer and offer the services, which can satisfy those needs. Branch level marketing strategy is the only option for dealing each and every customer personally. Author feels that branch managers are required to appreciate their roles as leaders of Strategic Business Unit. They have to be sensitive to all changes in socio-economic environment. It should be well appreciated that all such happenings, symptoms or changes, which have an economic implication today or tomorrow, are a potential source of business for a bank.

After the initiation of financial sector reforms in 1991, banking in general and commercial banking in particular, has undergone a metamorphosis. As a matter of fact the business of banking is being redefined. From mere acceptors of deposits and dispensers of credit, banks have now acquired the role of vibrant facilitator of economic growth. The competitive pressures, which were the consequence of globalization process, helped the Indian banks unleash their potential and emerge as strong players in the financial sector. During the past decade we have been witnessing the experiments in organizational restructuring, process re-engineering, innovative product-development, intensive market penetration, collaborations and

*Director, Lal Bahadur Shastri, Institute of Management and Technology, Bareilly.

acquisitions etc., all aimed at having the competitive edge. Technological developments have offered new possibilities of reach, diversity and integration, which have in turn provided strength to move on to perform as global players. Emergence and growth of new private sector banks, which were technology driven from day one, awakened some of the sleeping tigers. A good number of commercial banks have gained phenomenal strength and are in consolidation process; even few are envisioning to emerge as universal banks. But, the moment we compare the Indian banks with the stronger ones in the world, we realize that there is nothing to be complacent about. Actually now our competition is with the global players in this sector and our banks have to brace-up themselves with sharper strategic management skills which can sustain them in the intense multi-dimensional competition and realize their dream of emerging as universal banks.

While the transformation in banking scenario may largely be attributed to the dictates of the globalization communicated through Basel recommendations, and guidelines of international financial institutions' the major factors responsible for internal strengthening of commercial banks have been (1) markets as drivers of change (2) customers in focus and (3) people as creators, leaders and managers of change. While during eighties, most bankers even at top level, had no appreciation for the decisive role of marketing, the shake-out by the compulsions of government administered reforms woke up the banks and made them realize the emergent need to become market driven. The most difficult task was to communicate the urgency about fast promoting a marketing culture because the policy-makers themselves were used to perform in a so perceived sellers' market and having no concern for recognition of real income. In the realm of the environmental changes the entire approach of managing commercial banks has undergone a dramatic change. Top managements of all banks today are marketing-oriented. Customer has gained his due importance. The objective has shifted from providing satisfaction to creating delight and then to making the customer proud of his bank. Marketing activities including market research, market segmentation, new product development, product differentiation and strategic pricing etc., are gaining new momentum day by day. These processes have brought retail banking in the lime-light. To ensure that bank marketing accelerates the process of acquiring competitive edge in terms of larger market share and stronger bottom-line, it has become imperative that marketing culture percolates down to branch level and all branch level activities and functions are strategic responses to today's and tomorrow's needs of existing and future customers. Being sensitive to these emerging needs most progressive banks are trying to acquire winning positions in markets through Market Oriented Strategic Planning (MOSP).

At corporate or Central Office level, a bank's Mission statement is guided by its Vision and is drawn in term of the following basic questions recommended by Peter Drucker:

What is our business?

Who is (and can potentially be) our customer?

What is (and would be) of value to the customer?

What will our business be?

What should our business be?

Banks like all other business organizations have to raise these questions and try to answer them. Mission statement has an important role in providing a shared purpose, direction and opportunity to all employees across the bank: Vision and Mission are the pillars on which the entire edifice of strategic planning is built to facilitate outstanding business performance. The success of strategic corporate planning in banks largely depends on how the branches and other service centers are implementing the market-oriented strategies. With a view to ensuring that market-oriented strategies are being adopted at branch level, some major imperatives are discussed here.

BRANCH AS STRATEGIC BUSINESS UNIT (SBU)

In case of commercial banks, the entire organization needs to appreciate that branch is a SBU. Though during past several years, the treasury earnings which are resultants of treasury operations normally not conducted by branches, have grown faster than earnings from lending at branch, this trend is not going to sustain for long and efficient asset-liability management and strategic marketing of bank's products hold fundamental value to sustained growth.

Decades ago the process of Bank Marketing was described by Deryk V. Weyer as:

(i) Identifying the most profitable markets now and in future.

(ii) Assessing present and future needs of customers.

(iii) Setting business development goals and making plans to meet them.

(iv) Managing the various services and promoting them to achieve the plans.

(v) Adapting to changing environment in the market place.

It can be clearly seen that a bank branch has to play significant role at (ii), (iii), (iv) and (v) steps. It is at the branch level that all available resources are to be utilized optimally so as to satisfy the customer's needs and in the process maximize profits. Appreciating the importance of branch banking, successful banks strengthen their branches as SBUs and monitor and support their functioning for superior performance, which is essential for achieving corporate goals. An SBU in banking sector has following three characteristics:

1. It is a center managing a collection of related businesses of financial products and services, which can be planned for local potential independently.
2. It has its own unique local competitors.
3. It has a branch manager, who is responsible for branch level strategic planning and profit performance through strategic use of physical and human resources and funds.

Branch managers are required to appreciate their roles as leaders of SBUs.

ENVIRONMENTAL SCANNING AND POTENTIAL EXPLORATION

Environmental scanning is the process of trying to see the emerging symptoms in the socio-economic environment and analyzing their impact on future course of activities and developments. For example, the news of formation of a Vikas Parishad in U.P. which includes industrialists like Mr. Mukesh Ambani, Mr. Kumarmangalam Birla and Mr. Subroto Roy indicates efforts for inviting huge investment in the state and further Mr. Ambani's committing to install a power plant in NOIDA, is a clear message of high potential economic activity and linked future prospects in NOIDA. A keen understanding of dreams, plans and preferences of younger generation also helps in predicting the future environment. In the fast changing environment of business, branch officers have to be sensitive to all changes in socio-economic environment. It should be well appreciated that all such happenings, symptoms or changes, which have an economic implication today or tomorrow, are a potential source of business for a bank.

Potential exploration is the process of gathering knowledge of visible and invisible potential of business. Marketeers not only identify but also try to create a number of new needs of existing and innovative new products. Branch officers should actively participate in social and business gatherings. In fact they should interact with local chambers of commerce and industry, medical associations, various unions, trade organizations, village chiefs and all such sources, which can communicate about the future needs of people and organizations.

Environmental scanning and potential exploration will enable the branch banker to have an idea about present and future business prospects.

DATA WAREHOUSING

In the process of environmental scanning and potential exploration, a large amount of data is generated. It contains the demographic and socio-economic details of current and prospective customers. It also tells about emerging investment and spending patterns and preferences. To make an objective use of this data for creating real business opportunities, Data Warehousing has been developed as a computer-based technique of providing efficient, precise and relevant data for tapping the business potential at branch level.

Branch-level data warehousing will provide immense help in Customer-profiling, business forecasting, strategic planning and positioning. This has a strong potential to revolutionise business prospects in retail banking because continuous updating of data will enable the branch banker identify and select the prospective clientele, which needs to be approached through various marketing tools. The objective of establishing a frame of initiatives for strengthening and leveraging relationship banking will also be accomplished relatively smoothly with the aid of Data Warehousing at branch level.

ASSESSING AND UNDERSTANDING THE POTENTIAL OF BRANCH

Operational area is the geographic expanse where preponderance of bank's business today and prospects of marketing its products in future can be reasonably seen and forecasted. Unique features of products and quality of services keep on adding new dimensions to the operational area. Environmental scanning and potential exploration is the first set of research activities, which becomes the broader base for having a deeper understanding of the potential of the operational area. This has been discussed under preceding sub-heading. After having conducted this research on potential sources, the branch banker has to address following questions:

(i) What various factors form the criterion for selecting a bank by customers from different economic backgrounds?

(ii) What are the major attraction points that hold the image of the bank in distinct esteem?

(iii) What is the intensity of competition in terms of competitors' reach, competing products and other marketing efforts?

(iv) How much business potential in terms of selling liability products, lending and other financial services including De-mat, Investment advisory etc. can be foreseen?

The biggest source to help address above questions is the profile of existing and prospective customers. There are some other sources also which provide an insight into the potential of the operational area such as —

(i) Directories of professional associations viz; IMA, BAR Association, Contractors Associations, CA's local chapters, Chambers of Commerce and Industry, Trade associations, etc.

(ii) Telephone Directory and Yellow-pages.

(iii) Registration Bodies, Govt. Departments, Distt. Industry Centres, Lead Banks, Municipal and Panchayat records, list of societies etc.

The above list is only illustrative. It can never be exhaustive because innovative bankers continue adding new dimensions to such resources.

SEGMENTATION OF MARKET POTENTIAL

The operational area is composed of current and future customers having different type of felt and unfelt needs. These can be classified into various segments in terms of similarity of desires and needs. This type of segmentation, if done objectively would help the branch banker in targetting right type of segment in given environmental situations and in positioning the various products having different features. The major factors which help recognize different segments for banking business are: (i) current stage in the growth of a business organization (ii) stages in individual's life cycle viz. student, employed bachelor, young married, with school going growing children, approaching superannuation etc. (iii) social and cultural factors and value systems and (iv) individual's decision-making process. Since the business potential for a branch banker exists with (i) customers and (ii) in the given business environment, these two are the broader bases for segmentation . The customer dimensions needs segmentation on the bases of attitudes, preferences, interests etc. of individual customers and their demographic details. The environment includes patterns of availing banking services, number and variety of products, knowledge and market penetration etc. Segmentation of potential would lead to strategic positioning which aims at sustaining the present position and winning over the competitors in the operational area. To achieve this aim, the branch marketeer has to first create the best match between the specific needs of a segment and the product features and then devise strategic ways of reach, communication, convincing, delivery and services so as to outperform the competitors.

PLANNING AND IMPLEMENTING MARKETING STRATEGIES

Many branch bankers particularly in public sector banks think that drawing a plan for marketing is something to be done at corporate and zonal level alone. They feel that they have to do only directed activities and strive to achieve the given targets. The author hopes that by formulating market-oriented strategies as recommended through this article and implementing them with continued sensitivity to environmental changes, would lead them to surpass the given targets and take an exemplary lead. This will facilitate the attainment of organizational objectives at corporate level. It is recommended that guided by the Vision and corporate business guidelines and based on the SWOT analysis of the branch, a marketing plan should be drawn to tap the maximum potential on the strength of potential exploration and market segmentation through strategic positioning of the products and services.

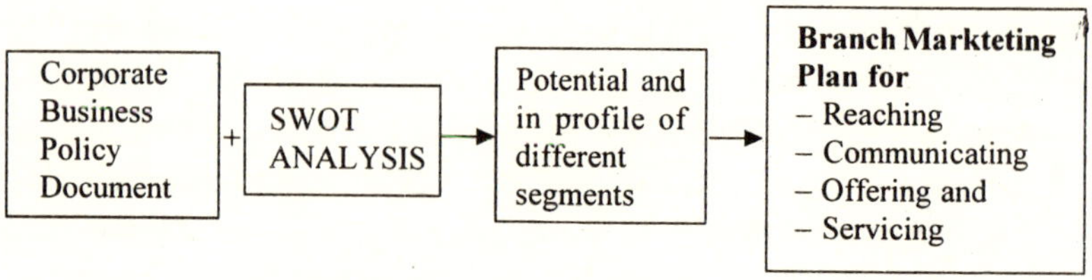

The branch marketing plan is an action plan which enables the process of identification, approach, persuasion and ultimately the sales and services. Such a plan will include different methods like telephonic contact, letters, addressing meetings, organizing and sponsoring meets and melas, local liaisoning,collaboration and various ways of presentation and recognition etc. Branch marketing plan is divided into quarters, months and weeks in terms of actions and the branch officers implement this plan with full zeal. Periodical reviews help in modifications and corrections in responses to changing business situations.

18

BUSINESS PERFORMANCE OF CENTRAL COOPERATIVE LAND DEVELOPMENT BANK OF J & K STATE

Nasrullah Bhat*
Rais Ahmad**

The role of land development banks in the context of agricultural transformation as a channel of institutional finance sanctioned by the National Bank for Agricultural and Rural Development (NABARD) is well recognized. Keeping in view this role the Reserve Bank of India set up a committee on cooperative land development banks to identify the problems of the banks and suggestions thereto. In case of Jammu & Kashmir state the committee observes that there was limited scope for providing long-term credit for farm mechanization and horticultural development. However, the bank successfully worked in financing for land leveling, reclamation of land, and water management like activities.

INTRODUCTION

In this paper an attempt has been made to examine the working performance of Cooperative Land Development Bank of J & K State. In Jammu and Kashmir, the Central Cooperative Land Development Bank was established in 1962 as a cooperative society for providing long-term credit to the farmers, and thereby accelerating the pace of

*Research Scholar.

**Reader, Department of Agricultural Economics and Business Management Aligarh Muslim University, Aligarh.

agricultural development and has completed 40 years in the service of rural population. The main objective of the Bank is to advance long-term loans to individual farmers and cooperative farming societies through its branches, for permanent improvement on land and for introducing better and improved methods of cultivation. The Bank advances loans to the farmers on the security of immovable property for one or more of the following purposes.[1]

PURPOSE-WISE LOANS

(i) Redemption of prior debts;
(ii) Purchase of land for cultivation;
(iii) Construction of wells, installation of tubewells and repair of old wells.
(iv) Installation of pumps and other water lifting appliances;
(v) Construction of bunds;
(vi) Fencing of agriculture land;
(vii) Raising of Fruit gardens;
(viii) Reclamation of " banjar lands ";
(ix) Purchase of tractors, allied implements, power tiller and power thrasher;
(x) Construction of godowns and cattle sheds;
(xi) Purchase of bullock cart;
(xii) Development of orchards;
(xiii) Purchase of cows, goats, sheep etc;
(xiv) Installation of gobar gas plants, fisheries, poultry, saffron, mules, dairy, bee-keeping, oil expellers, rice shellers, piggery and sericulture
(xv) Other purposes, relating to the development of agriculture and methods of cultivation as may be approved by the Board of Directors of the Bank and prescribed by NABARD from time to time.

The Jammu and Kashmir Cooperative Land Development Bank also proposed amendments to Cooperative societies Act for inclusion of 12 schemes under non-farming activities such as[2]:

- Establishment of processing units.
- Transportation of agriculture and horticulture produce.

- Development of fisheries.
- Production of animal and poultry feed.
- Setting up of small and cottage industries.
- Financing to rural artisans, craftsman etc. for establishing handicrafts units.
- Construction and repair of rural houses etc.

MAIN FUNCTIONS

Broadly the main functions of Central Land Development Banks are as follows:

(a) To float debentures on the security of mortgage bonds transferred by primary land development banks to it, and on such terms and conditions laid down in the Act and rules.

(b) To grant loans to primary land development banks or to the individual through its branches.

(c) To establish branches, offices or sub-offices or to organize new primary land development banks to facilitate its branches.

(d) To supervise and inspect the primary land development banks and verify utilization of loans.

(e) To encourage thrift and Cooperation amongst the ultimate members.

CONDITIONS FOR A SOUND LOANING POLICY

An essential aspect of cooperative finance is a sound loaning policy. A sound loaning policy of a Cooperative institution must ensure the following —

(i) Simplicity in Procedure: It must be simple in nature so that even illiterate cultivators may understand it. A lengthy and cumbersome procedure must be avoided in a sound loan policy.

(ii) Adequacy of Loan: Only adequate loans can ensure fuller utilization of credit and increase in production. If the credit supplied is inadequate it will not only fail to meet the need of the production, but also encourage misusing the credit for purposes other than production.

(iii) Timely Disbursement of Loans: It is said in Jurisprudence that, "Justice delayed is Justice denied". It is also applicable with equal force in relation to agricultural credit where 'Credit delayed is credit denied.' In other words, untimely loans not only defeat the purpose for which they are sanctioned but instances are not rare where the money so received was spent extravagantly.

(iv) **Production Oriented Loans:** The basis of Cooperative loans has been the status of the borrowing cultivator, which depends primarily on the value of land owned by him. This enabled the well-to-do farmers to garb the lion's share of the advances made by Cooperative institutions. Cultivators who owned little or no land were unable to obtain any loan at all or could get very meager amount. Hence, if the Cooperatives want to free the cultivators from the clutches of moneylenders, they must change their loan policy to production-oriented instead of security based.

(v) **Reasonable Cost of Credit:** The cost of credit should be reasonable while very low rates of interest may encourage unnecessary borrowing and very high rates fail to benefit cultivators.

(vi) **Credit Combined with technical Guidance:** The disbursement of credit must be combined with technical guidance related to various agricultural operations and scientific usages of various inputs. Such credit is called "Supervised agricultural credit".

(vii) **Form of Credit:** It has been generally seen that the loans given in the form of cash are very easily diverted to other purposes. Hence, as far as possible, they should be given in kind.

(viii) **Scientific Repayment Procedures:** The sound loan policy must ensure scientific repayment procedures. In other words, the amount given must be brought back. Proper recovery of loans is advantageous for institution as well as for borrower.

BUSINESS OPERATIONS

Jammu and Kashmir State Cooperative Land Development Bank has advanced loans through its 38 branches spread over the entire state during the last 40 years of its business operations. The purpose-wise classification of the loan advanced by the Bank is shown in Table 1.

Table 1 reveals that the disbursement of loans for making long-term improvements in agriculture, development of orchards, sheep breeding, purchase of land by the cultivators etc. are in list of productive activities of the Land Development Bank of Jammu and Kashmir state. The amount disbursed under various heads shows, generally, an upward curve though for certain years it was less due to exceptional circumstances. For instance, in 2001-02 and 2002-03, only a few application for loan were received from the members for buying pump sets, the amount disbursed was only Rs 1.46 and Rs 1.09 lakh respectively which is less than the amount advanced during 1990–91 to 2000–01. However, the amount of loan sanctioned in the purchase of tractors, farm mechanization, power tillers, and threshers has increased significantly except for 1990–91', because of abnormal conditions in the Kashmir valley. During this period, the amount sanctioned for all the purposes was poor. During 1991–92 and 2000–01, an amount of Rs 16. 27 lakhs and Rs 15. 921 lakhs was advanced for oil expeller, which comes to 3.39 percent and 3.6 percent respectively. For sheds/farmhouses, an amount of Rs 3.70 lakhs was advanced in 1991–92, but thereafter the amount disbursed decreased year after year and from 1997–98 onwards, no amount was disbursed for this purpose. Same is the case with amount sanctioned for levelling and bunding, it has decreased year after year and no application was received from 1996–97 to 2002–03. For saffron cultivation, Rs 1.18 lakhs was advanced in the year 1991–92. For poultry, the highest amount advanced was in the year 1991–92 to the tune of Rs 28.15 lakhs, which comes to 5.86 percent. In case of dairy, the amount disbursed increased year after year with certain fluctuations and the highest amount disbursed was in the year 1999–2000 to the tune of Rs. 40.91, which comes to 4.75 percent. In case of sericulture, the loan sanctioned for the only year (1994-95) amounted to Rs. 0.03 lakhs.

The authorized share capital of the Bank was Rs. 500 lakhs against which the individual share capital was Rs. 432.77 lakhs and State Government's Share capital was Rs. 137.40 lakhs. The total membership of the bank was 63580 thousand at the end of 2003.[3]

Lending/Achievements of Cooperative Central Land Development Bank

So far as achievement of the Cooperative Central Land Development Bank in Jammu and Kashmir is concerned, the below mentioned table

Table 1: Purpose-wise Classification of Loan Advanced by Cooperative Central Land Development Bank in Jammu & Kashmir From 1990-91 to 2002-03.

(Rs. in lakhs)

Purpose	*1990-91*	*1991-92*	*1992-93*	*1993-94*	*1994-95*	*1995-96*
Pump sets	2.97 (1.13)	7.89 (1.64)	15.25 (3.64)	6.53 (1.53)	23.56 (5.41)	12.05 (4.14)
Farm Mech. Power tiller and thresher	199.51 (76.48)	351.81 (73.33)	299.75 (71.54)	355.94 (83.52)	349.53 (80.35)	218.14 (75.08)
Oil expeller	4.04 (1.28)	16.27 (93.39)	9.10 (2.17)	7.00 (1.64)	12.64 (2.90)	6.69 (2.30)
Sheds / farm-house	1.40 (0.53)	3.70 (0.77)	3.53 (0.84)	0.79 (0.18)	0.60 (0.13)	0.18 (0.06)
Fencing	0.34 (0.13)	1.92 (0.40)	1.00 (0.23)	0.13 (0.03)	0.10 (0.02)	– –
Levelling and Bunding	0.66 (0.25)	0.58 (0.12)	0.32 (0.07)	0.32 (0.07)	0.29 (0.06)	0.73 (0.25)
Orchards	1.66 (0.63)	1.10 (0.22)	0.50 (0.11)	0.07 (0.01)	0.07 (0.01)	0.21 (0.07)
Saffron	–	1.18 (0.24)	0.10 (0.02)	0.11 (0.02)	– –	– –
Horse-carts	–	0.09 (0.01)	– –	– –	– –	0.12 (0.04)
Mules	–	–	0.41 (0.09)	2.03 (0.47)	1.61 (0.37)	6.00 (2.06)
Dairy	19.22 (7.36)	36.59 (7.62)	32.60 (7.78)	24.86 (5.83)	22.60 (5.19)	18.32 (6.30)
Poultry	22.00 (18.43)	28.15 (5.86)	24.52 (5.85)	8.27 (1.94)	10.00 (2.29)	3.41 (1.17)
Sheep	5.57 (2.13)	26.43 (5.50)	30.82 (7.35)	15.72 (3.68)	13.60 (3.12)	13.87 (4.77)
Purchase of tenancy right	– –	1.00 (0.20)	– –	– –	– –	– –
Rice sheller	2.84 (1.08)	3.05 (0.63)	1.00 (0.23)	4.21 (0.98)	– –	– –
Piggery /bulbs	0.64 (0.24)	– –	– –	0.16 (0.03)	– -	0.58 (0.19)
Bee-Keeping	–	–	0.05 (0.01)	– –	0.12 (0.02)	– –
Sericulture	– –	– –	– –	– –	0.03 (0.006)	– –
Fisheries	–	–	–	–	0.21 (0.04)	0.43 (0.14)
Purchase of truck	–	–	–	–	–	–
Total	260.85 (100.00)	479.76 (100.00)	418.95 (100.00)	426.14 (100.00)	434.96 (100.00)	290.51 (100.00)

	1996-97	*1997-98*	*1998-99*	*1999-20*	*2000-01*	*2001-02*	*2002-03*
1	10.73	3.93	5.23	10.31	6.352	1.46	1.09
	(3.26)	(1.07)	(0.01)	(1.19)	(1.22)	(0.001)	(0.01)
2	258.65	312.35	565.93	594.03	379.34	332.90	267.76
	(78.72)	(85.81)	(80.84)	(69.03)	(72.91)	(76.81)	(75.63)
3	9.21	5.22	13.13	3.54	15.921	7.80	7.98
	(2.80)	(1.43)	(1.87)	(0.01)	(3.06)	(1.79)	(2.25)
4	0.38	–	–	–	–	–	–
	(0.11)	–	–	–	–	–	–
5	–	–	–	–	–	–	–
6	–	0.10	–	–	–	–	–
		(0.02)					
7	0.12	0.05					13.58
	(0.03)	(0.01)					(3.83)
8	–	–	0.45	–	–	–	–
			(0.02)				
9	–	–	–	–	–	–	–
10	1.57	0.87	5.28	6.48	7.622	5.00	2.65
	(0.47)	(0.23)	(0.01)	(0.01)	(1.46)	(1.15)	(.01)
11	16.40	10.84	20.78	40.91	17.858	18.01	18.41
	(5.6)	(2.97)	(2.96)	(4.75)	(3.43)	(4.15)	(5.20)
12	5.51		0.27	0.25		0.49	
	(1.67)	–	(0.02)	(0.02)	–	(0.01)	–
13	14.73	9.24	11.89	29.06	15.01	6.27	11.41
	(4.48)	(2.53)	(1.69)	(3.37)	(2.88)	(1.44)	(3.22)
14	–	–	–	–	–	–	–
15	–	–	–	–	–	–	–
16	–	–	–	0.18	0.175	–	–
	–	–	–	(0.02)	(0.02)	–	–
17	0.29	0.05	0.25				
	(8.08)	(0.01)	(0.02)	–	–	–	–
18	–	–	–	–	–	–	–
19	0.37	0.57	–	–	1.75	0.12	–
	(0.11)	(0.15)	–	–	(0.01)	(0.02)	–
20	8.57	20.78	76.79	175.74	76.25	61.34	31.13
	(2.60)	(5.70)	(10.97)	(20.42)	(14.65)	(14.15)	(8.79)
Total	328.53	364.00	700.0	860.50	520.28	433.39	354.01
	(100.00)	(100.00)	(100.00)	(100.00)	(100.00)	(100.00)	(100.00

Note: Figures in parentheses show percentages.

Source: Compiled from the office records of Central Cooperative Land Development Bank Ltd. Srinagar.

shows that the Bank is busy in advancing credit facilities for various purposes. Out of the total loan disbursed, the major portion is utilized for purchase of tractors and farm mechanization. The bank has provided credit facilities to about 63000 families in the state for the following purposes:

Table 2: Purpose-wise Advancement of Loan of Jammu and Kashmir Cooperative Central Land Development Bank Ltd., Upto - 2003.

(*Rs. in lakhs*)

S.No	*Purpose*	*Amount Disbursed*
A.	**Loans Advanced under Normal Schemes**	
1.	Wells	26.25
2.	Minor irrigation (Pump sets)	90.43
3.	Tractors / Power/ Tillers	323.50
4.	Farm Houses (Sheds)	169.75
5.	Fencing of Orchards	87.98
6.	Orchards	87.17
7.	Sheep Development	196.33
8.	Mules	46.81
9.	Saffron Cultivation	71.96
10.	Bunding and levelling	73.33
11.	Purchase of tenancy rights	8.80
12.	Other loans (Piggery, sericulture, Bee-keeping)	56.06
	Total	1238.37
B.	**Loans Advanced under Normal Schemes**	
1.	Horticulture Dev. Scheme	125.00
2.	Farm mechanization, power tillers and threshers	5576.75
3.	Dairy development	485.65
4.	Poultry development	290.94
5.	Horse carts	7.87
6.	Purchase of Bulls	8.05
7.	Fisheries/Bee-Keeping	3.57
8.	Floriculture	2.10
9.	Oil Expeller	212.06
10.	Purchase of trucks and Mini-load Carriers	505.87
	Total	7218.86
	Grand Total (A + B)	8457.23

Source: Compiled from the office records of Cooperative Central Land Development Bank Ltd., Srinagar.

Quantum of Loan: The loaning policy of the Bank is essentially "Security Oriented". In other words, a farmer of big holding is in a position to obtain a larger amount of credit because of the large size of holding than farmer of small holding.

A farmer may obtain a loan from the Bank up to 50% of the value of the mortgaged land. However, the limit is 75% in case of small farmer; while in terms of project cost, the Bank generally provides 85% to 95% of the project cost as loan and the rest of the project cost is to be borne by the farmers themselves.[4]

The method of calculation of credit worthiness of the borrower, followed by Jammu and Kashmir Central Land Development Bank is explained below:

(i) Credit worthiness is determined on the basis of incremental income (incremental income = Net income of benefited land after proposed project minus net income before proposed project) of the farmer, or

(ii) 50% of the market value of the land to be mortgaged, or

(iii) 50% of land valuation (Land valuation is done on the basis of average sale statistics of the land in the area for the last 5 years).

The lowest credit worthiness on the basis of (i), (ii) and (iii) formulae shall be treated as credit worthiness of the farmer for purposes of loan. But in practice, the last formula (iii) is used by bank for determination of credit worthiness of the borrower.

At present, the maximum amount of advances based on unit cost prescribed by NABARD has been shown in Table 3. The Table 3 shows that the maximum loan available for the purchase of tractor is Rs.75,000.

Rate of Interest : The lending rate is determined by the Board of Directors in consultation with the trustee taking into consideration, the rate of interest at which the bank can raise money by floating debentures. The current rates of interest at which the Bank grants loans are:

(i) Up to Rs 25,000 —12% p.a

(ii) From Rs 25,000 up to Rs 2 lakh —14% p.a

(iii) Above 2 lakhs for reclamation of Land, dry farming — 14% p.a

(iv) Above Rs 2 lakhs for Non-farming Schemes (NFS) — 15% p.a.

Table 3: Statement of Maximum Credit Limit

S.No	*Purpose*	*Maximum Loan Limit (Rs.)*
1.	Diesel engines (according to H.P.)	4,000.00 to 8,500.00
2.	Pump sets / Electric Motor including accessories according to H.P.	4,400.00 to Rs. 10,000.00
3.	Tubewells (Diesel / Electric)	5,150.00 to 7.000.00
4.	Thresher (upto 5 H.P.)	1,400.00
5.	Cow (one)	2,500.00 to 4,000.00
6.	Goats (4 females and one male)	2,050.00
7. (a)	Sheep (20 Eves and one Ram in Hill regions)	5,650.00 to 6,200.00
(b)	Sheep (20 Eves and one Ram in plain Region)	3,600.00 to 4,460.00
8.	Dunlop-carts	3,200.00 to 4, 300.00
9.	Horse cart	5,000.00
10.	Gobar Gas plants	4,250.00 to 2,250.00
11.	Orchards	4,200.00 to 6,200.00
12.	Tractors	75,000

Note: H.P. = Horse Power.

Source: By the courtesy of Assistant Director, Central Cooperative Land Development Bank Ltd., Srinagar.

RECOVERIES AND OVERDUES OF COOPERATIVE CENTRAL LAND DEVELOPMENT BANK

An important test for evaluating the efficiency of any system of credit is the recovery of loans on due dates. The term 'Overdues' refers to the amount due for payment but not yet paid by the borrowers. We may now examine the recovery progress of the bank. The data pertaining to demand, recovery and overdues has been presented in Table 4.

Table 4 reveals that demand for finances has been rising consistently over the period from Rs 537.61 lakhs in 1990–91 to Rs 2223.74 lakhs in 2002–03. The amount of Overdues towards borrowers has been increasing year after year and has mounted to Rs 1266.76 lakhs, which comes to about 56.96 per cent of overdues to demand in 2002–03. The percentage of overdues to the demand has been the highest in the year 1996–97 that was about 68.95 per cent. The percentage of recovery to the demand has increased from about 40.25 per cent in 1990–91 to 43.03 per cent in 2002–03. It may be mentioned that the present political turmoil in the valley has badly affected the recovery performance of the bank.

Table 4: Progress of yearwise Recovery Position of the Cooperative Central Land Development Bank in Jammu & Kashmir State (1990-91 to 2002-03)

(Rs. in Lakhs)

Year	*Demand*	*Recovery*	*Overdues*	*% age of recovery to Demand*	*% age of overdue to Demand*
1990-91	537.61	216.43	321.18	40.25	59.74
1991-92	681.35	351.74	329.61	51.62	48.37
1992-93	858.08	391.00	467.08	45.56	54.43
1993-94	898.81	453.90	444.91	50.50	49.49
1994-95	1127.22	491.03	636.19	43.56	56.43
1995-96	1210.94	467.03	743.91	38.56	61.43
1996-97	1380.84	428.65	952.19	31.04	68.95
1997-98	1633.60	544.26	1089.34	33.31	66.68
1998-99	1779.84	655.53	1124.31	36.83	63.16
1999-00	1867.53	823.35	1044.18	44.08	55.91
2000-01	1969.32	755.29	1214.03	38.35	61.64
2001-02	2234.51	824.73	1409.78	36.90	63.09
2002-03	2223.74	956.98	1266.76	43.03	56.96

Source: Compiled from official records of Cooperative Central Land Development Bank Ltd., Srinagar.

In order to improve it's functioning, the bank has earmarked some new channels of business such as farm mechanization dairy farming/ sheep development and fisheries.

The commitment of refinance is 90 percent from National Bank for Agricultural and Rural Development (NABARD), 5 percent from Central Government and 5 percent from State Government.

The role of Land Development Bank in the context of agricultural transformation as a channel to provide agricultural credit sanctioned by National Bank for Agricultural and Rural Development (NABARD) and other agencies is well recognized. Keeping in view this role and anticipated participation, the RBI has set up a committee on Cooperative Land Development Banks to identify the specific problems of areas where there was need for improvement and the measures required to be taken for the purpose. The Land Development Bank's Committee made the following observation and recommendations with respect to the state of Jammu and Kashmir.[6]

(i) Loan Policy was more security-oriented than production orientated. No norms have been fixed for giving loans for various purposes. Maturity periods were fixed arbitrarily. No rational norms were adopted for valuation of hypothecate.

(ii) Defective loaning policies resulted in the mounting up of overdues. The other main reason for increase in overdues was inadequacy of supervisory machinery for verification of the use of loans of the ultimate borrowers.

(iii) The bank has a weak capital base, heavy overdues, poor management of funds and inadequate staff for appraisal of loan proposal and supervision.

The committee observed that there was a limited scope for providing long term credit for farm mechanization and horticultural development but the Jammu and Kashmir Cooperative Central Land Development Bank could play a useful role in advancing loans for land levelling, reclamation of land, water management, channels, etc. provided the state undertakes systematic and scientific approach for the formulation of suitable projects.

The committee was of the view that the weak financial position and lack of operational efficiency of the bank have resulted in a yawning gap between its performance and what was expected of it. Accordingly, it was that integrating the short-term and long-term credit structure will play an effective role in meeting the credit needs of cultivators for agricultural production and development.

REFERENCES

1. By-laws of the Jammu and Kashmir Central Co-operative Land Development Bank Ltd., Srinagar, 2 (5); p. 17.
2. By the Courtesy of Managing Director, Jammu and Kashmir Central Cooperative Land Development Bank Ltd., Srinagar.
3. By the Courtesy of Branch Manager, Jammu and Kashmir Central Cooperative Land Development Bank Ltd., Srinagar.
4. "Cooperative Agricultural and Rural Development Banks" Executive Summary, National Cooperative Agriculture and Rural Development Banks Federation Ltd., Mumbai; 1996.

5. By the Courtesy of Land valuation officer, Jammu and Kashmir Cooperative Land Development Bank Ltd., Srinagar.
6. Report of the Committee on Cooperative Central Land Development Bank in Jammu and Kashmir State.

19

INDIAN RURAL BANKING IN THE NEXT DECADE

R.C. Pandey*
P.C. Kavidayal**

The post-nationalization era witnessed phenomenal growth in banking in terms of quantitative, qualitative and spatial expansion reaching banking in almost every nook and corner of the country with a special bias for the rural and backward regions. There are many suppliers of financial services in rural areas such as, regional rural banks, commercial banks with branch network in rural areas, cooperative financial institutions and other providers of financial products and services. Each of these institutions can play its role better in rural development provided certain changes are made in their policies and operations. Author, is sharing his views on various areas of rural banking in India with special attention towards the problems and solutions thereof.

Indian banking system has played a crucial role in the socio-economic development of the country. This system is expected to continue to be sensitive to the growth and development needs to all the segments of the society. The outset of the financial sector reforms, which is in its second phase, has exposed Indian Banking to more competitive environment. Every organization is now vying with others in respect of innovative product lines, speed of decision-making, technology and providing customer delight. For this banks are even gearing themselves to ensure that the situation of "who moved my cheese?"

*Research Scholar

*Reader, Faculty of Commerce, Kumaon University, S.S.J. Campus, Almora.

does not happen. The banking system is expected to reorient its approach to rural banking. "Going Rural" could be the new market mantra. Rural market comprises 74 percent of the population, 41 percent of middle class and 58 percent of disposable income. Consumer growth is taking place at a fast pace in 17113 villages with a population of more than 5000. Banks approach to the rural lending will be guided mainly by commercial considerations in future.

Commercial banks, cooperative banks and Regional Rural Banks are the three major segments of rural financial sector in India. Rural financial system, in future has a challenging task of facing the drastic changes taking place in the banking sector, especially in the wake of economic liberalization. There is an urgent need for rural financial system to enlarge their role functions and range of services offered so as to emerge as "one stop destination" for all types of credit requirements of people in rural centers.

Indian rural banking has also witnessed radical changes viz. rationalization of branch networks, evolution of micro finance and farmer-friendly products like kisan credit cards, to mention a few. Information technology and communication technology are driving the growth of the banking sector, which will result in total transformation of our banking system.

In this paper an attempt has been made to reflect on the past and to visualize a future rural banking scenario, taking into account the present state of affairs in the industry. Let us see what is in store for Indian rural banking in the next decade.

RURAL BANKING SCENARIO

India has been fast developing, but the benefits of the development are yet to reach many. Quite large proportion of our country's population lives below the poverty line.

Table 1: Status of poverty in India

	1983	*1991*	*1997*	*Projection 2006-07*
% of population below poverty line	44%	35%	37%	–
No. of poor (million)	323	291	249	220

National sample survey data.

Various development programmes have come into existence since last five decades to cater the needs of several target groups in rural areas. In the post-nationalization era, the banks increased their networks in the rural areas.

Problems of Rural Branches: Most of the rural branches face the following problems:

1. Bank's lending formalities have been time consuming, which increased the transaction cost of the rural borrower viz. cost of repeated visits to the branch, cost for obtaining quotations for purchases out of the loan, cost for getting land ownership certificates from the authorities and so on.
2. Bankers, who have negative attitude, viewed the rural lending as a not profitable but a risky venture.
3. Some banks' systems and procedures are rigid and with less flexibility to cater the needs of the rural poor.
4. Many bankers insist on collaterals as additional security even from poor, whereas poor is assetless and the govt. has exempted abstention of collaterals up to a specified limit.
5. Timing of credit delivery is not assured and often delayed and defeating the very purpose of the loan.
6. Interference by middlemen in siphoning off the portion of loan amount from the rural poor, as they are not aware of the procedures.
7. Unrealistic target orientation in implementing government sponsored poverty alleviation programs.
8. Rural credit programmes are launched with the announcement from the top, without much focus on the felt needs of the poor.
9. High operational cost for the rural branch and poor volume of business as lending is not given thrust.
10. Manpower shortage in the rural and remote branches results in poor monitoring of the loan portfolio and deterioration of asset quality.
11. Increase in non-performing assets, requiring higher provisions and thereby affecting the profitability of the rural branches.
12. Due to the manual operation of the rural branches and because of low value of business, the per employee productivity is low.
13. In some cases there is double financing by cooperative banks and other RRBs leading to overdues in both institutions.

14. Gradual erosion of moral values and repayment ethics as the people had tasted the benefits of loan/ interest waiver offers.
15. Loopholes in enforcing the legal contracts on the willful defaulters.
16. Poor follow-up by the branch, as number of small accounts is more.

As the rural branches are facing the above problems, it affects their long-term viability.

Table 2: Network of rural branches of commercial banks

Year	*Total branches*	*Rural branches*
May 1993	61169	35389
March 1995	62367	33004
March 1998	64218	32878
March 2000	65412	32734
June 2002	66355	32394
June 2003	66514	32386

Source: IBA Bulletin Vol. xxvi No. 01.

The above table shows that even though the total number of branches has increased from 61169 in May 1993 to 66514 in June 2003, the number of rural branches has reduced from 35389 in May 1993 to 32386 in June 2003. This is the result of the branch network rationalization exercise being carried out in all banks. In coming few years also, the trend will continue and the number of rural branches will come down drastically. But it will not affect the prospects of rural lending as new rural credit delivery structures are evolving viz.

1. Self help groups
2. Federation of SHGs
3. NGO turned MFIs etc. which are cost-effective in linking banks with people.

According to National Sample Survey data, the poverty in India in absolute terms is increasing, even though it is coming down percentage-wise, in spite of the continuous efforts on the poverty alleviation programmes by the banks and successive governments. During the period 1991-97 the rural poverty has grown by 3.42%, whereas urban poverty has declined by 1.32%.

The eradication of poverty among rural masses is aimed either through implementation of wage employment or self employment programmes.The wage employment programmes are implemented either by central or state government which include Minimum Needs Programme, National Rural Employment Programme, Rural Landless Employment Generation Programme etc. The self-employment schemes which are mostly institutional credit linked schemes are aimed at providing self employment or for strengthening of productive capacity of the various target groups in rural areas such as IRDP, SEEUY, SEPUP, DOWCRA, PASMA, TRYSEM, SCAP, STAP, DRI etc.

In spite of implementation of such schemes throughout the country both by govt. and public sector banks during the last two decades, the objectives with which these schemes were launched remained unaccomplished. The important factors that are responsible for non-achievement of the objectives of poverty alleviation programmes include:

(a) Ill-defined Target groups
(b) Expansion of credit through subsidized lending programmes
(c) Loan melas
(d) Loan write-offs
(e) Risk of defaults
(f) High cost for monitoring the loan accounts etc.

In the present scenario of deregulated interest rates to farm and non-farm sector through institutional sources, a client looks for timely provision of credit instead of subsidized credit. Also, there is need for a sustainable credit dispensing system to suit the poverty struck target groups in different socio-economic settings across the country.

SHGs and MFIs

In India the SHG–bank linkage project was launched by NABARD in 1992 as a pilot project as a cost effective mechanism for providing financial services to the unreached and unserved poor. These groups are lent by commercial banks directly or through NGOs. Besides SHG–Bank linkage programme, a number of NGOs had started experimenting under Indian context or implementing various initiatives like replication of Grameen network with NGOs and financing through SHGs federations and cooperatives etc. This had paved a way for an orderly development of Micro-Finance (MF) sector and to adopt international best practices up to March 2003, all commercial banks put together linked 717360 SHGs with SHG bank loans of Rs 2048 crore cumulatively since the inception of the project. During the year 2002-03 alone, the banks disbursed SHG loans of Rs 1022 crore and registered a 99.6% increase in SHG loan disbursements, which is a solid proof that the bankers have recognized the SHG lending as a profitable and commercial opportunity with social objectives. NABARD has set an ambitious target of linking 1 million SHGs by 2008, which will be achieved well ahead.

CUSTOMER SERVICE IN RURAL BRANCHES

Customer service in banks is a continuing issue for discussion. What makes a bank customer friendly? Its overall service standards, rated for ease for opening an account; how courteous, accessible and knowledgeable its staff are; transaction time for services; how innovative the bank is in introducing products and services; how proactively the bank informs customers of changes in deposit rates or service charges; how quickly it redresses grievances; how likely it is to retain customers; and how probable it is that its customers will recommend the bank to others. In a deregulated environment customer's expectations keep rising, as they look for more convenient and flexible options available to them at competitive rates from many players operating in the field. But on the other side, the rural customers don't have any idea as to how much time is required for any type of banking services. The rural customers are not aware for what purpose the loans are available and how they can be availed. Customers don't know the complete rules, regulations and procedures of the banks and bankers preserve them for themselves and don't take interest in educating the customers.

Customer service is not merely the fulfillment of the Government's guidelines or the mechanical adherence to the time frames of services. It is a philosophy and an attitude of professional commitment, which believes in the ultimate satisfaction of each customer's wants. Now the country's top private sector banks have started entering in to rural areas, customer services will also improve.

VISUALIZING THE FUTURE OUTLOOK

The banks will roll out more customer friendly high tech products and services as the industry will shift from the seller's market to the buyer's market status, whereby the customer will be having more options to choose from at competitive rates. Technology would be the key to the competitiveness of banking and finance system. Indian players will keep pace with global leaders in the use of banking technology. In such a scenario, online accessibility will be available to the customers from any part of the globe. 'Anywhere and Anytime' banking will be realized truly and fully. At the same time 'brick and mortar' banking will co-exist with 'online banking' to cater the specific needs of the different customers. In the times to come the products and services range will be as follows:

1. Present Kisan credit card will be replaced by the high-tech smart card, which will be accepted in agro marketing outlets in rural and semi-urban areas.
2. Banks will bring out co-branded credit cards in association with the fertilizer companies and seeds companies. The farmer will be encouraged to use the cards issued by the companies by offering discount on the purchases made using the cards.
3. More off-site ATMs will be installed in marketing and agro processing centers. Banks will ensure that the thumb impression recognition systems are integrated in the ATMs, so that illiterate rural customers will also freely operate the ATMs.
4. Rural customers in remote areas will access the banking services through the Internet.
5. As the bricks and mortar branch infrastructure will not be available in many rural areas, the banks will utilize the services of the existing input/marketing outlets in rural areas to offer the deposit and loan products through the points of rate terminals installed in such outlets and connected online with the bank.
6. At present the crop insurance cover is available only for notified crops, but due to the fast development in forecasting techniques, the banks will launch crop specific insurance covers in association with the insurance companies. As the risk is covered, the banks will increase their crop loan exposures.
7. Banks offer infrastructure loan products to the Government for the creation of common facilities such as school, roads, electricity, health services, godown and so on in rural areas. In future, the banks will offer infrastructure loan products directly to local people's organizations. When it will be maintained by the LPOs, it will be put to optimal use and boost the credit off-take by the rural people.

8. At present the small loan documentation takes considerable time. Even for a small loan of Rs.10,000 a borrower may have to sign in many papers. Banks will shift to paperless mode of documentation and will rely on e-documentation, wherein the transaction cost will be greatly reduced to the banks.

In a competitive environment, one has to be effective to survive. So, our systems and procedures need to be fine tuned to cater the ever-increasing expectations of the customer. It is suggested that bank officials should be given frequent training with practical knowledge so that they can impart it at the branches. Meeting customers once a month at the branch with the customer committee will enable a branch to identify the issues to be addressed by the bankers. The banking industry is facing frequent changes and modifications; the staff should be given the required job enrichment training on a regular basis so that they can acquire the required knowledge to deal with customers. Various day-to-day changes, which are communicated by way of regular circulars, should be shared with staff members during staff meetings in order to keep them up to date with working knowledge. Even though the challenges ahead are many, the Indian rural banking system is optimistic in facing the challenges head on, by adopting proactive changes.

REFERENCES

1. Reserve Bank of India–*Trend and progress in banking* (1999–2002).
2. Ahluwalia, I.J. (1999) *The Indian Economy: Looking ahead in contemporary India.* Tata McGraw-hill.
3. Ahluwalia MS (1995) *India's Economic Reforms in Cassen*, Joshi, V (ed.) Delhi. OUP.
4. Mazumdar N.A. (2002) *Financial Sector Reforms and India's Economic Development*, Delhi Economic Foundation.
5. Venugopal Reddy Y (2002), "Monetary and Financial Sector Reforms in India". UBS Publications, New Delhi.
6. Promod Batra, 1994 'Simple Ways to Make Your Customers Happy (1st edn.)' New Delhi: Think Inc. Publishing house.

20

REGIONAL RURAL BANKS IN INDIA AND THEIR ROLE IN RURAL DEVELOPMENT

R. K. Agrawal*

On July 1, 1975, the Ministry of Finance, Government of India, Constituted a working group under the Chairmanship of Shri M. Narashimhan to examine in depth, the question of setting up of new Rural Banks to cater the credit needs of the rural people. The group submitted its report on July 30, 1975. According to the group, rational ideas for a Regional Rural Bank, oriented to rural credit, follows the identification of a specific region and functional gap in the present institutional structure. The group also felt that the existing institutions, as they are structured at present, wound not be able to fill up the gap within a reasonable period of time even with such an adaptation, reorganised and restructuring as may be considered. It is with this background that the group suggested the formation of State-sponsored, regionally based rural-oriented, commercial banks. The new institutions are intended to supplement and not supplant the other institutional agencies in the field, i.e., the co-operative and commercial banks.

The Government of India accepted the recommendation of the working group to set up Regional Rural Banks. Accordingly, the Regional Rural Banks Ordinance was promulgated by the President of India on 26th September 1975, for the establishment of Regional Rural Banks and came into force with immediate effect and extended to the whole of India. The establishment of Regional Rural Banks is a landmark in the history of Indian banking.

*Professor and Head, Department of Commerce, H. N. B. Garhwal University, Badshahithaul Campus, Tehri-Garhwal.

OBJECTIVES OF THE REGIONAL RURAL BANKS

According the Regional Rural Bank Act, the R.R.Bs. are to be set up mainly " with a view to developing the rural economy by providing for the purpose of development of agriculture, trade, industry and other productive activities in the rural areas, credit and other facilities, particularly to the small and marginal farmers, agricultural labourers, artisans and small entrepreneurs and for matters connected therewith and incidental thereto."

The Regional Rural Banks are set up mainly to benefit small and marginal farmers, agricultural labourers and rural artisans. The Regional Rural Banks are scheduled the commercial banks with the following distinctive features.

(a) Their areas of operation are limited to particular region comprising of one or more districts in any state.

(b) They grant loans and advances mostly to small and marginal farmers, agricultural labourers, rural artisans etc. To a limited extend they can grant loans to other farmers cultivating lands within the project areas approved for refinance by the NABARD.

(c) The Regional Rural Banks are considered to be a suitable institution to provide needed credit at their doorsteps on reasonable terms and conditions so that the weaker sections of people in rural areas could raise their standard of living.

(d) The share capital of a Regional Rural Bank is made up of 50 per cent from the Central Government, 15 per cent from the State Government and 35 per cent from the sponsoring banks.

CONSTITUTION OF BOARD OF DIRECTORS

The overall management of the R.R.Bs. is to be under a Board of Directors consisting of nine members including the chairman. The chairman is normally an officer of the sponsoring bank, but is appointed by the Government of India. In addition, the Central Government nominates three Directors belonging to various Ministries such as Finance, Banking, Revenue and Agriculture. The concerned State Government nominates two Directors. The sponsoring bank nominates three directors. The number of Directors of the Board can be raised up to fifteen with the prior approval of the Government of India.

CONCESSIONS AVAILABLE TO R.R.Bs

(a) Regional Rural Banks have been allowed to maintain a lower cash reserve ratio as compared to the other schedule Commercial Banks. At present this ratio is fixed at 3 per cent of total demand and liabilities.

(b) Regional Rural Banks can refinance at a concessional rate of 3 per cent below the bank rate from NABARD.

(c) Regional Rural Banks are allowed to offer ½ per cent higher rate of interest on all deposits except the deposits of 3 years and above.

(d) Regional Rural Banks are allowed to earn interest at the rate of 9 per cent on the current account balances maintained by them with the sponsor banks.

(e) Regional Rural Banks are required to maintain a lower statutory liquid ratio at 25 per cent as against 36 per cent by the Commercial Banks

(f) The training cost of the staff is born by the concerned sponsoring bank.

(g) In case the R.R.Bs. incurs heavy losses in excess of its paid up capital, the sponsoring banks may perhaps have to bear a part of its losses.

BRANCH EXPANSION

The Regional Rural Banks made their belonging with the establishment of five banks on October 2, 1975. Their details have been given in Table 1.

Table 1: Regional Rural Bank Opened on October 2, 1975

S.N.	*Name of the R.R.Bs. bank*	*Name of the sponsoring*	*District covered*
1.	Prathama Bank	Syndicate Bank	Moradabad (U.P.)
2.	Gorakhpur Kshetriya Gramin Bank	State Bank of India	Gorakhpur and Deoria (U.P.)
3.	Haryana Krishi Gramin Bank	Punjab National Bank	Bhiwani (Haryana)
4.	Jaipur-Nagpur Aanchalik Gramin Bank	United Commercial Bank	Jaipur and Nagaur (Rajasthan)
5.	Gour Gramin Bank	United Bank of India	Malda (W.B.)

Table 2 reveals that the total numbers of R.R.Bs operating all over India has reached 196 with 14454 branches spread over 448 districts in the country as against 6 R.R.Bs. with 17 branches spread over 12 districts in 1975, 85 R.R.Bs. with 3279 branches spread over 144 districts in 1980, 188 R.R.Bs. with 12606 branches spread over 333 districts in 1985 and 196 R.R.Bs. with 14450 branches spread over 372 districts in 1995.

Table 2 also reveals that the highest number of R.R.Bs., i.e. 103 with 9327 branches was established in India during the 5 year period (1980 to 1985). On the other hand, the minimum branches were opened during 11 year from 1990 to 2001. Thus, there had been slower progress in the number of R.R.Bs. and branches since 1990. During the 27 years period from 1975 to 2001, the number of R.R.Bs increased 32 times from 6 to 196 and the number of branches increased 850 times from 17 to 14454. Thus the growth of R.R.Bs in India has been quite satisfactory.

Table 2: Growth of R.R.Bs in India

S.N.	*Year*	*Name of the R.R.Bs.*		*Name of Branches*		*District covered*
		Opened during the 5 year	*Total at end of year*	*Opened during the 5 year*	*Total at the end of year*	
1.	1975	06	06	17	17	12
2.	1980	79	85	3262	3279	144
3.	1985	103	188	9327	12606	333
4.	1980	08	196	1837	14443	372
5.	1995	—	196	07	14450	448
6.	2001		196	04	14454	448

Source: NABARD - Statistical Reports.

MOBILISATION OF DEPOSITS

The most important source of the banks for enlarging their resources is the mobilisation of deposits. Deposits mobilised by the R.R.Bs. play a key role not only as an important source of fund for the banks but also as an instrument for promoting savings and banking habits among the rural people. The R.R.Bs. have to strive very hard for the mobilisation of deposits. They have even to make special efforts for this purpose. The advance and profits of a bank are significantly related to its deposits. Thus, deposits have a great significance not only for the R.R.Bs but also for the development of rural economy. However, in order to help the R.R.Bs effectively and enable them to compete with other banks, they have to permit to quote half a per cent more interest on deposits.

Table 3 shows that deposits increased from Rs. .20 crore in 1975 to Rs. 4150.52 crore in 1990 and Rs. 37027.00 crore in 2001. The average deposits per bank increased from Rs. .03 crore in 1975 to Rs. 21.18 crore in 1990 and Rs. 188.91 crore in 2001. The average deposits per branch increased from Rs. .01 crore to Rs. 2.56 crore between 1975 and 2001.

It may be pointed out here that although the deposits of the R.R.Bs have increased in recent years, yet the amount of deposits is not commensurate with the available potential for savings in rural area.

Table 3: Deposits of R.R.Bs in India

(Amount in Rs crores)

S.N.	*Year*	*Total Deposits*	*Per Bank Deposits*	*Per Branch Deposits*
1.	1975	.20	.03	.01
2.	1980	199.83	2.35	.06
3.	1985	1285.82	6.84	.10
4.	1990	4150.52	21.18	.29
5.	1995	11150.01	56.89	.77
6.	2001	37027.00	188.91	2.56

Sources: NABARD - Statistical Reports.

ADVANCES

In order to extent banking benefits to the maximum number of eligible persons and raise their standard of living, every Regional Rural Bank has undertaken the following types of loaning business

A Granting of loans and advances, particularly to small farmers and agricultural labourers.

B Granting of loans and advances, particularly to rural artisans and small entrepreneurs.

Table 4 shows that the progressive increase in the aggregate advance of R.R.Bs in India over the years. It increased from Rs. .10 crore in 1975 to Rs. 1407.67 crore in 1985, 6290.96 crore in 1995, and 15794.00 crore in 2001.

The purpose-wise classification of advances by R.R.Bs. in India is also shown in Table 4. The share of agricultural loan to total advances was 85 per cent which was highest in 1975 and the lowest, i.e. 45.63 per cent in 2001. The share of rural artisans and small entrepreneurs to total advances was 10.00 per cent in 1975 and became 17.55 per cent in 2001. A significant features which deserves attention is that loans for consumption and other purposes show an increased trend. They increase from 5.00 per cent in 1975 to 36.24 per cent in 2001.

Table 4: Advances of R.R.Bs in India

S.N.	*Year*	*Advances (in Rs. Crore)*	*Purpose of classification in* *	**	***	****	*(Per cent) Total*
1	1975	.10	85.00	10.00	5.00		100
2	1980	167.41	80.00	15.00	5.00		100
3	1985	1407.67	57.94	21.68	8.01	2.37	100
4	1990	3554.04	51.72	37.37	9.68	1.23	100
5	1995	6290.96	47.83	33.04	18.61	.52	100
6	2001	15794.00	45.63	17.55	36.24	.58	100

Source: NABARD – Statistical Reports.

* Agricultural Loan

** Rural Artisans and Small Entrepreneurs

*** Consumption and Other Purposes

**** Indirect Advances

Thus, the lending operations of the R.R.Bs. are definitely in line with the social objective of promoting economic development with social justice.

CREDIT DEPOSIT RATIO

Credit deposit ratio has been regarded as an indicator of the bank's performances in the matter of development of credit. Ratio between credit and deposit reveals the possibilities of utilisation of the available deposits in the form of credit. Higher percentage or ratio of credit ratio shows more benefits to the society through its credit mechanism in the context of rural areas or it reveals how much the R.R.Bs. have helped the rural development through credit. Similarly, the lesser percentage or ratio of credit deposits shows the lesser benefits to the society through its credit mechanisation and deposit mobilisation in the context of rural areas.

It was observed from Table 5 that credit deposit ratio of R.R.Bs in India has mixed trend. It was 50 per cent in 1975 and it increased to 135 per cent which was highest in 1980, thereafter became lowest, i.e. 43 percent in 2001.

Table 5: Credit Deposits of R.R.Bs in India

S.N.	*Year*	*C.D. Ratio*
1.	1975	50
2.	1980	135
3.	1985	112
4.	1990	93
5.	1995	59
6.	2001	43

Source: NABARD – Statistical Report.

PROFITABILITY AND REVIVAL MEASURES

The profitability of R.R.Bs were affected by the low capital base, poor recovery of dues and thin interest spreads. Besides the factor like limited opportunities for profitable investment of surplus fund also had a serious bearing on their profitability.

As part financial sector reforms, Government of India, Reserve Bank of India, and NABARD initiated various measures for improving the profitability of R.R.Bs. For instance, in the year 1994-95, the Government of India provided Rs. 150.00 crore for cleaning their balance sheets. In the year 1995-96, the Government of India provided a sum of Rs. 223.57 crore for the purpose. Most of the R.R.Bs relocated some of the branches to better location. The diversification of lending portfolio through housing loans and and loans for consumer durable have improved the profitability. This led to better utilisation of manpower and capital.

The financial results of R.R.Bs is shown in Table 6. Financial Result show that the number of profit making R.R.Bs has gone up steeply. The profit making R.R.Bs increase from 45 to 170 between the year 1987 and 2001.

Table 6: Profit Making R.R.Bs in India

S.N.	*Year*	*No. of R. R. Bs Amount Making Profit*	*(Rs. in Crore)*
1	1987	45	7
2	1992	23	13
3	1997	44	70
4	2001	170	676

Source: NABARD, Statistical Reports.

Lastly, we can say that R.R.Bs are developing rural economy of India by providing credit to agriculture, trade, industry and other productive activities. The R.R.Bs give more emphasis on small and marginal farmers, agricultural labourers, rural artisans and small entrepreneurs. In view of these objectives, directions have been given by the Government of India that R.R.Bs should confine their advances only to weaker section in rural areas.

21

ROLE OF COMMERCIAL BANKS AND FINANCIAL INSTITUTIONS IN THE DEVELOPMENT OF SMALL SCALE INDUSTRIES (SSIs) IN INDIA

K.S. Ramola*

The small-scale industry is always an important sector in all the countries. In the economies like Japan and America about half of the labour is employed in small industries. The SSIs are labour-intensive instead of capital intensive. So, they are more suitable for a country like India where capital is still scarce and credit is not easy. Further SSI is best fit for agricultural economies. This sector immensely helps tackling the employment problem. The institutional finance to SSI is provided by the SBI, Commercial Banks, Cooperative Banks, development banks, RBI, SFCs, NSIC. The govt support to this sector is given for long-term finance.

The liberalisation made the SSIs way difficult as the bigger domestic and foreign companies are producing the same product and they are in the competition. There is an estimate that more than 5 lakh units of small-scale sector have been closed resulting in unemployment of 25 lakh persons. The prime challenge before the SSI sector is the cost-reduction. The credit easy terms can help them reducing the cost of production. Thus, banks and other financial institutions have the key role in the survival and sustenance of small-scale industries sector.

*Dept. of Commerce, HNB Garhwal University Campus, Badshahi Thaul, Tehri Garwhal.

Small Scale Industries (SSIs) sector (consisting of modern as well as, traditional industries) has over the year developed as an important constituent of Indian economy in terms of its share in employment, output and exports. It has also made significant contribution to the development of rural and less-developed areas, widening of entrepreneurial base and providing ancillary support to large and medium industry. The contribution of SSIs sector to the national economy has also been well recognized by the various Industrial Policies of the country from time to time. Liberal policy of reservation protection and concessions has been extended to this sector so that the sector can thrive and prosper. Globalization has opened up opportunities, which the SSIs sector must seize to be globally competitive both in terms of price and quality. For this, they must improve upon the existing levels of technology, quality and market information (Mishra, 1997). In order to accelerate the growth and productivity of SSIs, the Government of India has set up a number of Boards/Commissions/Promotional Organization/ Corporation, etc.

These industries are considered labour-intensive. In 1999-2000 about 178 lakh workers were employed in SSI units, out of which 55 lakh job opportunities have been created during the post-reform period, i.e. between 1990-2000. A large chunk of country's population is unemployed and is forced to live below the poverty line. As per 55th round of NSSO-1999, 26.1 per cent population is living below poverty line. Therefore, the importance of SSI units, a labour-intensive technique, cannot be overlooked in a labour surplus country like India.

OBJECTIVES AND METHODOLOGY

Against this background in view, an attempt has been made in this research paper to examine the credit requirements particularly credit assistance to this sector in the new economic environment of liberalization, denationalization and globalization.

The study is basically developed on the basis of secondary data. Information is collected through personal investigation. In context of the credit assistance to this sector, the major emphasis is laid on the role of Banks and financial institutions in improving the credit delivery system in a liberalized policy regime covered under the present study.

DEFINITION

The definition of small-scale sector is broadened from small-scale industries to small-scale enterprises that include all business enterprises in the service sector which provide service to industrial sector in addition to SSIs. Taking into account all these factors, at present, RBI uses an expanded definition of SSI which includes: (i) small scale industrial undertaking which are engaged in the manufacture, processing or preservation of goods in which the investments in plant and machinery to not exceed Rs. 1 crore. These would, *inter alia,* include units engaged in mining or quarrying, servicing and repairing of machinery; (ii) tiny enterprises whose investments in plant and machinery do not exceeds Rs. 25.00 lakhs; (iii) power looms; (iv) traditional industries which require high workmanship and techniques as also village and household industries producing common goods of consumption predominantly by using simple tools; (v) the decentralized and informal sectors like handlooms, handicrafts, etc; (vi) the industry related to services/business enterprises which are notified as such; (vii) food and agrobased industries, and (viii) software industry.

GROWTH OF SMALL SCALE INDUSTRIES (SSIs)

The significant growth of the SSIs in India over the last five decades is on account of the high priority accorded to this sector by Government of India and RBI. Because of this, the growth of SSI sector in real terms stood at 10 per cent in 1994-95 as against 7.1 and 5.6 per cent respectively for the year 1993-94 and 1992-93. The number of SSI units have increased from 19.38 lakh in 1990-91 to 32.35 lakh in 1999-2000.

During the Eighth Five Year Plan, output of traditional industry sector like Khadi and Village Industries, handlooms, handicrafts, sericulture and coir industry rose from Rs. 24.228 crore to Rs. 53,716 crore recording an annual growth rate of 24.34 per cent. Employment opportunities provided by this sector also rose significantly from 279 lakh to 345 lakh during this period (Kulkarni, 1998).

The organized SSIs sector witnessed significant progress over the years, between 1992-93 and 1996-97, the number of units went up from 22.46 lakh to 27.50 lakh at an annual rate of 4.48 per cent while output increased from Rs. 209,300 crore to Rs. 40,324 crore.

Employment generation during this period recorded an annual growth of 3.73 per cent from 134 lakh to 159 lakh (Kulkarni, 1998). The value of production by SSI sector as a whole has increased from Rs. 155,340 crore in 1990-91 to Rs. 578,470 crore in 1999-2000. The exports from this sector has been significantly increased from Rs. 1643 crore in 1980-81 to Rs. 9100 crore in 1990-91 and further to Rs. 53,975 crore in 1999-2000.

The growth has been achieved through the total commitment and involvement of the central and state government, which is evident in introduction of various schemes and promotional efforts through financing, market support and development of required infrastructure in setting up of small units. At the apex level, there is Small Industries Development Organization that formulates, coodinates and monitors the various plans relating to small sector through a network of small industries service, branch service institutes, extension centers, etc (Kilam & Kataria, 1989).

ROLE OF BANKS AND FINANCIAL INSTITUTIONS IN A LIBERALISED POLICY REGIME

Finance is the lifeblood in the veins of the industry. Its adequate availability on easy terms is a basic requirement of the small-scale industries. Small entrepreneurs, especially in rural areas, do not have adequate resources of their own and have no access to raise capital in the market. SSI mainly needs to types of financial facilities, i.e. the medium term loans to acquire fixed assets and short-term loans to meet their working capital requirements and the cost of processing, marketing etc.

Government policy treats SSI sector as a priority sector for being provided with credit by banks and financial institutions. State Finance Corporations extend long-term and medium-term credit requirements and provide investment capital to SSI units. These industries also receive loan under the State aid to Industries Act though the quantum of loans is diminishing. Commercial Banks, Co-operative Banks and Regional Rural Banks provide short-term loans and meet the working capital requirements of SSI units. NSIC and SSIDCs at state level supply machinery on hire-purchase basis. Small Industrial Development Bank of India (SIDBI), National Bank of Agriculture and Rural Development (NABARD) and the Industrial Reconstruction Bank of India (IRBI) provide refinance facilities for financing SSI sector (Chopra, 1990).

At present the priority sector comprises agriculture, small scale industries, small road and water transport operators, retail traders, small business, professional and self-employed persons, self help groups (SHGs), housing consumption loans for weaker sections, government sponsored poverty alleviation and employment generation programmes etc. Within the priority sector, 10 per cent of net bank credit is required to be channelized to the 'weaker sections' which comprise small and marginal farmers, landless labourers, rural artisans, beneficiaries of special poverty alleviation programmes and the socially under-privileged classes. Banks have been extending finance to small scale industries (SSI) including the tiny sector of rural artisans/cottage and village industries. In view of the importance of tiny industries in the rural economy of the country, banks are required to "lend 60 per cent of their total SSI advances to the 'tiny sector' within the small-scale industries. Based on the reports of the Micro-credit Special Cell, which was set up in the RBI and the Task Force on Supportive Policy and Regulatory Framework for Micro-Finance set-up by NABARD during February 1999-2000. Two thousand banks were instructed to pursue vigorously the action initiated for main streaming micro-credit. Banks have been advised that micro-credit extended by them to individual borrowers either directly or through any intermediary would be reckoned a part of their priority sector lending (Joshi, 2002).

The available data regarding credit assistance to SSI sector under priority sector lending by commercial banks is given in Table 1.

Table 1: Credit Assistance to SSI Sector

(*Rs. in crores*)

Year ending March	*Net bank credit*	*Advances to priority sector*	*Advances to SSI sector*	*Percentage of SSI credit to*	
				Net bank credit	*Priority sector advances*
1995	169,038	61,794	25,843	15.29	41.82
1996	184,384	69,609	29,482	15.99	42.35
1997	189,684	79,131	31,542	16.63	39.86
1998	218,219	91,319	38,109	17.46	41.73
1999	246,203	107,200	42,674	17.33	39.81
2000	292,943	127,807	45,788	15.63	35.83
2001	340,888	146,546	48,445	14.21	33.06

Note:

1. Data are provisional.
2. *Inclusive of funds provided to RRBs by their sponsoring banks, loan to software industry, food and agro-processing sector and Self Help Groups, loan to food and agro-based processing sector and investment in venture capital, which are also eligible for inclusion under priority sector advances.

RECENT TRENDS IN SMALL SCALE INDUSTRIES

Sickness in SSIs

The growing sickness in the industrial sector, especially in the small-scale sector, is gaining new dimension every year. According to a survey conducted by the Federation of Indian Chambers of Commerce and Industry (FICCI), Rs. 50,000 crore were locked up in sick or weak industrial units, as on March 1994. Of this, the bank loan against the sick units including large, medium and small scale worked out to Rs. 15,000 crore. There were around 3 lakh sick or weak industrial units in India as on March 1994 out of which 99 per cent of these were in the small scale sector. The increase in the number of sick SSI units was 2 per cent between December 1988 and March 1992. From March 1992 to March 1994, the rate of sickness has increased to 3 per cent. During 1988 to 1992, the locked up funds in sick SSI units increased by 45 per cent.

Similarly, during the same period, the number of non-SSI sick and weak units went up by 8 per cent and 6 per cent respectively. The outstanding credit in these non-SSIs sick and weak industries increased by 53 per cent and 22 per cent respectively between 1988 and March 1992.

The industry-wise classification of sick SSI units showed the high incidence in the engineering sector (20 per cent) followed by chemicals (10.27 per cent), textiles (6.7 per cent), electrical (5.8 per cent), iron and steel (5.01 per cent) and rubber (1.62 per cent).

The state-wise sickness shows that West Bengal has the highest number of SSIs which are sick: 56,088; followed by Uttar Pradesh with 33,915 and Maharashtra with 21,350 sick SSI units. In terms of credit outstanding against sick SSI units, Maharastra has the number one position, i.e. Rs. 603 crore.

At the end of March 1990, there were 218,828 sick SSI units which increased to 268,815 by the end of March 1995—an increase of 49,987 units in a short duration of time of 5 years! Though the number of sick SSI units reduced in 1998 over 1995, still this number is very high. As on March 2000 more than 3 lakh SSI are categorized as sick units covering a bank credit of Rs. 4313 crore (Table 2).

Table 2: Sickness in small scale sector

(Rs. in crores)

Years ending March	Total credit (Outstanding)	SSI Units No. of unit (in lakh)	Net bank credit	Sick SSI Units No. of units (in lakh)	Bank credit	% of total bank credit
1990	95,132	19.38	159,89	2.18 (11.28)*	2427 (15.2)$	2.5
1995	169,038	27.20	25,843	2.69 (9.88)*	3547 (13.7)$	2.0
1998	218,219	31.21	38,109	2.20 (7.04)*	3843 (10.1)$	1.8
2000	246,203	32.25	48,483	3.06 (9.48)*	4313 (8.9)$	1.8

Note:

* Figure in brackets represent percentages to total SSI units.

$ Figure in brackets represent percentages to net bank credit to SSI units.

NPAs in SSI

The new concept of NPAs is based on the record of recovery of interest and installments, irrespective of availability of security and net worth of the borrowers. It is based on the Narasimham Committee on financial reform in 1991. Based on this committee, the RBI introduced prudential accounting standards for banks in April 1992. As per the prudential norms, the SSI advances will be non-performing when the borrower fails to pay the interest and instalments. The total NPAs in SSI was Rs. 7984 crore as of March 1997, which increased to Rs. 9959 crore as of March 2000 accounting for 6.18 per cent growth annually (Kulkarni & Shete, 2001).

The available data regarding NPL (Table 3) shows the trend of NPAs towards priority sector (43.6) and non-priority sector (53.3). There is thus a stage has come now to think and find alternatives for recovery of NPAs.

The RBI has come forward in this direction and introduced one time settlement of NPA. The banks have taken this opportunities and reduced NPAs to certain extant. RBI has also given permission to the banks to formulate its own schemes for recovery of NPAs. Some banks have taken to lead and introduced schemes for settlement of NPAs.

Table 3: Sectorwise comparison of non-performing loan (NPL) (for the year ending on 31st March, 2001)

(Rs. in crores)

	Priority sector	*Public sector*	*Non priority sector*	*Total NPA*
Nationalised Banks	15228 (46.2)	498 (1.5)	17257 (52.3)	32983 (100.00)
State Bank Group	8928 (44.2)	1213 (6.0)	10050 (49.8)	20191 (100.00)
Old Private Sector Bank	1591 (33.0)	123 (2.6)	3096 (64.4)	4810 (100.00)
New Private Sector Banks	243 (15.2)	—	1356 (84.8)	1599 (100.00)
Total	25990 (43.6)	1834 (3.1)	31759 (53.3)	59583 (100.00)

Figures in parentheses represent percentages of the total NPA.

Source: Trend and Progress of Banking in India, RBI Table Appendix II. 10 (A), p. 199.

CORRECTIVE MEASURES FOR GROWTH AND BETTER PERFORMANCE

To ensure adequate credit assistance to the SSI sector including those belonging to the cottage and village industries and tiny sector, the Government of India and the Reserve Bank have appointed various Committees and Expert Groups. The RBI had formed a committee under the Chairmanship of Sri P.R. Nayak in 1991 to examine the problems of credit, sickness and other related issues in SSI sector. Based on the recommendations of the Nayak Committee a special package of measures to ensure adequate and timely credit to SSI sector was announced in April 1993 and July 1993. The salient features of this package are:

(i) Banks should give preference to village industries and tiny units while meeting the credit requirement of the small-scale sectors.

(ii) Working capital finance to be made available to SSI units to a maximum of 20 per cent of annual turnover. This limit applies to those SSI units whose credit limit in the individual cases was up to Rs. 50 lakhs (since enhanced to Rs. 4 crores).

(iii) Single window clearance scheme of SIDBI should be extended to all districts of the country of meeting the credit needs of SSI units.

(iv) To set-up specialized branches for lending to the SSIs and rehabilitation of SSIs and SSI units have been concentrated.

(v) Setting up grievance redressal mechanism in banks for SSI units.

Nayak Committee was followed in 1995 by an Expert Committee headed by Dr. Abid Hussain on Small Enterprises. In 1997 this committee has recommended a set of recommendations for growth and better performance of small enterprises. The Abid Hussain Committee has pointed out that "India needs a new SSI policy framework that is much more promotional than protective; that will develop entrepreneurship, and be much more growth-oriented than in the past."

The GOI has also constituted a Informal Group to examine the bank credit to SSIs. The group has recommended a number of measures to improve credit flow to enhance the capacity utilization. The high level committee on credit to SSIs (Chairman Shri S.L. Kapur) appointed by the Reserve Bank of India had recommended:

(i) Strengthening of credit delivery system;

(ii) Policy matters related to pricing and adequate and timely availability of credit to SSIs so as to make credit delivery system more friendly for borrowers as well as banks;

(iii) Grievances redressal machinery and miscellaneous issues like marketing of credit facilities, access to technology information, software, corporatization of SSIs, micro-credit, women entrepreneurs, weaker sections, HRD, etc.

Recently, a Study Group on Development of Small Enterprises was set-up under the Chairmanship of Dr. Gupta, Member of Planning Commission (1999). The group had made several recommendations relating to definition and scope, reservation and other policy issues, legal framework, infrastructure and human resource development, financial and fiscal measures, and technological and marketing thrust for exports etc.

Reserve Bank of India in its mid-term review of Monetary and Credit Policy for 1999-2000, has advised banks and financial institutions to include flow of micro credit in their corporate strategy/

plan and to review the progress on a quarterly basis. In this credit policy, banks and financial institutions have been entrusted with special responsibilities for providing credit on reasonable terms to certain sector, particularly, agriculture, exports, micro-credit institutions, small-scale industries, and housing. In addition to improving the terms and volume of assistance to these sectors, an important priority is to improve and simplify procedures, reduce documentation requirements and decentralize decision-making to branch level.

In order to pass on the benefits of lower interest rates of SSIs sector the State Bank of India has announced an interest rate band of 2 per cent above and below the prime-lending rate. This has to be adopted by other banks too.

SOME ISSUES AND CONCLUDING OBSERVATIONS

Entrepreneurs in small-scale sector are reluctant to upgrade themselves to medium or large unit for fear of losing various concessions available to SSI. This effect is undesirable. Resulting in 1990, export of items produced by SSI, was at around $3 bn. in both India and China. By 1995, China's exports of these items jumped to $70 bn while that of India was around only $12 bn. In this context, policy measures, which aim to promotion of labour intensive industries, appear to have an undesirable effect of stunting their growth (Mohan, 2001).

However, RBI is playing a major role in checking sickness in the small-scale sector. It has created a special cell for information and also acts as a coordinating agency between the Government, Banks, Financial Institutions and other agencies. But, there is still lack of co-ordination between them due to which the small-scale units have to face a lot of problems. For this, the coordination between them is a must (Ramola and Negi, 1994).

Table 2 shows that the share of SSI advances to net bank credit and priority sector advances continuously reducing from 17.46 per cent in 1998 to 14.21 per cent in 2001 and 41.78 per cent in 1998 to 33.06 per cent in 2001 respectively. This trend underlines the need for vigorous effects in improving the credit delivery system in the SSI sector.

For achieving better results of credit and assistance provided to SSIs sector, field offers/branch managers need to develop greater contact with their clients through regular field visits so that identification of beneficiaries and appraisal of loan applications improve, post-sanction monitoring of credit utilization is strengthened and recovery of loan is pursued regularly and effectively.

An important task of the banking system in the coming years will be the management of the rural credit delivery systems and processes are also channels of credit flow to small and medium scale industries. Improving the credit delivery system of cooperatives is vital for reaping productivity and employment gains and to this end, strengthening of genuine co-operative credit structures is essential (RBI, 2001).

In the age of liberalization and globalization, the SSI sector must seize to be globally competitive both in terms of price and quality. For this, they must improve upon the existing levels of technology, quality and market information.

In India, e-commerce is just fledgling but its advantages and conveniences are soon to be realized. The SSI sector can enjoy the benefits of e-commerce in the upgradation of existing levels of technology and it is also helpful in taking market information's in time in the age of liberalization.

REFERENCES

1. Chopra, Kailash O. 1990. Village Industries and Role of SIDBI. *Financial Express*, New Delhi, August 8.
2. Joshi, Deepali Pant, 2002. Rural Credit. *Yojana*, Vol. 46, January : pp. 39-42.
3. Kilam, I.K. and Kataria, Neera. 1989. Financing: Role of Commercial Banks, *IBA Bulletin*, Vol. XI (12), December; p. 295.
4. Kulkarni, P.R. 1998. Employment Generation—SSI Sector. *Southern Economist*. Vol. 36 (23 & 24), April 1 and 15; p. 22.
5. Kulkarni, P.R. and Shete, N.B. 2001. Credit Flow to Small Scale Industries during the Post Reform period. *IBA Bulletin*, Vol. XXIII (II), November, p. 39.
6. Mishra, Gitanjali, 1997. Small Scale Industries - New Opportunities for Banks. *State Bank of India, Monthly Review*, June: pp. 326-327.
7. Mohan, Rakesh. 2001. Address at the 54th Annual General Body Meeting of Indian Banks. Association held on August 25, Quoted from *IBA Bulletin*, Vol. XXIII (10). October: p. 10.

8. Ramola K.S. and Negi K.S. 1994. "Sickness in Small Scale Industries: Some Basiç Issue in *New Trends in Indian Industries*" (J.S. Mathur, ed.) Allahabad. Chugh Publications, pp. 100.101.

9. *RBI 2001*. Indian Economy: RBI's Perspective. Quoted from IBA Bulletin, Vol. XXIII (10), October 2001: p. 24.

22

CORPORATE GOVERNANCE IN BANKS

J.D.S. Negi*
A.B. Thapliyal**

Corporate Governance is about promoting corporate fairness, transparency and accountability.

— J. Wolfensohn, President, World Bank

The business houses failures and scams in the corporate world led the evolvement of corporate governance standards. The corporate governance is said a system of running the business on certain ethical principles. It discourages frauds and mismanagement. The good corporate governance emphasizes on accountable leadership.

The accountability of banks to public is much more than in any other business because the maximum amount of deposits belong to public not to the bankers. The faith in monetary system can only be safeguard by sound health of banks, which includes solvency, liquidity and other operational efficiency parameters. It is imperative to ensure good corporate governance in every bank so that they could fulfill their obligations to their customers, shareholders and other stakeholders.

Most of the banks have started pursuing the international standards for good corporate governance. During last few years many urban co-operative banks failed. The corporate governance is of greater importance in co-operative banking segment where survival of banks rests on honesty and integrity of board members. The good corporate governance is only alternative there for restoration of public faith in urban co-operative banks.

*Reader & Head, Department of Secretarial Practice, HNB Garhwal University Campus, Badshahithaul Distt. Tehri Garhwal, Uttaranchal.

**Senior Lecturer, Department of Commerce, HNB Garhwal University Campus, Badshahithaul Distt. Tehri Garhwal, Uttaranchal.

In the present business environment increasing competition all over the world led to failure of a large number of companies. The demand to make the Board of Directors and Management accountable and the need for ethical practices in the corporate management and adherence to the law of the land were responsible for the emergence of corporate governance. Banks play an important role in the payment and settlement system of a country. As banks play a major role in maintaining confidence in the monetary system through their close relationship with regulatory authorities and the government, there is considerable interest in the well being of banks, in particular their solvency, liquidity and the relative degree of risk attached to the different types of their business. Therefore, it is necessary to implement a good corporate governance in the system of every bank so that banks will satisfy their customers, shareholders and other stakeholders.

CORPORATE GOVERNANCE: CONCEPT AND MEANING

It is very difficult to define corporate governance as it covers a large number of distinct economic phenomena. As a result, different people have given different definitions according to their special interest in the field. Generally, it is a system of running a business organization on certain ethical principles. It can be understood as running a company on principles of management, i.e. direction and control, using best policies and practices to achieve its objectives taking into account the interest of the stakeholders.

According to the report of Cadbury committee—"It is a system by which companies are directed and controlled".

According to Milton Friedman: The purpose of corporate governance is to conduct the business in accordance with owner or shareholders' desires, which generally will be to make as much money as possible, while conforming to the basic rules of the society embodied in law and local customs.

Organisation of economic collaboration and development (O.E.C.D.) experts define corporate governance as the system by which business corporations are directed and controlled. It specifies the distribution of rights and responsibilities among Board, Managers, Shareholders and other stakeholders, and spells out the rules and procedures for making decisions on corporate affairs.

The corporate governance is therefore about ensuring co-operative relevance and performance by connecting members, management and the employees to the policy, strategy and decision-making processes. It is about commitment to value and ethical business conduct and a high degree of transparency.

Thus, in brief, corporate governance is about a system, in which how a company fulfills its obligations to investors and other stakeholders. It can be said to be a means to maximize shareholders' value in the long term in a legal, ethical, transparent manner, ensuring fairness, courtesy and dignity in all transactions of the company.

NEED FOR CORPORATE GOVERNANCE IN BANKS

It is being a challengeable task to control effectively to a system of an organization, whose ownership in the hand of shareholders. So the management of this type of organization has performed by some selected peoples. In this situation to protect shareholder's rights and interests, the concept of corporate governance has established in banks also.

With liberalization of Indian economy since 1991 thrust has been linking the economy of India with that of the rest of the world. This requires privatization, contracting out and shifting the work from government to non-government executive agencies. Good governance depends on the cooperation and an involvement of a large number of citizens and organizations. These requirements are considered not only essential for good governance but also important for sustainable human development also.

The need for corporate governance has been much more realised in the banking industry because the public stake is very high as the maximum amount of deposits belongs to them in comparison to owners of the bank. Therefore, the accountability of banks to public is much higher. Besides this, the number and the magnitude of scams in the banking industry during the last few years and recent security scam and crisis in co-operative banks have rocked the nation and faith of the depositors which calls for a great need and sharper focus on corporate governance. The following objectives may be achieved through implementing a corporate governance in banking sector:

(i) To increase the capital interests of shareholders;

(ii) To ascertain transparency after providing proper, sufficient, clear and total information to all related parties;

(iii) To protect the interests of all the parties related to banks; and

(iv) To perform the best performance at all the level after fixing the responsibilities of higher authorities.

Recommendations of Various Committees on Corporate Governance

Although there are representatives of Reserve Bank of India and financial institutions in the board of directors of every bank in India and they are responsible for improvement in governance of banks, as well as to perform their duties with transparency, yet different committees have given their recommendations and suggestions to banks for improving their performances. The recommendation of various committees in brief are as under:

Cadbury Committee (1991): This committee investigated accountability of the board of directors to shareholders and to the society. This committee suggested that the Bank's Chairman and Chief Executive Officer (C.E.O.) must be appointed by independent individuals so any decisions may be taken impartially in the public interest. Committee further suggested that nobody can be a director for more than ten companies at a time.

Kumar Mangalam Birla Committee (May 1999): In 1999, SEBI constituted a 18 members committee, chaired by the industrialist, Mr. Kumar Mangalam Birla, on corporate governance, mainly with a view to protecting the investors' interests. The committee made 25 recommendations, 19 of them mandatory in the sense that these were enforceable. The main recommendations were related to Audit Committee, Compensation Committee, accounting standard, effective use of rights, etc.

Basel Committee (Sept. 1999): This committee suggested that it is the responsibility of the banking supervisors to ensure that there is an effective corporate governance in the banking industry. The committee highlighted the need for having appropriate accountability and checks and balances within each bank to ensure good corporate governance, which in turn would lead to effective and more meaningful supervision.